STREET SAINTS

STREET
SAINTS

Renewing America's Cities

Barbara J. Elliott

Templeton Foundation Press

Philadelphia and London

Templeton Foundation Press
Five Radnor Corporate Center, Suite 120
100 Matsonford Road
Radnor, Pennsylvania 19087
www.templetonpress.org

Templeton Foundation Press helps intellectual leaders and others learn about science research on aspects of realities, invisible and intangible. Spiritual realities include unlimited love, accelerating creativity, worship, and the benefits of purpose in persons and in the cosmos.

Designed and typeset by Kachergis Book Design

www.streetsaints.com

LIBRARY OF CONGRESS CATALOGING-IN-PUBLICATION DATA

Elliott, Barbara J.
Street saints : renewing America's cities / Barbara J. Elliott.
p. cm.
Includes bibliographical references and index.
ISBN 1-932031-76-6 (hardback : alk. paper) 1. Social service—United States—Case studies. 2. Volunteer workers in social service—United States—Case studies. 3. Volunteer workers in community development—United States—Case studies. 4. People with social disabilities—Services for—United States—Case studies. 5. Church charities—United States—Case studies. I. Title.

HV91.E433 2004
361.7'5'092273—dc22
2004011003

04 05 06 07 08 10 9 8 7 6 5 4 3 2 1

To my husband, Winston,

whose pursuit of the true, the good and the beautiful

makes all things new through love.

Philippians 4:8

Contents

Contents

Part IV. The Big Picture: Faith at Work in America's History
The Beliefs That Motivate Street Saints Today

Foreword

Some of the most inspiring work in America is being done quietly in our cities, without much fanfare. There are courageous, motivated citizens reaching out to their neighbors in need with authentic compassion. These "street saints" are among America's great unsung heroes. The work they are doing in serving the least, the last, and the lost brings renewal that comes from the deepest well of human change: the human heart.

Years in public service have taught me that there are many things government can do well. The terms I spent in the House and Senate of the United States presented many opportunities to be a part of initiatives that have made a difference. But I have not forgotten an encounter I had in a government hearing in 1984 in Macon, Georgia. It was a defining moment when a humble pastor said to me, "What you do in Congress has limits. You can put a roof over our head, and food on the table. You can provide material aid. But you can't touch people's heads and hearts. You can't touch the spirit and the soul. Unless you deal with the whole person, you can't help them." That statement launched a journey over the past twenty years that has led me to think differently about these issues, and to seek out the people who can go deep enough to change lives. There are some things the government can do, and others it simply cannot.

That encounter pointed me toward agents of healing who can reach the whole person: body, mind, and spirit. Street saints are working as mentors in neighborhoods across America, providing encouragement for neglected youngsters. They are helping families find work or leave addiction. They are encouraging men released from prison to lead productive lives and to never return to crime. These people of faith are taking neighborhoods back from the drug dealers and creating oases of peace with the power of conviction. Experience has shown me that the best thing we can do is to foster their work of renewal of individual lives.

The issues that afflict our cities are not limited to the poorer neighborhoods. There is a poverty of spirit that affects America, cutting across boundaries of income, race, education, and geography. Social maladies know no borders, and the human wreckage that is left behind as families implode and moral standards evaporate cripples rich and poor alike. Addiction and unruly adolescents are not determined by zip codes. America's cultural decay indicates that we are no longer the shining city on a hill that we once were. The kind of work that reaches not only material need, but also the human heart, is necessary to renew the soul of the nation.

One of the manifestations of the modern mind is to seek policy solutions to human problems while ignoring the deeper motivation of human lives. It is clear that despite all our well-intended efforts, many of the efforts to eradicate poverty and heal the social maladies in America for the past forty years have not been successful. Some of these policies have actually made the problems worse. I saw this up close in Chicago just after my undergraduate studies, when I worked for a consulting firm charged with implementing President Johnson's Great Society programs. I went door-to-door in poor neighborhoods trying to convince the residents that it was a good thing that their apartments were going to be bulldozed and replaced with high-rise public housing. Some of them wept at the news. I didn't understand why they preferred their chaotic neighborhood to the clean new high-rises in the photographs I showed them. But their objections proved irrelevant. The bulldozers came and the new, sterile buildings the people were forced to move into became uninhabitable over time. The human misery that resulted from that social experiment shaped my understanding of government in a profound way.

Whatever antibodies that community had to combat its social maladies were crushed—not only by the bulldozer, but by the hubris that claims that governments can remake human beings. We replaced a generation of fathers with welfare checks, which has left whole pockets of our cities fatherless. When government took over the care of the poor, private charities were often crowded out. And as we centralized our social services in the government, the private voluntary sector shrank. We are still trying to undo the damage that was done, which now stretches into the third generation in our cities.

The failure of these policies to lift people from poverty is obvious to many, regardless of their political affiliation or race. Some of the most outspoken critics have been those afflicted themselves. And while some are still fixated on formulating the ideal government policy to try to solve these problems, others are thinking about what a compassionate alternative to government largesse looks like. There is an important place for both public and private solutions. A truly compassionate alternative seeks a greater engagement of the private sector, as well as the removal of political obstacles for the practitioners at the street level.

The Welfare Reform Act of the Bill Clinton administration and the Faith-Based Initiative of the George W. Bush administration are two different but related efforts to return the care of the poor to the people closest to them, in their own states and neighborhoods. Decentralizing care moves the interaction closer to the recipients, and to a human face. The current Bush administration has taken strides to level the playing field for faith-based groups working at the grassroots to compete for government contracts to provide social services on even footing with secular providers. Faith-based providers of human services who seek government funding for the portion of their program that is faith-neutral in nature should not be discriminated against. Because faith-based groups are able to solve some problems that have not responded to any other solutions, they should be given a chance to compete fairly for funding to do their work, which fulfills an important civic purpose.

Faith is an agent of change, and that change has a civic value. Every group that reduces the recidivism of prisoners is reducing crime, lowering the public cost of incarceration, and returning parents to nurture their children, making those children less likely to follow their parents into jail. Every group that helps people leave drug addiction returns citizens to work as taxpayers who can lead productive lives, no longer driven by the compulsion to steal to support a destructive habit. Every group that convinces teenagers to abstain from sex before marriage prevents illegitimacy, sexually transmitted diseases, and child poverty. People of faith have a persuasive track record in these areas, and they are contributing to a better quality of life for our fellow citizens. Their work has a clear civic value—serving the common good, demonstrated in the lives that are changed for the better.

Another thing we can do is to encourage private support of faith-based organizations by expanding the charitable deduction for contributions to nonprofits. This puts the giving power back into the hands of individual citizens, who are free to seek out the street saints in their own communities and support their work. The best solution for funding faith-based organizations is for neighbors to support privately the successful efforts in their own towns with their own money, time, and talent. The more private giving that is released, the healthier our nation will be.

I believe that every neighborhood has been gifted with strengths for its own healing. The talents and convictions of people whose own fates are affected by their actions are best applied to solutions they devise themselves. The one institution that has remained solid in our cities is the church. Many of the neighborhood healers who have the strength to revitalize the city around them are motivated by their faith. How can we—creatively but not intrusively—strengthen faith-based organizations working at the grassroots level in our cities? It is an important question, rooted in the paradox of our free institutions, which rest on the fruits of faith but cannot produce them.

So much of the recent debate on faith-based organizations has centered on the relationship to government funding. But the question that has not yet been fully answered is: What can the private sector do to foster the growth of the faith-based groups? The answer to that question provides a meeting point for thinkers who have stepped outside conventional approaches, left or right, to find truth that transcends political ideology.

The deepest renewal does not come from public policy, but from neighborhoods, families, churches, and local institutions. The best thing government can do is to foster the growth and health of these little platoons, and then get out of their way. Government can remove obstacles and provide incentives to encourage private support of their activities, but no government can ever take the place of the engagement of individuals in face-to-face encounters. As individuals in churches and charities across the country are caring for their neighbors, they are renewing the soul of the nation.

Although this kind of activity is not as common as it was a generation ago, it is still producing cohesiveness in a culture that is centrifugally disintegrating. Participating in civil society is like exercising a muscle: if you do not use it, it atrophies. The civic muscle of contemporary America has lost its earlier prowess. But if it can be further strengthened, its potential is a mighty force for renewal.

For free institutions to function well, America depends on the personal strengths of individuals. Founder Samuel Adams wrote, "Religion and good morals are the only solid foundation of public liberty and happiness."[1] But the government itself is incapable of instilling the virtue necessary for our country to thrive. Although we depend on the social capital of voluntary associations, government cannot create them or make them flourish. This is where street saints, working at the grassroots level of our communities, are effective and necessary: they are building up civil society. As we participate in the care of our neighbors, we are training the moral habits of the heart. Alexis de Tocqueville said if this activity "does not lead the will directly to virtue, it establishes habits which unconsciously turn it that way."[2]

Faith is the most powerful source of motivation for the care of one's neighbor. I believe the root of the solution for renewal in America is in the end spiritual. The people who are living out their faith in compassion are beacons of light, illuminating the landscape around them. They are transforming our cities one person at a time, while building up civil society. The remarkable people who are doing this kind of work are worthy of our attention and support. I have been privileged to meet many of them, and invite you to do the same in the following pages with Barbara Elliott as your guide.

Daniel R. Coats
April 2004

Daniel R. Coats has been the U.S. Ambassador to the Federal Republic of Germany since 2001. He represented the state of Indiana in the U.S. Senate from 1989 to 1999, and in the House of Representatives from 1981 to 1988.

Acknowledgments

This book is the fruit of many seeds, which have been planted and tended by many other people laboring in this vineyard. My heartfelt thanks to mentors Bob Woodson, Marvin Olasky, Amy Sherman, and Virgil Gulker, to whom I owe gratitude for their wisdom and willingness to teach me. To Father Donald Nesti for imparting the spirituality and theology of compassion, as did Henri Nouwen, Dallas Willard, and Richard Foster through their writing. To Brad Birzer and Gleaves Whitney for conveying the intellectual underpinnings of America's founding while encouraging me through their friendship. To Reid Carpenter, John Stahl-Wert, Larry Lloyd, Howard Eddings, H. Spees, Kurt Madden, Art Erickson, and many others in the Leadership Foundations of America who engagingly conveyed the charisms necessary for city renewal. To Adam Meyerson for providing opportunities to write, speak, and convene others on these topics for thoughtful discourse. To Cathy Lawdanski, Alison Tunnell, Christy Wills, and Alex Taylor, whose capable assistance was indispensable. To Irma Moré, Karen Minyard, Clint and Catalina Brand, who provided a pillar of strength. To Charles Harper and Arthur Schwartz of the John Templeton Foundation for the generous grant to do the research for this book, and to the Templeton Foundation Press for publishing the result. To Jay Hein and the Hudson Institute for their support as the writing was being completed. To Dan Hales, John Mundy, Robert McNair, Peter Forbes, Paul McDonald, George Strake, Dick Wendt and the American Institute for Full Employment, Houston Endowment, and the many others who have made the Center for Renewal a learning lab for civic renewal through their support. To Landon Short, under whose wing I entered this field in Houston. To the Capital Research Center for publishing excerpts from these findings. To the hundreds of people who spent thousands of hours with me, entrusting me with their stories. A special thanks to Rufus Smith, Sylvia Bolling, Freddie and Ninfa Garcia, Joe Hernandez, and Prince Couisnard, all of whom welcomed me with trust, and taught me to see with new eyes. To Father James Moore, Vincent Uher, and the parishioners of Our Lady of Walsingham for prayer and encouragement. To my mother, Phyllis, Regnum Christi members, and the many other prayer partners who have carried this project. And above all, to my husband Winston, and our children, Stephanie, Tommy, Winston IV, and Morgan, who have all borne the brunt of many research trips and long hours at the computer which kept me from them. *Gratia Deo et gloria.*

Introduction

Come on a visit into a world so hidden away it's almost invisible. It could be in the city where you live, and you may have driven past it for years. It's both beautiful and tough, heartbreaking and inspiring. It's the world of street saints. Street saints are on the front lines of our communities, serving the broken, the forgotten, the abandoned, and the abused. They are binding the wounds of battered women and children, feeding the hungry, and leading addicts out of captivity.

A street saint is someone who is willing to go where there is pain and suffering and be a presence of healing with love. Street saints are walking into drug-infested neighborhoods to broker truces between gang members. They are scooping up heroin and crack addicts from our cities' streets and loving them back into wholeness. They are giving a hand to families in transition from welfare into work and productivity. They are coming into schools to put their arms around and mentor at-risk children. Street saints who are victims of crime are walking into our prisons to confront prisoners face-to-face so they will not commit crimes again. They are giving immigrants language skills and entrepreneurial training so they can support themselves. Street saints are renewing the soul of America's cities.

Street saints are very different kinds of people. Bob Muzikowski is an insurance executive who loves baseball and founded a league and a school for the kids in the inner-city neighborhood he moved into. Freddie Garcia left his heroin addiction and now helps thousands of others to do the same. Kathy Foster is a nun who cares for abandoned and abused children. Wilson Goode is a former mayor whose father was imprisoned; he has founded a mentoring program for children of prisoners. Gib Vestal is an investment banker turned construction boss for an athletic facility for inner-city kids. Brian King was a gang member in shootouts—he now counsels parents whose children have been killed. Sylvia Bolling is a speech pathologist now renewing the impoverished neighborhood she came from.

Street saints are doctors and jazz musicians, teachers and preachers, stockbrokers and manufacturers. They may be Latino, African American, Asian, or Anglo. Some are Presbyterian or Pentecostal, Roman Catholic or Mennonite, charismatic or Baptist, Nazarene or nondenominational.[1] Street saints are reconcilers among the races and bridges over denominational chasms, offering unity where there is division in an increasingly balkanized country.

There is no single educational background to equip them. Ivy leaguers with Ph.D.s find themselves working side by side with savvy high school dropouts, former addicts, and ex-drug dealers who have an education from the streets no doctoral program could ever offer. Some street saints stayed in the neighborhoods they came from and are effective because they know the people, the problems, and the dynamics there. Others have relocated from the suburbs into the inner city, taking their families with them, in order to be close to those they serve. They have found that living in the same zip code gives them authenticity.[2]

Street saints are modern-day manifestations of the Good Samaritan. When they see a person who has been damaged, instead of walking by, they stop to bandage his or her wounds and provide care until he or she can stand again. The wounds may be physical, psychological, or emotional; in any case, they are crippling. The people who help alleviate the pain heal with faith as their motivation and love as their method.

Americans sprang into action when the hijacked planes smashed into the twin towers of the World Trade Center in New York on the fateful September 11 of 2001. The flames seared our souls as people leapt from windows to a ghastly death, and as firefighters heroically charged up the stairwells laden with sixty pounds of equipment to rescue others at the expense of their own lives. We cheered for their heroism with a lump in our throats and with a deep admiration that we had almost forgotten in this jaded age.

Something was still smoldering, deep in the American soul, which was reignited by the fiery explosions of September 11. Embers of resilience and greatness were lit again, blazing forth in heroism and sacrifice for others. Our sense of unity, fractured by many "isms" and numbed by complacency, was recovered. Ashes covered our faces, and we were no longer black or white or brown, but one shade of gray. In that moment, there were no more hyphenated Americans. We prayed together in grief, one people, crying out to God in a wail of incomprehension. Our political representatives stood shoulder to shoulder before the Capitol, joined hands over their party divisions, and sang "God Bless America" with one voice. Suddenly, we were one nation again.

An outpouring of compassion and generosity swept in a vast wave from across the nation to embrace the victims. Churches swelled to overflowing and, for a moment, we stopped and paused to reevaluate. People prayed, and married, and conceived children, and did things they had put off, because time suddenly seemed precious. *Everything changed*, we said. And for a time it did. But only for a short time. Within a few months, the seared mind of the nation was no longer conscious of the jagged wound— except in New York, as people walked by Ground Zero. And as the war against terrorism with its daily carnage continues, most of us have sunk into our old ways again.

But what that experience made clear is that the American soul may have atrophied, but it is not dead. The American soul—which since our founding has cared for neighbors with generosity, respect, and compassion—has not been extinguished by modernity. America has always been a country with an extraordinary degree of compassion and good will. Anyone who has lived elsewhere in the world is struck by it when they come to these shores. And even as tattered as the social fabric of America has become in recent years, this remains true. But today, the pain in our own country does not tug at the heartstrings because we do not hear the people in our own communities who suffer quietly. And yet, these victims of violence and neglect, both physical and emotional, are in every town. It's not a question of which neighborhood. They are all around us, among us.

The problem is that so many of the victims around us are almost invisible. The more than two million children who have a parent incarcerated aren't even a blip on the screen for most of us. We don't know their names, or where they go to school. Sometimes even their own teachers don't know of their plight, because the children are ashamed to admit that they have a parent behind bars. Yet these forgotten children are seven times more likely than their classmates to follow their parents into jail because of the kind of life they are thrust into, through no fault of their own.

The same invisibility blankets the working poor, the single mother who has left welfare only to discover that it's not possible to feed her children and pay for an apartment with one minimum wage job, and that she has to work two . . . while patching together care for her offspring. The mentally ill who wander the streets in the ranks of the homeless are virtually unemployable. Nobody wants to adopt HIV babies, and yet many are among us. The health needs of the uninsured fester quietly. This is the soft underbelly of an otherwise affluent nation.

The modern mindset points us toward the government to provide solutions. But as Ambassador Dan Coats has pointed out, there are some things the government can do and others it cannot. The most important question is not what should the government do, but what should we as individuals do? It is far easier to debate the first question. But where the rubber hits the road is where we put our own convictions into action in our own communities, with our own time and money. No new political policy edict can take the place of the soul of a nation. And that soul is very much in peril.

The problems of the nation's soul go far beyond the issue of material wealth or poverty. We live in a country of "down-and-outers" and "up-and-outers." We hear more about the "down-and-outers"—somebody who seeks solace in a needle or a rock of crack. Or the rebellious teenager who runs drugs or sells her body. The kid who finds a sense of family in a gang that pummels him with steel-toed boots in an initiation rite. The single mom who goes to jail, leaving behind a six-year-old to take care of a toddler. Whole sections of cities where no one lives with a father. These are the bitter fruits of our contemporary culture for the "down-and-outers" of the inner city.

But let's look at the "up-and-outers," a more perplexing phenomenon. The driven business executive who sells his shares for an early retirement, only to discover the family he wanted to spend it with has imploded in his chronic absence. Or the male midlife crisis that roars full throttle into a hot sports car and a new woman. Or the teenager who gets a new Mercedes convertible for her sixteenth birthday and blows out her brains with her father's handgun. These are the "up-and-outers"—people of means who have discovered that what they own or earn does not fill their hearts.

What do these two worlds have to do with each other? The answer to that question is one of the keys to renewal. We live in a culture that is relationally impoverished and spiritually crippled—for both the "up-and-outer" and the "down-and-outer." What we all yearn for in the depth of our souls is relationship. There is a universal need that transcends the boundaries of race, geography, and income. One thing that heals a shattered life is the touch of another human being who is a vehicle of divine love. Relational one-to-one bridges can heal both the "up-and-outers" and the "down-and-outers."

The maladies of our country do not all come from our material circumstances. They come from a poverty of spirit. Too few hands move swiftly enough to give where there is need. Street saints build relational bridges to heal the souls of the people whose lives they touch. The healing that takes place is reciprocal.

What is the scope of faith-based work in America? Sociologist Ram Cnaan has devoted the past ten years to finding out what religious congregations in America provide. The Israeli-born social scientist, a secular Jew, admits candidly, "I didn't get into this field because of my religious beliefs. I moved into studying religion and social work . . . almost by mistake. My academic interest was in how society provides social services."[3] He was flummoxed to discover that America doesn't provide these services through the government, as is usually the case in the European countries he had written about. In the European model, the government taxes and gives the money to local authorities, who provide services.

When he came to the United States, he asked people, "Who provides social services?" No one knew what to answer. So he said, "Six o'clock in the evening, you've been evicted from your home, you can't eat, where would you go?" People would pause and say, "Well, to a homeless shelter, or I'd go to a soup kitchen." He assumed these were government agencies. When he found out how many of them were run by religious congregations in the private sector, he was intrigued.

Cnaan has documented that there are approximately 350,000 different congregations in the United States.[4] Religious congregations spend $36 billion providing services in America today. Many such programs address the needs of children, the elderly, the poor, and the homeless, while others are involved in housing projects or neighborhood renewal, pastoral care, aid for the ill, or counseling. Some offer financial assistance, health care, or educational programs. Cnaan estimates the annual value of the work each congregation provides in helping others is on average $184,000. He found that 93 percent of religious congregations provide at least one program of service for the community.[5] And, most often, the beneficiaries were poor neighborhood children who had no affiliation with the church.

After a study of more than 14,000 congregations, the Hartford Institute for Religion Research concluded that "nearly 85 percent of US congregations are engaged in soup kitchens or food pantries, emergency shelters and clothing pantries, and with financial help to those in need."[6] Beyond these services offered directly by churches are a plethora of stand-alone nonprofits that churches have spun off, or which were founded as fully separate organizations.

Are faith-based organizations making a difference? A growing body of research indicates that some faith-based programs are making headway in treating social maladies that have resisted all other attempted cures. Some faith-based prison programs are reducing the rate of recidivism of released convicts, ordinarily 50 percent or more, to as little as 8 percent.[7] Mentoring programs for at-risk youth are improving academic performance and decreasing disciplinary infractions.[8] Faith-based drug and alcohol treatment programs are releasing addicts from their life-crippling habit; one program has a success rate as high as 84 percent.[9] Much more remains to be done to validate the results of such programs through serious sociological research on the "faith factor." There are many wonderful stories, but, as the sociologist John DiIulio likes to remind us, the plural of anecdote is not data. However, as the sociological evidence continues to come in, it validates that faith is a force to be reckoned with.

This book will take you on a journey into the cities of America to experience the people, programs, and strategies of the street saints today. As the programs are introduced, their best practices are highlighted for those people who would like to emulate their successes. Where studies have been done, the research is summarized. An online directory at www.streetsaints.com provides contact information for all of the groups profiled.

Think of this journey like a filmmaker would, starting with close-up shots of individuals, gradually pulling back to a medium shot of groups of people, and finally, seeing a broad panorama of the landscape. In Part I, you will meet some of the street saints face-to-face in close-up portraits. They are diverse: a former gang banger, a Wall Street broker turned social entrepreneur, a third-grade dropout who has fathered a national movement, a heroin addict now freeing others from addiction, a nurse who has reclaimed an entire inner-city block from drug dealers, and a pastor who walks into gang confrontations to defuse them.

Pulling back the lens to a wider angle, in Part II we move from the people to the programs. The tour takes you behind the bars of prison to see: programs where street saints are transforming criminals so they won't return; mentors for the angry children prisoners leave behind; and an innovative way to protect the infants of convicted mothers. You will visit a home that cares for abused toddlers and a partnership that mobilizes thousands of mentors for at-risk children, pairing one church with one school. You will see the genesis of a youth center that is transforming an entire neighborhood, as well as two successful models of inner-city schools raising the bar on education. You will see the transformation of homeless people and drug addicts into productive citizens.

Then the tour turns to social entrepreneurs finding creative ways to work, like combining the care of street kids with marketing coffee on the Internet. You will meet a priest who is transforming immigrants into entrepreneurs. We visit mentally and physically handicapped people supporting themselves with micro-enterprises. We go into several of the nation's most successful homeless shelters, which are transitioning residents into a new life. And we see drug treatment and welfare-to-work programs that have moved people out of dependency into self-sufficiency.

Part III pulls the camera lens back even further, to give a view of entire cities. Taking Nehemiah as the biblical paradigm for mobilizing people in renewal, you will meet two contemporary Nehemiah figures working today in Washington, D.C., and Philadelphia. The tour continues through three American cities—Pittsburgh, Memphis, and Fresno—where strategies embrace a vision as big as the city and mobilize people of faith and resources to "transform geography into community."[10]

Finally, Part IV shows us the big picture, the historical framework to put all of this activity into an even broader context, within which America has defined its soul since its founding. The concluding reflections point upward, providing a glimpse of the spiritual reasons people engage in this kind of work. There you will hear the voices of people like Henri Nouwen as the "wounded healer" and Mother Teresa, whose life as a street saint was a "pencil in the hand of God."

My own journey into this world began in 1989 with a prayer. I had never really asked God what he wanted me to do with my life, and if you ever pray that prayer meaning it, look out. You may get something you are not expecting. The answer I got was one word: refugees. It was the summer before the Berlin Wall came down, and the first 300,000 people had fled Communism through snipped barbed wire on the border of Hungary, streaming into West Germany, where I lived. If they got out with a small suitcase, they were fortunate.[11]

It was clear that not just someone should do something about them, but that I should. A friend and I launched a small initiative to care for those we could, with blankets, clothes, help finding a job or an apartment, and tutoring for their children. Over the coming months, we had opportunities to listen for hundreds of hours, to love these people through the transition, and to encourage others to do likewise. Neighbors came to my door, unasked, to press a check into my hands or to donate warm coats. My friend and I would drive to the shelters, having prayed and picked an address that morning from our list and having loaded a few things in the car. We would invariably discover the one family that had just arrived the night before, and we would have exactly what they needed in the car. If ever God was at work despite blind and fumbling human efforts, that was such a time.

I later experienced people of faith who were rebuilding in the ashes of the collapsed Soviet empire, and I marveled at their courage and the disproportionate effect they had on the wreckage around them. A small amount of money given to one honest Russian Orthodox priest would produce medicine for an entire wing of a children's hospital, and a visit a month later would reveal children demonstrating the first blush of returning health. A modest sum would allow a Russian street saint to feed scores of homeless people and rescue teenage girls from prostitution. The amounts of money friends asked me to deliver were not nearly as critical as finding the trustworthy people who were genuine agents of renewal.

My past eight years in America have taken me into homeless shelters, prisons, drug treatment centers, inner-city churches, and some neighborhoods that have caused my husband consternation. Through the Center for Renewal, I have worked with a number of these groups with enough intimacy to know, and sometimes to share, their bruises. What I have found through my encounters with nearly a thousand organizations and in more than three hundred interviews is a remarkable diversity of people who amaze me. They are genuine agents of renewal, modest saints at work. Their humility, contagious joy, and invincible spirit keep drawing me back, particularly when I am spiritually hungry. I know that where they are working, there is always evidence that the aroma of Christ is present.

Come and meet some of them.

Barbara J. Elliott
Pentecost 2004
Houston, Texas

part i

THE PEOPLE

Portraits of Street Saints

chapter 1

American Street Saints in Action

"It's important to strengthen our communities by unleashing the compassion of America's religious institutions. Religious charities of every creed are doing some of the most vital work in our country—mentoring children, feeding the hungry, taking the hand of the lonely."—President George W. Bush, State of the Union Address, January 20, 2004

Kirbyjon Caldwell: Windsor Village and the Power Center

Although he didn't know it at the time, when Kirbyjon Caldwell showed Governor George W. Bush the Power Center in Houston in 1997, it lit the fuse of a paradigm-busting vision to renew the soul of America. The man who soon thereafter became the president of the United States saw up close what could happen to transform a gritty strip mall into a haven of health and hope and transform a community from the inside out.

When Kirbyjon Caldwell took over Windsor Village United Methodist Church in 1982, it drew only a dozen stragglers on Sunday. He launched an incendiary renewal that now attracts more than thirteen thousand members and deploys them in a hundred ministries throughout the community, aiding battered children, drug addicts, and people seeking work. Intrigued by an article about Caldwell in a Dallas newspaper, then-

Governor Bush met him and later came to Houston to speak at the Power Center. The governor saw what happened to a community when an abandoned K-Mart and an auto repair shop became a 104,000-square-foot humming hive of small businesses, a bank, executive suites, a hospital health clinic, a K–8 school, a vast conference facility, and a community college technology center.[1]

It was no coincidence that Caldwell was asked to introduce George W. Bush at the Republican National Convention or to offer the invocation on Inauguration Day. The president saw that leaders like Kirbyjon Caldwell hold the keys to renewal of their own neighborhoods. He had seen the power of the faith community in action, and he wanted to unleash more of the same. Kirbyjon's meteoric ascent drew flak, however. Some folks in the African American community fired potshots when Kirbyjon, a political Independent, stepped forward on behalf of a Republican. His parishioners caught more shrapnel than he did, but the damage seems not to have been lethal.

When Kirbyjon Caldwell answered the call to ministry, he did not set out to create a multimillion-dollar enterprise. But as it has turned out, he has relied on both financial and theological training, as one of the few pastors who holds an MBA. Of course, it doesn't hurt that he is articulate, intelligent, and dynamic. He claims he's an introvert, but it's hard to believe when he's throwing off sparks in a riff from the pulpit. He has become highly visible both locally and nationally.

Kirbyjon Caldwell, named after his two grandparents Kirby and John, grew up in Houston's Fifth Ward, the son of a tailor who made classy suits for such notables as B. B. King and Ray Charles. His neighborhood was pocked with pool halls, pimps, and prostitutes, and he watched his father patiently clean up the broken glass every time his shop was broken into. But Kirbyjon broke out by attending the Wharton School of the University of Pennsylvania, earning a ticket to Wall Street, where he became a bond broker on the fast track to a six-figure income. He hobnobbed with investment bankers and drove a sleek gray sports car. He had a bright future in the financial world.

That is, until one Monday afternoon in 1978 at two. In a call as clear as a phone, but more urgent, Kirbyjon realized that his gifts, his education, and his experience were all necessary for what he was to do next. And although he did not know exactly what that was to be, it was clear that God was urging him to follow this "locomotion that overrode all logic"[2] and enter the ministry. When he announced his decision with a firm voice, his boss on Wall Street, his coworkers, and even his family all told him he had lost his sanity. No one in his or her right mind gets that high into the upper stratosphere of success and parachutes out. If they had known he was headed blindly for seminary and then to pastor a dying church with twenty-five members, only twelve of whom showed up on any given Sunday, their howls of protest would have been even louder.

What Caldwell believed in was a different kind of vision of the Kingdom among us. Long discontented with the kind of preaching that looked at salvation merely as "a passport out of hell," he believed that we are charged with modeling our lives after the Kingdom in the Lord's Prayer. Here and now. He believed that "Jesus gave us clear examples in the parables to show us how to model a family, a business, and a community after Kingdom principles." And he was convinced that "one of the keys to renewal is found in the original sense of the word salvation," which in Greek connotes total wholeness. A Kingdom vision would include a "holistic approach to renewal, both internal and external."

The boy who had a stutter overcame his disability, and Kirbyjon proved to be quite a preacher. His persuasive message, verbal pyrotechnics, and personal dynamism swelled the church membership, and he urged them to move out of the sanctuary and onto the streets. Starting with the talents of the original twenty-five members and the needs of the community around them, Windsor Village United Methodist Church mapped out a strategy for holistic renewal. They saw people in need of drug treatment and founded a ministry to assist them. They saw battered children who needed a place to be safe and created a shelter for them. Parishioners were mobilized into lay ministry, admittedly partly because the needs outstripped the budget. But Caldwell quickly realized that one of the most powerful tools for discipleship is giving people Kingdom responsibility, so he nudged them out the door. He found that "as people engage in service, they discover they are being changed underway." Together they were becoming what their pastor calls "a lean, mean, Kingdom-building machine."

The spiritual heat that had been ignited in the neighborhood drew the attention of the local Fiesta grocery store, which owned a strip center with an abandoned K-Mart and auto repair shop. The manager asked Pastor Caldwell if he had any ideas on how to renew the blighted area. It's probably better that neither one of them had a clue about what was to come, or they would have stopped right there. Little did the Fiesta managers know that they would end up giving the church $4.4 million worth of property. And Kirbyjon Caldwell couldn't have guessed then that what he thought was a $2 million project—which was bad enough—would turn into a $6 million one, which at the beginning would have seemed utterly impossible. Today it's all paid for.

Although it is only fifteen minutes south of the fashionable Galleria area in Houston, this neighborhood was beyond the great economic divide. Caldwell found it had no bank, no learning center, no clinic, no place to incubate businesses, too few jobs, and too little investment. So the Power Center was born—a holistic approach to neighborhood renewal. Caldwell's ability to move with ease between the pulpit and the boardroom helped him succeed in bringing partners into the project and landed him on the front page of the *Wall Street Journal*.[3] Leasing space to a range of providers like the Chase Bank of Texas and the University of Texas–Hermann Hospital Clinic provided income for the nonprofit project, and the vision became reality. Today the Power Center is hopping with conferences in the city's third-largest banquet facility, serving up meals in a thriving catering service, assisting 6,000 in a Woman-Infant-Children's center each month, and schooling 450 kids in the private K–8 Imani School.[4] The Power Center has created 560 construction jobs, 372 other jobs, and pumps an estimated $17.5 million annually into the Houston economy.

The ministries spawned through the church cut a wide swath through the community's needs: job preparation, drug treatment, AIDS ministry, singles groups, prison ministry, teen groups, parenting, and life skills. While the church's traditional ministries are run strictly through the church, the community is being served by the nonprofits created by the church, as well as by the faith component of the church's outreach. The religious and the civic entities are clearly separate but complementary. The *Wall Street Journal, Newsweek,* the BBC, NBC, and others have looked at Windsor Village and the Power Center and hailed them as "an entrepreneurial incarnation of the twenty-first-century Church."[5] Caldwell says he got the idea from Wal-Mart, the mega-market with everything under one roof. He wanted to create a center that provided the means for spiritual and economic renewal in one location, one-stop shopping for body and soul.

Daring to have a big vision is essential, says Caldwell, as is the willingness to take risks. He and his team prayed first, then sat down and thought big, as if money were no object. "Divine visions attract dollars," he assured them. And judging by the results, that would seem to be the case. The combined budget of Windsor Village church and the eight nonprofits the church has created is now $14 million. Affordable housing was the next need on the wish list, and the Pyramid Residential Community Corporation was created to realize Caldwell's big dream "to provide an intergenerational place for help, hope and healing." A whole community is being created in the Corinthian Pointe Subdivision, which will include 452 single-family homes, a Family Life Center, a YMCA, a 20-acre community park, two catfish ponds, an 8,500-square-foot Prayer Center, a public school, two museums, a skating rink, tennis courts, and a commercial park. More than two hundred families have already moved into the attractive homes. The entire community, valued at $109 million at its completion, is to be finished in 2006.

Interestingly, most of the work of the Power Center and the other non-profits it has spun into existence has been done without significant government funding. Pastor Caldwell offered a private bond to his own parishioners to finance much of their first project, the Power Center. From a total of $6 million, only $200,000 came from government sources. A housing firm has collaborated with the group to build the 452-home Corinthian Pointe project, which has not applied for any HUD funding. Caldwell says a newly formed drug treatment center may apply for a slice of federal funding appropriate to its mission, but private funding has been found for virtually everything in this sweeping renewal project. It wasn't a political or ideological issue for him—Caldwell just preferred to find private financing and was capable of doing so. He is convinced that faith-based initiatives like this one are about people of faith renewing their own communities and producing a common civic good.

It would be easy to let the sheer magnitude of the Power Center's community development projects eclipse the spiritual part of Windsor Village's mission. But the external community renewal is an outgrowth of internal spiritual renewal; as Caldwell tells it: "The story of Windsor Village is prayer coupled with action, and proof of the incredible power of this combination stands one mile from our church: the Power Center."[6] Caldwell asserts that prayer is essential for what church members do—foster the renewal of individuals and, through them, the community. "The Word became flesh and dwelt among us," he explains, as he challenges believers to put their faith into action. "The invisible became visible, and our faith should do the same. Someone who does not know the Kingdom should be able to peer into the church and get a glimpse of what the Kingdom is like. If believers cannot point an onlooker in the direction of the Kingdom, we're not doing our job."

White-hot holistic renewal of the individual and of the community drives the Windsor Village church and the nonprofits it has started. "God wants to save souls, but also communities," says Kirbyjon Caldwell. "Faith is not just about personal transformation, it's about transforming communities. Jesus called men and women to be the light of the world. He's asking us to do the same. It's not enough to talk the talk. We have to walk the walk."

Best Practices: Windsor Village United Methodist and the Power Center

• Launching church ministries to meet spiritual needs in the community first

• Training and deploying laity to serve their neighbors

• Jumpstarting economic renewal with an entrepreneurial center

• Mobilizing participation of business, public and private sectors

• Spinning out separate nonprofits and small businesses to deepen the work that complements that of the church

• Fostering holistic renewal, both spiritual and economic

Results

• Church growth from twenty-five to more than thirteen thousand

• One hundred new ministries to meet local needs

• $17.5 million produced for local economy annually

• Seven new nonprofits created

• Affordable housing development with 452 homes

Freddie and Ninfa Garcia: Victory Fellowship of Texas

The years Freddie Garcia spent as a heroin addict on the streets would seem to make him an unlikely candidate for sainthood.[7] A hustler and sometime thief, he tried scores of detox programs but kept going back for another fix. He had a moment of reckoning in 1966 as he fumbled to shoot up heroin in the men's room of a gas station, his infant daughter swaddled in toilet paper on the filthy floor. He had taken her along on holdups. He looked at her and for one lucid moment wondered what kind of father he was. *There has to be a better way to live,* he thought.

Freddie had lived on the streets for years, stealing to support his drug habit and losing his last shred of dignity. After flunking out of every drug program he tried, he decided to try the faith-based program Teen Challenge in California—more out of desperation than hope. What he experienced there was like putting his finger into an electrical socket. The jolt of power blasted him into a whole new life.

No one was more surprised than he was. Well, maybe his common-law wife, Ninfa. He asked her to marry him. She thought he was *loco*, considering she was already the mother of his children—one of whom they had abandoned, another of which they aborted, and a third they were neglecting between bouts with drugs. They definitely qualified as a colorful couple: on their first date, she drove the getaway car while he robbed a convenience store. But after Freddie's experience at Teen Challenge, she plugged into the same spiritual power he had discovered and stopped popping pills. The two of them straightened up and launched an outreach to addicts that has created ripples throughout the country and beyond for the past thirty-five years. With a wellspring of experience like theirs, there is no one who can talk to addicts with more conviction. They can say, "I've been there. I made it out with God's help, and so can you."[8]

What allowed a hard-core addict to kick drugs after a chain of failed attempts? Freddie says it was his conversion. He looked at the needle scars on Sonny Arguinzoni as he spread his arms wide, preaching, "I don't care how much drugs you've shot or how many sins you've committed. Just come forward and ask Jesus to forgive you for all of your sins, and you'll be a drug addict no more. Jesus wants you to change your life right now." Freddie had ridiculed others who had gone forward before, but that day a desire to go prompted turmoil within. He stumbled forward and sank to his knees, saying, "Lord, I'm tired of using drugs, I'm tired of the life I've lived. Forgive me."[9]

Freddie and Ninfa founded Victory Fellowship of Texas as a refuge for addicts that helps them leave drugs through faith. It's not only a program—it's a complete change of life for addicts, prostitutes, gang members, and ex-convicts. It is multifaceted: a church, outreach to gangs, prison visits, youth programs, apartment ministry, and street evangelization, with a strong dose of community building. In the past thirty-five years, this ministry has blossomed into a network of seventy affiliates, twenty-five in the United States and the remainder in eight Latin American countries.[10] They have helped more than thirteen thousand people leave addiction and get their lives on track.

When you walk into the Victory Home in San Antonio, heroin addicts may wander in at the same time, still half high but coming down. They want help. Someone there will take them in, listen to them, and promise to stay with them no matter what until they are through detox. For the next hours, or days if needed, there will be someone to sit with them, wipe their foreheads when they get the sweats, hold a bowl when they vomit, talk to them when they can't sleep, and pray them through the pain. Every single person helping the seventy addicts in care at Victory Fellowship in San Antonio knows exactly what the detoxers are going through, because they have been there themselves: they are all former addicts. They offer a structured life in the homes, based on love, authority, supervision, and discipline. Schedules are firm; order is mandatory. Participants stay in a home from six months to a year. House parents who live there model a Christian life round the clock, slowly transforming character. Based on its internal tracking, Victory Fellowship finds that 70 percent of those who stay to finish the program stay off drugs.

Freddie is crystal clear about the difference between reforming and transforming an addict: he combats addiction with spiritual transformation. "If you treat an addict with a drug rehab program, all you have is a reformed junkie," he says, seated at the kitchen table of his home, which serves as the hub for his ministry. "If an addict meets Christ, he is transformed. He's a whole new person." Freddie has a straightforward approach to dealing with addiction that flies in the face of our therapeutic culture. "Drugs aren't the problem," he says. "Drugs are a symptom of the problem." The addict-turned-pastor is just getting warmed up. "Everybody's got an explanation for the problem. Psychologists call it emotional disturbance. Sociologists call it the product of our environment. Educators call it the lack of education." He drives home his conclusion: "Sin is the problem. Jesus Christ is the answer."

On a given afternoon, you will see former addicts in small clusters in front of the home, their heads bowed over Bibles in one-on-one scripture study in the hot Texas sun. Ninfa takes a break from teaching the women participants to stir a huge pot of beans in the kitchen, one that is always simmering to feed the hungry hordes that show up at the front door. Across town in one of the apartment complexes, one of Freddie's protégés is talking to a kid who has taken refuge in his apartment there, trying to escape the crossfire of warring gangs in the barrio. The apartment that has been given to Victory Fellowship is a sanctuary for people trying to escape a bullet or a beating at the hands of an abuser. It also serves as a ministry incubator to train people who later go into other communities to do outreach for Victory Fellowship. This learning lab for new members of the ministry provides hands-on experience with domestic violence, gang intervention, and all the other maladies they will face. It's not exactly the kind of training you'd get at divinity school or in a sociology department. "Our people may not have Ph.D.s," Freddie says, "but they have an education you can't get at Yale or Harvard."

When a somewhat timid-looking group of well-heeled philanthropists disgorged from buses to experience Victory Fellowship in San Antonio not long ago, they were ushered into an auditorium-style building for a presentation. "It's a good thing they don't know who's in here with them," Freddie chuckled. "I'll bet they've never been in a room with this many murderers, thieves, pimps, and prostitutes. The only requirement you have to get into my program is to be some kind of criminal," he said with a mischievous glint. "God has raised up an army of rejects." The ex-addicts choir thundered in wearing combat boots and fatigues to give a heart-rending performance of gospel music with a *Tejano* flavor. Traces of their dissolute lives were still visible in their faces. Under the direction of the Garcias' son Jubal, who is being groomed for leadership, former gang bangers presented a drama depicting life in the barrio that was wrenchingly real.

At the end of presentations like this, Freddie tells the audience: "Listen to me, folks, the miracle that took place in our lives didn't happen when we called upon the name of Socrates, Charles Darwin, Karl Marx, or Sigmund Freud. This transformation took place in our lives when we called upon the name of our Lord and Savior Jesus Christ. It was he who broke the shackles of sin and drug addiction and set us free."[11]

Victory Fellowship takes the message of transformation to the streets.

Former addicts go out at night, walking right into the middle of drug transactions and gang confrontations. These are the same guys who may have trafficked in that exact neighborhood before they changed. Now they are there trying to save the lives of anyone who will listen and leave that way of life. To the addicts who refuse to listen, they just shrug and say, "That's okay. We'll come visit you when you're in jail."

A remarkable number of the addicts who succeed at Victory Fellowship stay on to become a part of the work. A whole generation of disciples has been equipped, trained, nurtured, and deployed to expand Victory Fellowship, which is serving primarily the Latino population in Texas, with outposts in Mexico and Central and South America. In each of the seventy locations, a drug program and a church are planted to work side by side. Initially Freddie sent his leaders to Bible school, which he had completed, but he concluded they needed a more specific education tailored to the kind of work they would be doing. Freddie puts future leaders through his own three-year program in San Antonio, which includes study of the Bible and leadership skills along with face-to-face discipleship. Once the new leaders are launched, they continue to come back for additional training and can access crisis intervention help if needed; they always work within a framework of accountability.

One of Freddie's protégés, Joe Hernandez, heads a Victory Home in Houston, for example. As an addict, Joe found his way into Victory Fellowship several years ago, taking refuge while healing from a gunshot wound. He says he "had hit rock bottom but still thought he was pretty slick" and didn't really need "any of the religious stuff they were talking about." But his interest was piqued by the authenticity of this unusual outfit. Joe stayed, and eventually committed his life to Christ; he has become a preacher and ministry leader himself. The home he now heads in Houston can house fifty men in transition from addiction to sobriety and employment. It is immaculate and run with military precision. The small church Joe pastors cares for the families of the addicts as well as for people in the neighborhood. He and his wife return to San Antonio intermittently for training and interaction with their counterparts.

Victory Fellowship operates on a frugal budget with a wing and a prayer—they never charge participants anything. All the affiliates face the same problem of trying to raise money in a sector of the community that's chronically poor. Even Freddie Garcia, who has been honored in the White House Rose Garden and has a wall full of plaques in his living room, ekes out funds for his ministry. Good work does not necessarily equal money. It's a typical problem for street saints, who are fully focused on their mission and are neither professional fund-raisers nor in a position to hire one. They serve a population that's burly, tattooed, and scarred— too rough to attract most socialite gala organizers. But Freddie Garcia and the scores of former addicts he has inspired to become street saints like him are too busy to be concerned. Their mission is to do the hard work of transforming a tough population. The proof of their success is in more than thirteen thousand changed lives.

What happens at Victory Fellowship has the capacity to move people, if they will just go and see it. A group of businesspeople in San Antonio were so captivated that they recently pooled their resources to help Freddie and Ninfa purchase seven acres of land, where three future dormitories and a multipurpose building are being financed by these anonymous donors. "We never could have done this," Ninfa says. "We don't know how to begin, and don't know these kinds of people. It really has to have been God at work."

Best Practices: Victory Fellowship

- Ends drug addiction through intentional spiritual transformation
- Immerses recovering addicts in a structured program to change their character as well as their behavior
- Church and home for recovering addicts work in tandem to address the needs of their families as well
- Three-year training program fosters replication of Victory Fellowship's work in other cities
- Continued education and accountability stabilizes leaders of new affiliate programs

Results

- More than 13,000 participants have left addiction
- Seventy affiliates in the United States and five countries

Cordelia Taylor: Family House

Renewal in America's inner cities is sometimes sparked by one person who demonstrates the courage to face down drug dealers and reclaim the neighborhood, one block at a time. It is not a task most people would take on if they have made it out of the poverty of that neighborhood, overcoming obstacles to acquire an education and a profession. Once you've moved into the suburbs and tasted the fruits of success, coming back into the inner city is much harder, especially if you have eight kids to raise. Cordelia Taylor has demonstrated the grit that it takes to do that. The petite woman in a stylish suit and heels steps out as adeptly from a meeting in an elegant hotel as she does over the broken glass on the street. The Family House she runs in a tough neighborhood in Milwaukee has expanded since 1987 to encompass almost the entire side of a city block. Cordelia Taylor has stepped across the barriers of poverty, race, and hatred to become one of America's street saints.[12]

Cordelia's father was murdered by two white men in a small town in Tennessee in 1947. She recalls the night: "Two men followed my father home. They broke his neck with a two-by-four and threw him in the ditch. Then they came back to town and bragged about it." When her mother and grandfather sought a lawyer, locals threatened to take the farm. To preserve their property and to have a place to raise and educate the children, her grandfather and mother opted not to pursue murder charges. "So I grew up a very bitter, very racist young woman," says Cordelia. "I was looking for revenge. But my grandfather, Joe Thompson, chose not to do anything. He was trying to teach me that love and forgiveness are the way to go, and that if you carry hatred, it would harm you more than the person you were hating. But I didn't understand that for a long time."

Cordelia carried the hatred with her into adulthood. When she and her husband moved to Milwaukee, she joined open housing marches that crossed the dividing line between blacks and whites. Bricks and bottles hailed down on her, and she seethed. The night that Martin Luther King was killed, the group stormed into downtown Milwaukee. Cordelia picked up a huge rock as the group marched. "I threw that rock and I broke a window in a department store," she says.

> It seemed like glass fell for an hour. I thought the glass would never stop falling. It came to me clearly that I was not marching for the right reasons. The hatred had built up in my heart, and I was doing anything I could to get relief. That night God spoke clearly to me and said, *This is not what I want you to do. This isn't truly from me. You have to do it my way.* I have been free since the evening I broke that window. I have not marched another march. I have never again looked at anybody with hatred in my heart because of the color of their skin. And I thank God for it.

While the hatred abated, the resentment resurfaced when she and her husband would travel with their small children to visit relatives in the South, and they would be refused use of restrooms in service stations, and could only buy hamburgers from the back door. "That's when the anger would come back. But I understood that God loved these people the same as he loved me." Undaunted by the burden of raising eight children, Cordelia went back to school to study nursing at the age of thirty-seven. The administrator discouraged her from applying, telling her she would never make it through with that many children, because she could only miss three days. In fact, Cordelia only missed one hour. Several years later she returned to school again, this time to get her RN degree, borrowing the money to pay her tuition and outperforming her classmates.

Cordelia later took a job in a large nursing home, hoping to make a difference in the way poor elderly people were treated. She saw "people who had a sparkle in their eye when they came in, but they lost the motivation to live." She saw arbitrary rules for residents that were convenient for the staff but hampered the quality of life for the elderly. She saw care driven more by costs than by caring. Frustrated at the nursing home administration's lack of responsiveness to her suggestions, she vented to her husband, who challenged her to open her own home.

Cordelia accepted the challenge. She set out to create an institution for elderly people that would be more like a real home, and make care available to them regardless of their income. At the time, she and her family were living in an elite suburban area of Milwaukee in a lovely house they cherished. It had been the fruit of their hard work, and represented a lifetime of overcoming racial and economic boundaries. Reversing the direction of all logic, Cordelia and her family chose to be downwardly mobile, moving back into the inner-city neighborhood she had left years before. They fixed up their broken-down house room by room, living in the midst of the crime and squalor they had escaped. She says she worked with indefatigable energy because "It was a mission God had given to me." When they opened Family House, eight residents moved into the home with them. During the first five years, Cordelia worked another part-time job to buy groceries.

Two rival gangs had shooting matches at night, with bullets zinging over the backyard of the house. The elderly residents hid under their beds. The local police were unresponsive until one day when Cordelia, fed up with the warfare, drove down to police headquarters and told them that unless they took action, she would take her plight to the local television station. By the time she got back, there were police cars swarming the neighborhood.

Drug dealers shamelessly trafficked on their street, counting on the fact that blacks living in the neighborhood wouldn't report them to the police. A building in the alley behind her home had a drive-through drug pickup. Cordelia was incensed with their brazen trafficking and walked out boldly to tell the dealers to take their business elsewhere. One man pulled a gun on her. "I told him to go ahead and shoot. He'd just get me to heaven faster than I had planned to go." She fixed him with her steady gaze, and he slowly lowered the gun. Then he put it in his pocket and said, "I won't be back, lady. You can have this neighborhood."

The fact that Cordelia had the courage to face down the drug dealers changed the climate of the neighborhood. What started out as one Family House has expanded, as Cordelia has bought one adjacent house after another. The Family House now encompasses one side of almost an entire city block. It has become a home for the elderly with the feel of a genuine home rather than an institution. The residents each have their own rooms with their names on the doors. Hand-made quilts are thrown across the chairs. People are free to go to bed when they want to, watch night baseball if that's their passion, and linger at the table after meals. A fountain graces the wide open yard they all share behind the adjacent houses, where residents can sit on benches. In the garden plot, neighbors grow vegetables and children learn about plants from the seniors. Residents with Alzheimer's or dementia can amble safely in the enclosed common yard. While the houses remain freestanding, they are all connected at the rear with wooden decks accessible to wheelchairs, which also lend themselves to basking in the sun and chatting with a neighbor. An old grocery store across the street has been transformed into a clinic. Now Cordelia has hopes of taking over the liquor store on the corner that just closed, renovating the bullet-pocked building and adding it to her home.

Family House now has fifty-eight people living there, with a staff of forty-five caring for them round the clock. Residents are fifty-five or older, and may not be violent or actively using street drugs or alcohol. Many of them pay only a portion of their cost, but no one is turned away if they cannot pay. The current budget is $2 million, and Cordelia has to raise two-thirds of it each year. A team of registered nurses, medical technicians, and certified nursing assistants handles the medical care, while other staffers prepare meals and keep the homes spotless. Five of Cordelia's eight children work there with her, and they are being groomed as future leaders.

Family House, a multigenerational ministry, has become an anchor for the community. Responding to local needs, Cordelia has added elements to Family House to nurture the neighborhood. Food, medical care, job training, and after-school help for neglected kids are all pressing needs. So Family House has responded to those creatively. Cordelia's son, James, often found youngsters sitting on the steps as he brought in groceries. He tossed them an occasional piece of fruit, but soon concluded he would do more good if he asked them first if they had done their homework. The kids' requests for help led to launching an after-school program, which now serves fifty-one children.

A food pantry was added to provide nourishment for the local residents, and is feeding three to four thousand people each year. Cordelia gives young mothers grocery staples and teaches them how to shop economically and prepare food. There's an acute need for jobs in the neighborhood, so entry-level positions on the staff have gone to a number of young people who were welfare recipients. Cordelia sees this as an opportunity to teach the disciplines of employment while imparting marketable skills.

Medical needs face not only the elderly, but all local residents. So Cordelia converted a grocery store into a medical clinic that offers care for anyone who walks in, regardless if they are insured. She dispenses pharmaceutical samples to fill prescriptions for free. The clinic also serves as an entry-level teaching facility to groom young women for the nursing profession: Cordelia teaches them how to take temperatures, monitor blood pressure, and administer basic medications. And the clinic is used to teach neighborhood residents the essentials of nutrition and preventive health care while giving them a better option than an emergency room for primary care. The clinic handled more than two thousand visits in 2003.

A wall full of plaques indicates that Cordelia Taylor and Family House have garnered much attention. She was "discovered" by Robert Woodson, founder of the National Center for Neighborhood Enterprise, and has been given national visibility through his organization. Several Milwaukee foundations have generously supported Family House, as have other donors. Not all inner-city ministries are as fortunate, she admits. Being able to present her story the compelling way she does gives her an advantage. "I am one of the blessed people to have an education along with my mission. There are a lot of small missions that have the vision and great ministries, but don't have the educational background. They have difficulty articulating what they do, and don't have the relationships outside their neighborhoods."

While a number of people have come to Family House to see if they could replicate its success, the most unusual visit was a delegation from Georgia in the old Soviet Union. They had come to America on a fact-finding mission to find models for medical care. The upscale medical college they visited struck them as unattainable in their present economy, but its president recommended that they take a look at Family House as a more approachable model. The Georgian minister of health was enthusiastic, and they are now emulating Cordelia Taylor's example in a very unlikely place: in the ashes of the collapsed Soviet empire.

Cordelia credits faith with the fruits her work has yielded. "It's not because of me, but because of the vision God had for me, and the plan He wanted me to take on. Then He sent people into my life to make it work." Determined but modest, she says, "All of us have gifts. If we put our gifts to work, and have faith in God, we can make changes not only in our own lives, but in the people's lives around us." As the drug dealers in the neighborhood discovered, don't get in the way of a woman on a mission from God.

Best Practices: Family House

- Buying adjacent properties to create a critical mass in the neighborhood
- Providing care for the elderly in a financial model that absorbs costs of those who cannot pay fully
- Maintaining the dignity of the people served
- Meeting multiple needs in the community as they emerge—food, medical care, job training, after-school programs—without losing focus on the mission
- Using opportunities to teach local residents health basics and nutrition

Results

- Facility serves 58 elderly, indigent residents with 24-hour long-term care
- One entire city block reclaimed from drug dealers and disorder
- Decreased crime in the neighborhood; jobs provided for residents
- Medical care provided in 2,000 visits to clinic in 2002

- Food pantry feeds 3–4,000 neighbors annually
- Fifty neighborhood children served in after-school program

Eugene Rivers: Ten Point Coalition

Frustration can foster clarity. Fed up with the crack addiction, drive-by shootings, and stabbings in the neighborhood, Rev. Eugene Rivers once took on a drug dealer in Boston and asked him what he was doing wrong as a pastor. Why was he losing the battle for the kids on the street? "It's simple," the drug dealer replied. "When Johnny goes to school in the morning, I'm there and you're not. When he comes home from school in the afternoon, I'm there and you're not. When his grandmother sends him out for a loaf of bread at the corner store, I'm there and you're not. I win, you lose."[13]

It seemed so obvious. The Pentecostal preacher who had been in a gang as a kid growing up in South Chicago and North Philadelphia grasped it immediately. Unless pastors could take it to the streets, they were never going to have a chance to capture kids' hearts and push back the tidal wave of violence engulfing the 'hood. The Harvard-educated man not only had academic training, he had enough street smarts to know that the drug dealer was onto something.

What grew out of that encounter was an initiative that mobilized pastors in the Boston neighborhood of Dorchester. Rivers, as the pastor of the Azusa Christian Community, had found himself smack in the middle of confrontations. His house had been shot into twice and burglarized more often than that. He teamed up with other pastors from three dozen churches to form the "Ten Point Coalition" and joined forces with the local police to take on the local troublemakers. If the police would handle the one kid in ten who really needed to end up in juvenile justice as a violent offender, they would take on the other nine. They got alternative sentences and community service hours for them, beefed up educational offerings, and found mentors, jobs, and drug treatment for the young offenders. They organized neighborhood patrols. Cops and clergy made a common cause to keep kids from being killed.

The results were impressive. In less than a decade, the crime rate dropped 77 percent. Instead of the twenty juvenile homicides per year that had become the norm, there were none for five years running.[14] The phenomenon became known as the "Boston miracle." Now Rev. Eugene Rivers and his wife, Jacqueline, are taking the approach to other cities. The National Ten Point Coalition has successfully mobilized strategists in cities including Indianapolis, Gary, Memphis, Tulsa, and most recently, Los Angeles. Other cities are seeking to emulate the model, and several major foundations have stepped up to fund its replication.

Pastor Rivers is passionate about the cause and doesn't care who he offends in saying so. "We have a generation of young people drowning in their blood, looking for their fathers. God wants us to wake up the black church and do something. He's challenging us to stop looking for a hand-out. He's challenging us to do something new." Impatient with the political jockeying that has gone on regarding faith-based initiatives, Rivers confronts believers, asking: "Are we more committed to Republican or Democrat ideology or Jesus Christ?" He has drawn praise from conservatives who like his self-help approach, but also from liberals, who approve of his seeking government support for his initiative. Unfazed by either, Rivers steers an independent course. He roasts the churches that have become so sanctimonious they don't welcome sinners. "It's easier for a girl to find refuge in a crack house than a big inner-city church," he thunders. But no pushover for kids, Rivers doesn't shy away from telling parents their fourteen-year-old son is a sociopath, if he is. Impatient with the hesitation of the philanthropic community to get behind his effort several years ago, he gave a meditation like a flamethrower one Sunday morning at a conference, where a wealthy Christian businessman sat. "Until I see something better than the rich young ruler who wouldn't let go of his wealth, I'm not going to be convinced of anybody's authenticity," he said pointedly. "If you want to go and play in your sandbox with your other friends having a midlife crisis, fine. But don't play with me."

This confrontational streak can offend, and sometimes does. But the fire behind it is a zeal to change lives and neighborhoods. He wants to intervene, and his urgency is great. Since the number of young black males killing each other has exceeded the death tally of the Ku Klux Klan, it is time for action, says Rivers. Disciples need to step up and put their faith into action. "Our faith has to be incarnational, visible in the willingness to save the poor. The world is looking for authenticity, people of God to model the thing. Kids need to see the common spirit of servanthood among God's people. We, the body of Christ, have to make good on our profession of faith."

Ten Point Coalition Strategy to Mobilize Churches

1. Establish "adopt-a-gang" programs to serve as drop-in centers and sanctuaries for troubled youth
2. Commission advocates and ombudsmen for black and Latino juveniles in the courts
3. Commission youth evangelists to do one-to-one evangelism with young drug traffickers
4. Establish community-based economic development projects, including micro-enterprise and worker cooperatives
5. Link suburban and urban churches to provide spiritual and material support
6. Initiate crime-watch programs near local churches
7. Collaborate with health centers and local churches to provide pastoral counseling for families in crisis, drug abuse programs, and abstinence training
8. Convene Christian black and Latino men and women to develop rational alternatives to violent gang life
9. Establish rape crisis drop-in centers and services for battered women
10. Develop a black and Latino curriculum for churches focused on the struggles of women and poor people[15]

Results

Seventy-seven percent drop in crime in Boston in the targeted area over a decade

chapter 2

John Perkins

Raw Violence and Reconciliation

John Perkins has a distinguished pedigree as a street saint. "My people in Mississippi were bootleggers and gamblers as far back as I can go," he says.[1] The third-grade dropout from a sharecropper's family grew up in a tense time in a Mississippi rife with violence and racism. From that background he has risen to become a reconciler and a leader who has fostered the community development movement now changing America's impoverished communities from the grassroots up.

Perkins has overcome major obstacles. His mother died when he was seven months old, and his father gave him to his grandparents to be raised. John grew up sleeping on a shuck bed with seven people in it most nights. His brother, Clyde, returned from defending America in World War II only to be killed by a U.S. marshal outside a movie theater in a small town in Mississippi—as he defended himself in a fracas with racial overtones. John had every reason to want to escape this brutality and futility.[2]

"As blacks after World War II we had just three choices," John recalls in his autobiography. "We could stay in the state and become dehumanized . . . and accept the system. We could go to jail or be killed. Or we could leave rural Mississippi and go to one of the big cities. My family decided it was no longer safe for us in Mississippi, so most of us left and went to California" (17). He made a good living there, as did his wife, Vera Mae.

Although he had previously dismissed religion as useless, while he was in California, John became a changed man through conversion and began to immerse himself in scripture. The last thing he wanted to do was return to the backwater of poverty and racial tension, but God had something else in mind. In a voice audible only in his spirit, John sensed these words: *My desire for you is that you go back to Mississippi, because your people have a zeal for God, but it is not enlightened.*[3]

In obedience that defied all logic, John and Vera Mae returned to Mississippi. There they plunged into work in the grassroots of the community in Mendenhall. He settled his wife and children into a house with a tin storefront for $60 a month, lived off groceries and gas money donated from churches where he spoke, and was grateful to have plumbing. As a preacher, John rallied the youth in schools and organized evangelistic tent meetings. While John's evangelism was effective, he became aware that the needs of the community were so deep that preaching alone could never get to the deepest issues of most people's lives. John's approach was holistic: he wanted to meet their needs for basic necessities to live, but he also wanted to share the message of the Gospel. "If a person is hungry," he says, "you've got to keep him alive until faith comes."

John and Vera Mae decided that meeting physical needs would be at the center of their ministry. "We were reminded daily of where people were hurting. We would watch the roaches crawl up and down their walls. We ate their cornbread and milk even when it was the only thing in the house. We felt the wind as it came through the cracks in the walls. And what we discovered was that God's love in us created real responses: we wanted to counsel, to get food, and to fix homes" (64).

People began to come to them for advice on how to get a loan, or where to get medical care for a sick child. "You have to start with the person's own defined felt need, to understand them and identify with them," John explains. "Then that person is more apt to respond to you in a more loving and wholesome way. Christianity is the offering of God's love in reality." He discovered that the best vehicle for communicating the Gospel is to put love into action through relationship, "and when programs emerge they have to emerge out of that person's felt need."

Getting at the Roots of Poverty

As John worked with families in Mississippi, he concluded that poverty is more than the absence of money; it is a condition of the mind and spirit as well. It's a mentality that can infect an entire culture. John saw, for example, Miss Hester and her children tearing wood off the outside of their house to start a fire to cook in the summer, oblivious of the fact that winter would descend in only a few months. "You could look right through the floor and see that the wood blocks that held the house up had been cut on, time and again to get splinters to build a fire with. Eventually you could see through the whole house." John realized that for "Miss Hester and many folks like her, poverty had moved beyond her physical condition to claim her whole mind. For the real poor, poverty means thinking just for the moment. It is the inability to think about the future because of the total demand to think about survival in the present. It is a culture, a whole way of life. A little money can't help much" (82). Poverty of this kind is passed on through generations, as evidenced by one of Miss Hester's daughters, Mamie, who later lived with her malnourished children in a rat-infested two-room shack, huddled around a trash-can fire to warm them in the winter.

John understood that it was going to take deep changes in both the mindsets of the poor and in the community to produce whole, responsible people. What grew out of this awareness took shape in Jackson through the Voice of Calvary in 1972, in its holistic approach to healing a community. Over time, the Voice of Calvary began to provide day-care programs, food for needy children, adult education, and a medical clinic. John and Vera Mae invested a great deal of their efforts in children, teaching them the Bible to shape their characters and minds early.

Breaking the Cycle

John was frustrated by the shoddy housing, unsanitary living conditions, malnutrition, lack of medical care, and poor education of rural Mississippi blacks. He saw a cycle of hopelessness linking malnutrition to dropping out of school, because children couldn't concentrate. He saw the lack of education was clearly linked to unemployment, and poor housing was linked to disease. Racism and violence blocked the exit from the cycle. Whites paid blacks lower than minimum wage for jobs, and threatened those who didn't play along. John pulls no punches in criticizing the white church for neglecting the plight of blacks. He claims,

> With a few exceptions—some preachers during the Great Awakening, the small heroic minority of people involved in the Abolitionist movement, and later those few white protestants who helped develop a handful of black schools—there has been, since the original enslavement of the black man in America, no systematic, concerted effort on the part of evangelical white Christians to evangelize or to develop any sort of community uplift in the black community. (97)

John says today, "The white church has lived so long with the injustice of a black person that it's difficult for them to think of black concerns being equal to their concerns." He is highly critical of "cheap involvement," the kind that meets "some random symptoms a person has without getting down to the real needs, without asking those difficult questions about why those needs are there, what causes them, and how we get down to the root of the problem" (100). Both government welfare and church charity have failed, says John, because they don't reach the root causes of poverty, nor do they train local people to develop communities from within.

John Perkins's efforts through the Voice of Calvary came at a time when racial tensions were increasing across the country. Recall the climate of the time. In June 1963, Medger Evers, the field secretary of the NAACP, was killed. Two months later 200,000 people marched on Washington, D.C., in a massive protest for civil rights. President Lyndon Johnson signed the Civil Rights Act into effect in July 1964, just weeks before three civil rights workers were murdered by the Ku Klux Klan. In the summer of 1965, Los Angeles burned in the Watts riots, which left thirty-five dead and nine hundred injured and seared the heart of the country. Churches in Mississippi went up in flames. In April 1968, Martin Luther King Jr. was assassinated on a hotel balcony in Memphis, and the bold dream he had for the nation was all but extinguished. A man who was committed to peaceful means for change had been killed by the violence he wanted to end.

John Perkins wanted change, but he was convinced it must be peaceful. He was firmly convinced that the real energy for change had to be mobilized from within the black community. He saw that lifting the heads of those who were bowed with a victim mentality was necessary. He knew that ownership of a solution was crucial for its implementation, and that unless individuals participated in formulating a plan, they would never buy into it at the deepest level. As he put it, "people defend what they help create" (132). Anything less than a community-based solution could never accomplish what was needed.

John believed that ownership lifts human dignity while fostering responsibility. He was inspired by a black Catholic priest, Father Albert J. McKnight, who introduced him to the concept of cooperatives. McKnight had been frustrated by his inability to penetrate Louisiana poverty through literacy programs, and had hit upon the idea of forming cooperatives to help people purchase fertilizer and farm supplies, set up bakeries, and establish gas stations. McKnight invited John to become a local affiliate to establish a similar effort in Mississippi to give blacks the economic means for self-help by developing ownership.

Part of the change came in moving people from a consumer mentality to one of ownership. "Exploited people consume far more than middle-class people," says John. "We buy more furniture, more cars, more clothes" (134). He discovered by setting up cooperatives that the mindset changes when people take responsibility for themselves. Local people can create their own capital with a credit union. Once they begin to save, they begin to create an economic base. And with that base comes independence. "Unless people can help themselves," says John, "nothing will break the mindset of dependency that's behind poverty."

Confrontation Has a Price

In 1969, the black community in Mendenhall was seething under mistreatment. Black drivers were stopped and harassed, black workers were paid less than minimum wage, illegal searches and arrests were common, and hostility and verbal abuse was frequent. Their pleas for paved streets, access to desegregated recreation facilities, and decent-paying jobs fell on deaf ears. John received death threats for his activism, calls at night, saying, "If you want to live, you'd better get outta' town." When the local constable hauled in two black men one day in December 1969, John had had enough. He and a group of seventeen went to the courthouse to check on the fate of one friend, and into the local jail to see whether another was being beaten. He had been, and the whole group decided to stay in the prison as a protest.

"I figured that things had reached the place in our town, and other small communities just like Mendenhall all over Mississippi, where in the end someone from each of these communities would have to be willing to give up his or her life in order to stop the machinery of injustice from just continually grinding people up. There in jail, I decided that I was willing to be one of those persons" (158). John went to the second-floor window of the jail and spoke to the people gathered in the darkness outside. He called for a boycott of the local stores in the Christmas rush as a protest against the injustice. The black community rallied behind him.

He led marches every week throughout February, which began to attract students. An incident erupted on February 7, 1970, that turned violent. A highway patrolman pulled over a van of participants from the march alleging reckless driving. With guns drawn, patrolmen from four to six cars swarmed over the passengers, handcuffed them, and arrested them. The driver was beaten on the way to the jail. Once inside the jail, John Perkins and two other leaders of the civil rights march were "beaten with blackjacks, kicked, punched and verbally abused," according to the court brief filed later. Two of the leaders had their heads shaved, "and the sheriff himself pour[ed] moonshine whiskey over one of them." One of them had his head "split open with a blackjack."[4]

John spent the next week healing from the severe beating. But he was determined to march again. The Saturday after his release, demonstrators were to gather again in front of the co-op building. But the city refused to issue a parade permit, and the highway patrol set up a roadblock. Vera

Mae got a nervous call from a woman who worked downtown. "Sister Perkins, you can't march today. There's about one hundred National Guard and highway patrol up here at the armory, and they all got guns. You tell Rev. Perkins not to go out there. They gonna kill him" (163). But John was determined, despite his lumps and bruises, not to give in. "If we didn't march, it would look like we had lost. So we were determined to march, even if it meant physical abuse or death."

A group gathered at the cement brick building that day not knowing if it would be their last march, but they were not cowed. There was determination crackling in the air. People came who had never been there before, swelling their ranks to nearly two hundred people. They began to sing:

> My Mama, she done tole me;
> She tole me on her dyin' bed—
> She tole me, "Son, you'd better get your freedom,
> Or I'd rather see you dead."

John linked arms with Vera Mae and the other leaders, leading the crowd out of the tight circle they had formed together. He gives a riveting account of the showdown:

Like a rope uncoiling, the marchers left the co-op, wound down Center Street in front of our white house and Bible Institute building, turned right on Circle Street and followed it around to Dixie Street. We marched down Dixie Street, spilling over both sides of the street, past the tin store-front that had been the Fishermen's Mission and the tarpaper shacks that lined both sides of the street. As we marched, all the people knew the plans of not allowing us past the end of the street. They had seen the highway patrol and the sheriffs armed with shotguns and riot guns. And so they knew (or at least they thought they knew) that we were marching to our deaths. That was the power behind the march. That was what sent women screaming into their houses when they saw us coming down the street—they were afraid of what was going to happen to us. Yet for some strange, instinctive reason, masses of people joined the march. . . . We picked up momentum. . . . We marched up to the place where they were going to stop us and kept going. . . . When we finally got up to the tracks all seemed eerie and unnatural as a squadron of sheriffs, highway patrolmen, and National Guard armed with shotguns and tear-gas rifles blocked our progress. Our group wound itself up in a knot right there in front of them. (164)

John faced the crowd, which contained both black and white faces, and spoke forcefully: "What it comes down to is that we demand our freedom. We demand the power to determine the destiny of our community. Black people will not be free until we are able to determine our own destiny. Let's all join together. Let's pray for these men standing here protecting something that is destroying them and us too. Let's pray . . ." (164–65). And in that act of prayer, a power was unleashed that diffused the anger, suspended the justified resentment, halted the fingers poised on the triggers, and against all odds dispersed the crowd peacefully. No one was shot. No one was jailed. Not a single person was beaten. The forces for peaceful change had won that day.

A week later, they were granted a permit to march. And as the group began to circle the courthouse, John witnessed a scene that has been seared in his memory ever since. "The black women were cooking for the whites in their houses," he recalls, "wearing their white uniforms and aprons. The cooks and maids were usually the last people to resist because their whole life depended on that. When we were walking around the courthouse and got to the top side of the courthouse, Miss Womack came running from the house where she was a maid, with her white dress on, pulling off her apron. She couldn't hardly wait to join that march. It was like her one chance in a lifetime to express the depths of her desire for freedom." That image burned into John's brain, and the heat of her conviction scorched the whites watching. A local man who was there told John recently, "We saw in that group of black people marching that you had decided that death would not stand between you and what you wanted. And that was frightening."

The personal toll on John was severe. Over the coming months, his body showed the strain of the previous struggles. He suffered a mild heart attack that summer and major ulcers the next year, which necessitated the removal of two-thirds of his stomach. He lost thirty pounds. His civil rights struggle was far from over, as he had to face down charges of disturbing the peace for that night in the Mendenhall jail. As he sat outside the courthouse one day, dejected, a woman came to him whom he did not know, but who left an indelible impression on him. As he sat alone, his head in his hands, she embraced him and said, "Stand up, young man. You're standing for a whole race of people." He never knew her name, but he has never forgotten her words.

Raw Violence

John's confrontation with raw violence wasn't yet finished. When a group of students were arrested in nearby Brandon, John went to post bail. "There were three of us," he recalls. "They started beating us when we got in there. And then in there the sheriff began to curse us and say 'this is a new ball game now. This is not Mendenhall. You are in my county now.' And they began to beat us and torture us. One of the sheriffs took a pistol and cocked it and put it to the side of my head and pulled the trigger. . . . In my mind I was a dead person."[5]

In that split second as he was sure he faced certain death, John was pleading with God. He looked into the eyes of the people torturing him and saw their hate. "I said, 'God if you'll let me out of this jail, I really want to preach a gospel that is stronger than my race, that is stronger than my economic interest. I want to preach a gospel that can reconcile.'"[6] As the hammer of the pistol landed, there was a click. There was no bullet in the chamber. He exhaled with profound relief. But his ordeal was not yet over. One of his jailers took a fork and bent prongs on it and shoved it up John's nose until blood gushed out. More violent torture ensued. He hovered "between the reality and the insanity, between the consciousness and the unconsciousness that would sweep across my dizzy mind, between my terror and my unwillingness to break down, between my pain and my fear, in those little snatches of thought when in some miraculous way I could at once be the spectacle and the spectator, God pushed me past hatred. Just for a little while, moments at a time" (190).

"I saw these people no longer as normal human beings. I saw them as animals, as demons, and that's what pushed me past hatred. I saw the sinfulness of sin," John says today. "How could I hate when there was so much to pity? How could I hate people I suddenly did not recognize, who had somehow moved past the outer limits of what it means to be human? It would have been different if the men had been in control of themselves. But the realization that kept pressing in on my mind was that these men were infected, hopelessly sick, possessed by something which caused their faces to lose that ingredient that made normal features look human" (190).

"I saw that hate and that hate scared me. And during those days after my beating in the Brandon jail, the pain and the agony being in the hospital . . . I could almost sense that it was a weight on me." John had physically survived the ordeal, but the damage he sustained was not only from the abuse, but from experiencing the hatred of his jailers. John began to think about Christ's admonition that "unless you can forgive those that trespass against you, how do you expect your heavenly Father to forgive you. I began to see that forgiveness was my way of shedding the reaction of hatred in my own life. It's not so much for the sheriff. . . . It is really for myself."[7]

How could he find the strength or willingness to forgive? He says today, "I think it had already been the grace of God in my life that had prepared me for that moment. When I was first converted, I was discipled by whites and blacks together in an environment that I thought was the nature of Christianity. There was not a time that I did not believe that the Gospel was stronger than race. I experienced it, and did not want to lose that freedom."

Misfired Attempts to Eradicate Poverty

John has worked with both blacks and whites in the years since to reconcile the races and renew communities. He is critical of many government attempts to aid the black community, and says the past forty years are lit-

tered with failed attempts to eradicate poverty. While John embraces President Bush's Faith-Based Initiative today, he blasts earlier "cheap forms of
involvement that don't have any impact and in fact damage people in the
black community." He says, "We have seen the failure of one program after
another as we have worked in the community. In the poverty program and
other programs of cheap involvement, we have what I would call the failure of liberalism" (146). The food distributed in the commodity program
wasn't the kind of food the people ate, so it ended up being fed to their
hogs. The food stamp program didn't alleviate the problem of hunger, but
did benefit the white storeowners. "One reason other poverty programs
failed was that they would never allow for community ownership. If you
started a black self-help program with government money, you could rent
buildings and you could rent furniture; you could lease cars, but you
could not own anything. And it was supposed to break the cycle of poverty. But ownership is the way to break the cycle of poverty" (147).

John is just as critical of the half-baked attempts that have come out of
the white church community:

> For many white Christians, strategies for involvement in the community are
> based on a volunteer or charity mentality. Our white society's concept of
> charity is one of the main stumbling blocks to real community development.
> This is because in white society, charity can blind people to reality and sub-
> stitute cheap action for expensive action. And when I say this to my white
> brothers and sisters they get very uncomfortable. But charity blinds us and
> keeps us from seeing that our whole system works methodically against the
> development of certain people—economically, educationally, spiritually, and
> socially. The white person who is part of that system and benefits from it uses
> charity in order to cleanse his or her conscience and in order to have a means
> for not dealing with the big issues. (148–49)

John is convinced that people of Christian conviction need to step out
to fulfill the vision God gives them, even if it's not comfortable. "A vision
comes when God looks down and sees the aches and pains. He gives it to
an individual and God says 'do you see what I see?' A vision is when you
see it. A leader is simply a person with a vision beyond, that interacts with

the pain God sees in the society."[8] Because John Perkins was willing to see the pain in the community and was open to approaching it with a fresh vision, he was instrumental in launching a grassroots approach to community renewal. It builds upon the strengths and capabilities already present in the community, mobilizing and bolstering them. Rather than bringing in solutions from the outside, it brings together the stakeholders to chart their own course, giving them ownership of the process and its outcomes. It stresses personal responsibility and fosters economic ownership. The legacy of John Perkins's work in Mendenhall remains in a church, farm, health center, and school he founded there. In Jackson, a health center and a housing development corporation he planted are meeting local needs.

In 1983, John founded the Harambee Christian Family Center in Pasadena, California, which has a very different demographic profile than rural Mississippi, with its Californian mix of Latinos and African Americans. Targeting a twelve-block area adjacent to the center, he embarked once again on developing the community from the grassroots up. The corner where the center is located was known as "blood corner" because of the number of drive-by shootings. The neighborhood had the highest daytime rate of crime in California. But now there's a prep school grooming youngsters for academic success, and an after-school tutoring program for neighborhood kids is giving them a leg up. What John and Vera Mae Perkins launched was continued by their son, Derek, and by Rudy Carrasco, who now serves as its executive director. Most of the staff and volunteers for the award-winning program live near the center in order to be incarnational leaders who serve their neighbors.

John founded the John M. Perkins Foundation for Reconciliation in Jackson in 1983. He also founded the Spencer Perkins Center for Reconciliation and Youth Development, which focuses on the spiritual, academic, and social development of local young people, offering them Bible study, tutoring, and summer day camp. It also serves as a training center in Mississippi for high school and college students who come as work groups or interns. Some come for a week; others stay for an entire summer or even for several years. It's hands-on training for at least 350 students every summer. And most recently, he has founded Inside Out, a prison ministry to reduce the 85 percent recidivism rate in Jackson.

Lessons Learned from a Street Saint

Stepping back and looking at the overarching principles of community renewal that have characterized John Perkins's work, three Rs emerge: reconciliation, relocation, and redistribution. Racial reconciliation is essential for renewal because it unites. He saw in Mendenhall that the Lord was at work creating more than a program:

> He was creating his church, the Body of Christ. I saw the deep unity between black and white brothers and sisters and remembered Paul's words in Ephesians: "For he is our peace who has made us both one, and has broken down the dividing wall of hostility . . . that he might create in himself one new man in place of the two, so making peace, and might reconcile us both to God in *one body*, thereby bringing the hostility to an end."[9]

That kind of reconciliation "has to happen in the context of involvement in the life of that person," John says today. "It's a process, not an intellectual thing. It's contextual theology, with the people there."

John calls for redistribution, not the kind that uses federal taxes to redistribute wealth via a Washington program, but a locally rooted kind, one that transfers skills that lead to personal and economic development. He means a structured response of an entire community "to develop people and to allow them to begin to determine their own destinies." John says, "It's education to transfer the skills to save, invest, and own. These skills lead to success, an investment that produces money, but if you just give the money first, instead of the skills, it doesn't help." His primary concern is meeting the needs of the whole person through Christ, not a political agenda. "I'm a Christian social activist," he says, "not a social activist and a Christian. It anchors our sociology in Christianity, instead of liberalism or socialism."

Key Principles of John Perkins's Work

- Start with a person's felt need
- Relocate into the neighborhood served
- Redistribute skills; transfer knowledge
- Reconcile the races
- Eradicate poverty through ownership
- Lead through love

Based on his years of experience, John is convinced that "because leadership must come from the community and must have a central unifying commitment, *it is almost required that the organizer live in the community, with the people.* Commitment is more caught than taught, so association is crucial" (130). Relocating into the community is one of the essential qualifications for effective work of this kind. "Relocation brings you into the same environment with the people you work with. You see their pain. It brings you into the same realm, brings you into humanity with humility and prepares you for service."

One vibrant manifestation of both reconciliation and relocation is the deep and trusting relationship that grew between John Perkins and H. Spees, who came from an upper-middle-class suburban California background for a summer and ended up spending the next eleven years at John's side. H. and his wife Terry had their children in Mississippi and made the deepest kind of commitment there is—for H. to stay as co-laborer and as a living presence of reconciliation. Through the tutelage of John and the years of experience they shared in Mississippi, H. Spees became one of the most effective leaders now making an impact in community renewal.

The kind of renewal they embody illustrates the principles of a Chinese philosopher John likes to quote in a poem called "Serving the People."

> Go to the people.
> Live among them.
> Learn from them.
> Love them.
> Serve them.

Plan with them.
Start with what they know.
Build on what they have. (125)

John Perkins discovered, through the toughest trials and abuse, principles of renewal that have now spread throughout the country. Thanks to his wisdom and experience, the Christian Community Development Association has been created and now convenes thousands of practitioners from America's cities every year to learn from each other and to build relationships with other street saints working on the front lines. The depth and breadth of the movement is growing.

"Suffering Sharpens Us"

For someone who has as many scars—physical, emotional, and psychological—as John Perkins does, he would seem to be a very unlikely spokesman for racial reconciliation. But that is exactly what he has become, and in the years since his experience at the hands of violent jailers, he has become a tireless advocate for reconciliation. Precisely because he bears the stripes on his own body, his message is powerful. With a voice that speaks from the depths of experience, John says, "When I was almost beat to death, I saw the futility of racism. I believe that suffering sharpens us. We need to be a model of God's reconciling people. Jesus intended the church to be black, white, Jew and Gentile together. Racial reconciliation is not everything, but it's a big part of what God is doing."

As the ethnic dynamics of the United States have changed in the past thirty years, John's vision of reconciliation has expanded in an increasingly multi-ethnic country. "We need to raise up Hispanics, blacks, whites, Asians, people who do not forsake their racial identity, but don't let their race interfere with their mission in society. We've got to live beyond race. The world will know there is a miracle if we can do this together."[10]

His stirring message has taken John to audiences not only throughout the country, but elsewhere in the world. He found himself in the Holy Land on the eve of the new millennium, addressing representatives from the three monotheistic religions, Jews, Christians, and Muslims, who had gathered together as children of Abraham to pray for peace and reconciliation.[11] John spoke on the same podium as Tommy Tarrants, a former member of the Ku Klux Klan, and they shared the story of their reconciliation through faith. Others addressing the gathering were a German aristocratic couple who were devoting the final years of their lives to apologizing to Jews for the inaction of the Germans in protecting them during World War II. Jewish parents of a girl slain by Palestinian terrorists were reconciled to the parents of her killer. Gandhi's great-grandson was among the participants. All of the people taking part in this conference met in a hotel and visited sites that had been targeted by Al Qaeda, we later found out. Al Qaeda operatives were arrested the day before the gathering began. The international message of reconciliation was threatened but not snuffed out by terror, and the need for it is as acute today.

Now, as John moves further into his seventies, he is fixing his sights on two Bible verses, one for his mission, one for his method. Acts 1:8 says: "But you will receive power when the Holy Spirit comes on you: and you will be my witnesses in Jerusalem, and in all Judea and Samaria, and to the ends of the earth." John reflects that while the neighborhood work he has done is important, the "greater mission is to carry the Gospel to the world. But I've seen that people are coming to us from all over the world and carrying it back with them." He lights the torch that they now carry. The verse that sets his method is 2 Timothy 2:2: "And the things you have heard me say in the presence of many witnesses entrust to reliable men who will also be qualified to teach others." John's main focus now is to teach and disciple those who come to him in Mississippi—high school and college students, members of different churches who have been flocking to hear him. Some come for a week, others for a month, a summer, or a year. As he shapes them, he communicates the wisdom of a lifetime as one of America's authentic street saints. He is equipping them to go and do likewise.

chapter 3

Brian King

A Gangster Disciple

Brian King got involved with the Gangster Disciples in Chicago when he was eleven.

His life in the gang was not much different from that of many young guys drifting in America's cities, environments rife with drugs and violence. The first time he went to jail he was

in the seventh grade. After Brian had seen 130 of his friends die, he didn't expect to survive

to the age of twenty. His family had given up on him altogether, and he woke up next to a

dead man on skid row. Brian's life has changed now, taking him to the front lines of the city

in a very different life. This is his story, in his words.[1]

I grew up on the South Side of Chicago in a pretty tough neighborhood, between two of the worst housing projects in the city. It was a big gang environment. My father was a Cook County sheriff, and he had a drinking problem. He would get drunk and it would escalate into violence against my mother. When me and my brother were eight or nine years old we woke up one night because our mother was hollering and screaming, and we ran out to see what was going on. It was my father attacking my mother, and we were scared. He told us to just go back in the room. I told my brother, "Man, next time it happens, I am going to try to do something."

Things got back to normal, maybe about six months, and he did it again. We had bunk beds, with the little slats that hold the bed up. I grabbed one of them and ran out there telling my father, "If you whip my mother again, I am going to hit you with this and I am going to kill you." I was eight at the time, and there I was standing toe-to-toe with my father. We lived in the middle of these projects, in the roughest neighborhood in Chicago, and had to fight to get home from school, and here I am standing toe-to-toe with the dude that is supposed to be protecting us from all that—and I'm protecting us from him. It had a psychological impact on me.

I could see that with no protection from inside the house, it got to come from somewhere. And so that year, I joined up with the gang in our school and I became one of the Baby Ds, the Baby Disciples. That allowed me to have protection in the streets or wherever I'd go. If something would come up where one of my buddies got into something, I had to step up and make sure that I had his back. I knew that I had to be a part of it because it meant my survival in the neighborhood. But this real fine protection and status kind of goes to your head, and it went to mine. We thought we could just about do what we wanted to because we got so many people that got our backs.

We hung out at the drug houses, and the guys started to invest in us to bring us along. Some of them had already been in jail, and they knew that if they had some young guys out there if we get caught as juveniles, the police would just give us a slap on the wrist. By the time I was eleven, the older guys used us to get stuff from the drug houses to the playground. We would make $100 a day, and at eleven years old that is some real good money.

I didn't know at the time that there was any way else to live, because everyone else in my environment lived this way. By now my father was gone—he left when I was eight. My mother was trying to do the best she could to take care of me and my brother with her job, then she got sick and had to have an operation. She had to go into semi-retirement and we had to move in with my grandmother, who worked every day. My grandmother would leave in the morning to catch the bus almost twenty blocks to get to work at five. My mother was trying to go back to school to learn how to be a beautician so that she could earn some type of money, so we were basically left to ourselves.

In the process of going to the drug houses we would see all the guys smoking marijuana, so we started to smoke marijuana. These were the only cats that took interest in us, and I think where we all got screwed up is that we came from an environment where everybody was out there looking for the same thing. Even the older guys who never had it were trying to give us some type of male role model to set an example. I think all of us were looking for acceptance from our father that wasn't there, and we went out on the streets looking for it and it wasn't there either. So we made up our own concept of what it is to love and respect and mentor the younger guys, which was screwed up.

One day as I was taking some of the drugs back to the drug house, we were going up the stairs and these three guys we knew made us knock and get the guys to open the door. They wanted to stick up the drug house and forced their way in. None of our buddies went for a pistol and the one guy killed a good friend of mine. I decided I wanted to have revenge on these guys. I been in a lot of shootouts since then.

I used to get in so many fights at school, I was in and out of a lot of schools. They kicked me out of public school and I had to go to these "bad boy" schools. I committed my first armed robbery in the seventh grade. The officer told my mother, "We're going to let him go now, but he'll be back." And he was right. From then on, I was in and out of jail.

I started doing heroin when I was about twelve. One of the older guys knew that I was able to get to the drugs because I was in the gang house when they bag it up, and they trust me, and they leave, and I could always take two or three bags and nobody would never know it. This guy used to be a big-time dealer, and was an addict now. I don't want to see him sick so I steal a few bags for him. I had been snorting heroin, but he showed me how to shoot it.

The drugs in my life started to escalate to the point that I was a full-blooded heroin addict. My drugs and my drinking got so bad my mother kicked me out of the house when I was thirteen. She would just push some sandwiches out the window to me. My whole community had written me off. They all said, "This cat won't live to be sixteen."

My drinking and drugging had got so bad by the time I was twenty-one that my family was gone; then the gang had turned their back on me. I was an alcoholic and a drug addict and I was living in anybody's house that would let me in. One day found myself on Madison Avenue, walking down skid row. Just twenty-one years old and I was just ready to die, man. I didn't even want to live another day.

My uncle had showed me this nice suit he had bought. He said, "This is the last time you'll see this suit, because the next time I'm going to be wearing this suit it's gonna be at your funeral, man. I am going to hang it up in the closet right now." And he was right, because I had involvement in really nothing. I was just one of them young guys on the street that's out there today, they're stoned, they don't care. They have no real understanding of life, they really have no ambition, no dreams, they have nothing.

I was on skid row, sleeping one night. When I woke up the man next to me was dead. I said, man I gotta do something. So I got into detox. While I was in detox, for some strange reason I went into a chapel. My mother had been talking about church, but I told her, "I'm not going to no church and doing none of that type of stuff." But here I was. It was a real small chapel. There was just a little bench, a little rail, a little altar, and a Bible. I sat on my knees and I was crying and I said, "God, please help me, man, I don't want to die." Then all of a sudden the door to the chapel just slammed and I hear a big, giant wind. It was the strangest thing because there wasn't a window or anything, but there was this wind. I just put my head down and I didn't want to look up. I was just crying, "Please, please

. . . I don't know nothing about God, I don't have no knowledge of anything spiritual. All I know is that they said Jesus is the son of God." I was
just scared to death. I asked God to please clean me up. I didn't understand what was happening. But something happened. Then I got up.
When I went back after being in that chapel I wasn't drinking or drugging
anymore. I haven't taken a drink or a drug since that day. I was twenty-one
then, I'm forty-one now.

So I cleaned up. I wasn't doing no more drugs. But I didn't get it with
a relationship to God. I wanted to start making a little money, like the
eleven-year-old boy I used to be who thought he was sharp, and could
make all this money selling drugs. So my idea was to go back to selling.
And since I didn't get high, I was thinking clear when everybody around
me was in euphoria. So I left that detox center and signed in a ninety-day
Salvation Army program. I was just staying there so I could get my
strength and my health back. So I stayed there for the ninety days, got my
hair cut, built me up a little wardrobe, and I'm going back to the street and
taking my corner back. I called my mother and I said, "Hey I'm clean, and
I want to come home for a little while." She was like, "Man, I heard this a
thousand times." By this time, I had been in about every institution in Illinois, every jail, every detox, every everything.

Before I went to the Salvation Army, I had misused women. I had
started messing with a girl, so when I got out I moved in with her and so
we were living together. I started running into people who know me from
my younger days. So this one guy and I, we really started trafficking. We
had another buddy that was with us that we used to send out there to LA
from Chicago to get cocaine because it was cheaper and we would get a lot
and take it back and break it up. I got in a group of older men that were doing things, and before I knew it we were in the projects and we were making $16,000 to $20,000 a day.

We had all the projects that stretched for miles, you can't even see the
end with the naked eye. Most of the people in the projects used drugs. In
the community it was 100 percent African American, 98 percent unemployment, 99 percent drug addiction. They was giving out welfare checks

alphabetically, so if you was like an Adams or Blackman you would get your check between the first and the third of the month, names beginning with C or D on maybe the fourth or fifth. So every day somebody's getting a check. And this whole thing of unemployment and public aid and drug addiction is in there, so it's so easy for you to get that money on a daily basis.

We were the Gangster Disciples, and it was like 100,000 of us. There was so much terrible stuff going on, so many buddies being killed. One night I decided to count all the friends I been through. I think I was up to 130 or 140 people dead. When I looked at the cause of death, besides my uncle and grandmother and maybe five others, mostly everybody had been killed, or OD'd on drugs, or drank themselves to death. I could re-member going to double funerals, two or three caskets there. I got so numb. Every day it was like, okay, you're next. I would leave the house and not know if I'm going to make it back. And I would go out and be ready to die. Because that's all I ever seen or known. I just decided okay, I'm gonna die here. This is it.

There was so many brothers getting killed and families being de-stroyed. I had two boys and a girl, by three different women. One of the guys told me, "Hey man, you know what goes around comes around again." He was insinuating someday somebody's gonna be out here selling drugs to my kids. That really worked on me because I tried to keep some conscience. I was around a lot of guys that didn't have no conscience at all. It wouldn't be nothin' for me to be in the room with seven, eight guys and six of them had already murdered somebody. So many unsolved homi-cides, nobody gonna tell the police nothing, none of them.

This one guy got out of prison and started a youth service, and he would always come down there and try to get me to come. And I'm like, "Why do I wanna go to your youth service, man? I'm out here getting thousands every day. I'm driving what I wanna drive, I'm wearing what I wanna wear, I get any girl I want, what you gonna give me in your youth service? I mean what y'all got down there?" And he would say, "You come down and see, man."

There was these three officers that really wanted to send me to prison forever. They knew I was one of the bigger drug dealers in the neighborhood. I said, man I'm getting away from down here. It just so happened that about then this guy with the youth service said to come on down. It looked good, four or five miles away. So I said, "All right, let's go." So me and four or five other guys went down. This cat got an office with my name on it and some business cards. And I'm like wha'? So I go and sit in the office, I'm looking out the windows, spinning around. I'm like, "This ain't half bad, man. I kind of like this here." He like, "Yeah, that can be yours, man." But in my mind I'm thinking, *This would be a real nice place for me to set up operation and sell drugs.*

This cat got us involved in all different types of stuff. He took us to a school in our community, and he was giving a presentation about the dangers of being involved in gangs. And he says, "Mr. King can talk about what can happen to you when you're in a gang." I'm like wha? I never knew nothing about giving no workshops. I went up there and I was telling them what was really going on, about how a brother could die, and how they got choices. They never heard a presentation like that in the raw about what's really happening. Then he took us to another seminar where he was talking with lawyers, people from probation and different law enforcement. And he had us give another presentation.

We went to schools, and one of the little guys came up to me afterward who was just going to join a gang, and he said, "Thanks, man, that really helped me." And I'm like, oh man, we helping the little guys. But the conscience is struggling, because when we leave the youth services at night, we go back on the streets. It started an internal struggle. I'm struggling like mad. I'm thinking I gotta get away from this youth service thing. And this man continues to invest in us, getting us to do things that we never imagined that we would do. He was genuine. He had been through the gangs. He knew where we were headed and he was trying to stop us from self-destructing.

He gave us the idea for a football team down there, raise some honest money, do a talent show to get a playground and buy uniforms. So we did our first "Boys in the 'Hood" talent show and raised money for our pee-wee football team. Man, this cat went even further. He said, "You need to go and join the police steering committee." I said, "Man, let me tell you something. I've had some bad experiences in those places. I don't think I'm going." But he says we need to go. We was the youngest people there. It was mostly made up of seniors who was scared and police officers and officials. One of the senior ladies said, "I'd like to hear from some of those young people that just came in." I stood up and told them we were down here trying to get in the loop to figure out what to do to make the community safer. I said, "We'd like to join this steering committee and plan with you guys." And they all clapped, and was excited they had us with them.

So now as this is going on, the drug business is taking a nosedive. No matter what I did, nothing would work. I could have some of the best drugs in the city and they wouldn't sell. They wouldn't do nothing. And I was losing interest and my buddies was like, "Hey Brian, come back and take the helm back." We had enough drugs to make at least $300,000 but I didn't really care. The guy with the youth service was working on a shoe-string budget and out of cash. He said, "It's easier for a kid to join a gang than it is gonna be for me to get somebody to help me keep these doors open." We were like, "We'll go hit the streets and shake something up and make some rent." He said, "No, you can't do that. It would destroy us. We're trying to do things legit." I had been volunteering at the youth service almost three years, and I felt so good about myself. But he called us in and said, "We don't have no more money. We got to close down." And I thought to myself, *God, I do not want to go back to the streets.* I really didn't know Christ, but I just knew there was a higher power. I was saying to him, "God, please, I really don't want to go back to the streets."

My buddy Tyrone was working out in Fresno, where he got a basketball scholarship in '79. He said come out to California. So I came out for a two-week Christmas vacation in '93. I still had a lot of that Chicago wild mentality in me. Tyrone—we called him T-Bone—said, "Man, get yourself together. I'll help you get a job and you can bring your family out here. Brian, I ain't letting you go back." So I stayed out here and had the rest of my clothes shipped out. They was starting a men's group where his wife worked, and they asked me to go be a part of it.

So I got there, and I thought these were some squares. These cats was talking about things that were real foreign to me. Stuff like you had to be the head of the household. And that don't mean that you sit back on your throne and point fingers and tell your woman, "Go get me this and that." I said, "It don't?" They was telling me it means you go out and make sure everything is taken care of—that you become the provider. I'm hearing this stuff, but I had so much hurt and anger and pain in me from living thirty-two years in that jungle that some of this stuff sounded real foreign to me. But it started registering.

I can remember the first time Tyrone took me to a park when he went to pick up his kids. People were swinging on swings and mothers were pulling kids in little red wagons. And I just started crying. The park flashed back to where I came from, where no kids was playing. It was nothing but grownups, dopeheads everywhere, and kids can't play in the park because there's guns and drugs.

These cats invited me to church, but I said that's going too far. But because they had been so nice, I did. And when I went to church with them the first time, I sat down and heard the Gospel. I heard about Jesus healing the blind man, and it just registered. It was the first time I heard the Gospel for real. I'd heard my neighbor saying I was going to hell, but I never heard anything about grace. I was saying, "Oh God, please." I was crying uncontrollable tears. *If this is what you say Jesus is, I want Jesus.* It had to be the drawing fire of the Holy Spirit that snatched me out of my seat. I went forward and I found myself standing at the altar crying, asking God to take me. You talk about relieved, man. I got so excited. I gave my life to Jesus and just started running for him.

I called one of my buddies that I had brought out of Chicago and said, "Man, we need to start our youth service again." We picked up what we learned in Chicago. So we started giving seminars to the sheriff's department. We started going into high schools. We went to all the different agencies, doing major events. We were feeding people and adopting the poorest families at Christmas.

There was a murder here. An innocent kid, a football player, was going home from practice and he got killed. There was people crowing all over and flapping around his mother. I didn't even know her, but after a while all the publicity died down and she was by herself. So I went and said, "I'm not a counselor or nothing, but since I see that nobody's calling you, if you want I'll meet with you once a week." Pretty soon, there's another mother whose son got killed, and I told her I'd meet with her once a week. So now I'm meeting with all these mothers, and they start telling other mothers, and soon I've got a group of families who have lost kids to senseless violence. And I'm seeing how God is using me—one of these same drive-by shooters—to bring families together who have lost kids to the same thing I used to do.

And things just started happening. It was crazy. Ever since, God has been placing me in spots where people are real broken and hurt, and I work with people coming through the things I experienced. He gave me a key to go into those places where his heart is—with the poor, in prisons, with widows. It's like a Green Beret, going into those dark holes and bringing people out. Getting kids out of gangs, working with families who lost kids through senseless violence, working with fathers to try to mend their families.

Now I'm working with incarcerated youth and with high-risk kids. We partner with high-risk kids and match them with mentors. We go out into the churches and bring in Christians to come alongside young men and women in the system to help them build a foundation and have an opportunity, instead of going back to that same environment. Fresno is unique in that we have a mayor that's a Christian, a police chief that's out praying with the mothers, and when there's another homicide, you can really sincerely see his brokenness. I think we gonna be able to make a major difference in this whole community because we're able to present opportunities. We're partnering with the police, taking the gang bangers on fishing trips and into the mountains. We're building a relationship with them where they see the police now, they say, "Hey, it's my buddy, Officer So-and-so." They're looking at these guys now as role models and mentors instead of what they were being told about them.

And I do a victim of violence family camp, where I'll take the whole family up to the mountains and start the healing process. We get counseling for the families in our community that can't afford counseling. We did a prayer vigil for the city, where the police chief, police captains, and residents from the community that have lost kids through senseless violence come out and light a candle for each of the homicides.

The first time I did the family camp, one of the mothers got up and said, "You know, the most innocent son in the world was killed, Jesus Christ. He said I wish this bitter cup could have passed away from me, but let his will be done and not mine." You know when you hear those mothers say things like that, you be so glad that you just being used. I be just sitting back wondering *God, why you putting me in these spots?* I think what he's doing is allowing me to build my conscience back.

I was somewhere speaking to a group of ladies, and man, I was bawling out of control. And I had to explain to them that I couldn't cry for a long time before. I told them, "I remember when I was looking at my grandmother in her casket and started to cry. One of the gang members tapped me on the side and said, 'Man, you can't cry—they looking, man.' I wasn't allowed to cry for this woman who cried for me, who fed me when I couldn't feed myself, who prayed for me when I couldn't pray for myself. And I couldn't cry for her." So I'm in front of this group of ladies, and I said, "I'm crying today because Jesus was able to save me, and he's allowing me to get my conscience back."

The dudes in my old neighborhood used a strategy to stop any success by planting a lie. They say, "Man, don't go downtown and try to get a job, because them white boys ain't gonna do nothing for you. They don't like us, man, you better not like them. They don't care about giving you no job. Don't trust them, don't do nothing with them. Ain't nobody got to tell you what to do. They gonna keep you enslaved." They created a false hatred in me, a prejudice against white people. But when I came out to California and I meet new people from everywhere, I said, "Those dudes sure lied to us, man." I found out you got good people from everywhere. All races, all colors, all backgrounds. They lied to us, but it was easy because it was 100 percent African American—my high school, my grocery store, my liquor store, my library, my fire department. Everywhere it was just African American. When God comes in, you start learning the truth.

I was talking to my mother and she was excited because I had won the NAACP Image Award for youth involvement and a number of other awards from senators and things like that. She said, "Brian, I know you thought I had really just thrown you away. But I'm telling you, I turned you over to God. I went into my prayer closet and I turned you over to God when you were eleven years old." I started to really meditate. And I thought about it. I thought about my uncle when he had that suit in his closet he said he was gonna bury me in. Then God is telling me, *The one thing he forgot is that your momma has a closet too—a prayer closet. And she went in and prayed, and I saved you. And now here you are, and you're saved, and you're filled with my Holy Spirit.*

When I gave my life to Christ, the only thing I knew how to do would either get me killed or sent to the penitentiary for the rest of my life because I had thirty-two years of straight garbage in my life. And then after I found Christ, he started adding and subtracting things, and putting people in place. Every time, I'd take a little bit of them with me, guys like H. Spees, who took time out for a season to allow me to see their hearts and learn. And now I take that back to the community along with all that God has given. So the message comes back like a universal message that's able to snatch a lot of kids out of the fire. And I'm sure we're doing something right every time I see some kids walking forward who are walking in the light. And it's awesome.

part ii

THE PROGRAMS

What Works and Why, as

Street Saints Change Lives

chapter 4

Rescuing America's At-Risk Kids

Youngsters all over the country are going home today to pockets in our cities where life is fractured. Maybe Dad's in jail. Mom may have a drug problem. Kids in the neighborhood are in gangs. There's shooting outside their door, and they know people who have been killed, even kids their own age. They wonder if they're going to live past eighteen. They don't know many families where two parents share the same home, or are even married for that matter. Hardly anybody has a hands-on, good dad they spend time with. They've scarcely been outside the neighborhood, let alone the state. Their school is a joke academically. They don't know many adults with a real job. Poverty is normal. And there's no reason to hope things are ever going to be better. These are America's at-risk kids. There may be as many as 8.2 million, but no one knows for certain.[1]

These facts illustrate the scope of the problem.[2]

- Child abuse and neglect have more than doubled in the past decade.
- One in four children under the age of six lives in poverty.
- Nearly four of ten children are being raised without a father.
- Seventy percent of long-term inmates and 75 percent of adolescents charged with murder grew up without fathers.
- A teenager in this country is killed every five hours.
- A preschooler is killed every thirteen hours.

The one thing at-risk kids are desperate for is a stable relationship. Street saints all over the country are walking into their lives to give them just that. There are a rich variety of faith-based programs to care for at-risk youth. Mentoring programs are linking one caring adult to a youngster in need. New schools are being planted in urban neighborhoods to offer a solid education and a ticket out of poverty. After-school programs abound to supplement education and to offer safe places for recreation. Youth entrepreneur programs are building character and marketable job skills. Abstinence programs like Best Friends and the Silver Ring Thing are reducing teen pregnancies. Gang intervention programs are helping kids leave, or avoid, a destructive life. Young Life, a popular program for suburban youth, is now reaching scores of kids through its Urban Youth Life. There are faith-based programs that focus on sports, or on micro-enterprises. Some bolster academics, while others like Homeboyz teach teenagers computer-programming skills and get contracts for them to produce work.[3]

But at-risk kids don't always come from urban environments. Curt Williams heads Youth-Reach Houston, a home that takes in the most troubled kids, the ones everybody else has given up on, including some frustrated suburban parents. These kids, most of whom have dealt drugs or been kicked out of school, appear to have been headed for a coffin or jail. In a rigorously structured program with high disciplinary standards, Curt and his round-the-clock staff remake the character of these derailed youngsters. If they stay—and not all of them choose to—they are slowly transformed.

Small churches in inner-city neighborhoods do significant work reaching kids who are endangered by their environment. Some pastors like Prince Couisnard in Houston open up their home in the 'hood, and are inundated with kids in a "hanging out" approach to ministry that disciples by example. Inner City Youth, which Prince began in 1992, has produced a new generation of young leaders who came through the program and are now working with the youngsters full time. Whiz Kids in Denver mobilizes seven hundred tutors from churches throughout the city and deploys them in forty urban churches for evening sessions of academics, games, and exposure to the Gospel. Sylvia Bolling founded Aldine

Y.O.U.T.H. to serve inner-city kids, but soon discovered she needed to address the needs of their families as well. She leads a dynamic neighborhood center with a multigenerational outreach, where everyone is asked to give their time and talent, rather than receive a handout.

What follows are other examples of faith-based programs for at-risk youth that are producing truly changed lives.

Casa de Esperanza: Loving Fragile Children into Wholeness

The most vulnerable among us are newborns born to addicted mothers, toddlers who are abused, and children with AIDS. These are the children to whom Kathy Foster and Bill Jones wanted to give refuge when they founded Casa de Esperanza de los Ninos (House of Hope for Children) in Houston. This residential program takes in medically fragile and emotionally disturbed children and places them in homes to be intensely nurtured in a family-like setting saturated with love.

As a nun and a social worker, Kathy was managing a halfway house for the mentally ill. Bill was an infant development specialist. The two of them saw the turmoil of families in crisis, and the abuse by parents under stress they could not manage. With $500 in donated seed money, the two of them took a small house in Houston's Third Ward that had been gutted in a crack cocaine fire, with dumpsters on one side and an abandoned vacant lot on the other. They thought it was perfect. Some friends put up sheetrock, others painted and fixed the plumbing. Another friend who was a pediatric nurse agreed to help care for children on the day shift. Babies began to come to them, some left in phone booths, others in dumpsters. Social workers warned Kathy, "You're taking the worst children in the city." She replied, "That's exactly what we hope to do."

Children require emotional attachment almost as much as they need food and water. The hunger they have for human contact and interaction is programmed into their natures from birth, and if attachment is inadequate in their early formation, the damage can be as traumatic as malnutrition or prenatal drug exposure.[4] To be successful human beings, newborns must develop attachment skills. If their families cannot give them adequate care, they desperately need substitute caregivers.

———————————————————————

Kathy Foster tells the story of a baby she cared for:

We received a call from CPS (Children's Protective Services) asking us if we had room for a newborn. The baby's mother did not want him. So we went to the county hospital to pick up this four-day-old baby. The baby was a very tiny, little boy. He looked so fragile, almost lifeless. Although the hospital had told us that the baby had been examined and was okay, the baby was not well. The baby would not eat. He actually refused to eat, would not suck, and when we would force-feed him, he would throw it back up. Our volunteer nurse came to see him and discovered signs of drug withdrawal. We took the baby in to San Jose Clinic.

When the doctor examined the baby, he had this grim look on his face and asked, "Sister, can you tell me a little about this baby, what is his background?" I told him that the baby's mother had been raped, that she had tried to abort the baby, and had done drugs. The doctor then stated, "Sister, this is a failure-to-thrive baby." I understood what the words, "failure" and "thrive" meant, but it was still mind-boggling. I asked the doctor what exactly he meant. The doctor, very straightforwardly and rather bluntly, said, "In other words, Sister, this baby wants to commit suicide; he does not want to live because he knows that he was not wanted from the time he was in his mother's womb." I choked up and looked at the baby. Then I asked the doctor what we could do to save this baby. The doctor stated that even if we were to use IVs to feed him, we could still lose him since he did not want to live.

The doctor said, "You are going to have to convince him that he is wanted, that he is loved. You will consistently hold him and literally make him feel that you love him. Love him so much that he will want to live."

When we returned to Casa, everybody was eager to hear what was wrong with the baby. I explained to the staff and volunteers what the doctor had told me. With heavy hearts and some with tears in their eyes, they all vowed to love this kid so much that he would know he was loved and wanted. From that moment, little (for confidentiality's sake, I'll call him Daniel) Daniel was cuddled, talked to, held close at night, and just loved so much that he lived and grew into a beautiful child.

Daniel became a radiant child, beaming with joy and love. We were told that this child, because of his mother's drug use during his gestation, would probably have mental and maybe even physical abnormalities. [Despite that] a very loving family adopted this child. This child will be graduating from college soon. It is no wonder the great Apostle St. Paul writes in his letter to the Corinthians, "In the end there remains, faith, hope and love. And the greatest of these is love."[5]

A recent report from thirty-three research scientists, pediatricians, and mental health professionals concludes that failure to thrive is increasing in our nation's children, and that neither drugs nor therapy can make up for the serious deficits that are caused by this damage.[6] The report, titled "Hardwired to Connect," summarizes the results of a study that was jointly sponsored by the Dartmouth Medical School, the Institute for American Values, and the YMCA of the USA. Allan N. Schore of the UCLA School of Medicine says, "The idea is that we are born to form attachments, that our brains are physically wired to develop in tandem with another's through emotional communication, beginning before words are spoken."[7] The way people around a child meet this need interacts with "gene transcription and the development of brain circuitry," according to the report. The way an infant's brain develops is a product of human interaction, or the lack thereof, and the social environment "imprints into the developing right brain either a resilience against or a vulnerability to later forming psychiatric disorders," says Schore.[8]

After twenty years of working with young children in crisis, Kathy Foster and Bill Jones have concluded that the earlier they can intervene, the better. This recent scientific research confirms their experience that the critical formative period is very early. "Consistent and constant interaction with a newborn from the first moments of life affects virtually all that makes us human as adults," says Kathy. It determines "empathy, emotionality, language and abstract thinking, impulse control, attention, memory, sensory information processing, the ability to be social . . . the ability to love."[9]

Since 1982, Casa de Esperanza has been offering intensive, full-time intervention in small houses in the Third Ward of Houston, where children live with house parents twenty-four hours a day, seven days a week. There are now nine houses in which Casa has cared for a total of two thousand abused, neglected, and HIV-infected children. At any given time, there are fifty children, ranging from newborns to six-year-olds, in the residences and in community homes. Some of them have been taken from their parents by Child Protective Services because they were being abused or neglected. Others have been given up with the hope that they can be adopted. Some of the HIV-positive babies come from hospitals where they have been left with no one to care for them.

The heart of Casa de Esperanza is its family-based care program. Once a child arrives at Casa de Esperanza, he or she is put into the intake and assessment home, where trained staffers determine needs and begin comprehensive care. Once the child has been stabilized, he or she might be moved to another home for longer-term placement. Two adults are in each home to care for four to six children there. Their job is to give the children a safe, regular environment, with so much love that the children feel wanted. Trained volunteers come to interact as well, rocking babies or reading to toddlers. Some children will eventually be reunited with their families, while others are placed in foster homes with families that have volunteered through Casa. Over the years, 153 children have been placed for adoption.

As the experience grew at Casa de Esperanza, so did the organization's programs. It became clear that the children who were coming had special medical needs because of prenatal exposure to drugs and alcohol, for example. So an in-house medical clinic was started. Children who had been abused had emotional and developmental problems, so a development center was founded. The educational needs of these children demanded a flexible educational environment, so an integrated preschool/

school/after-school program was put into place for them. Children who were put back into their families were more likely to thrive if their families received some assistance as well, so a parent after-care program was initiated. And for the families that were adopting, Casa began to offer education, psychological services, and crisis intervention as adoption and post-adoption services.

The enthusiasm to adopt has rippled through Casa de Esperanza's volunteers and staff, and even into their relatives. Bill Jones, the co-founder, has adopted four special-needs children and is raising them as a single parent. As people come in as volunteers, some of their hearts are captured and they become foster parents, then adoptive parents.

One of the most challenging tasks the agency faces is caring for HIV-positive children. In 1986, Casa de Esperanza was the second institution of its kind in the country to open its doors specifically to these children. Several of its residential homes have been set aside to care for children who need long-term care. Some of the children have been orphaned or abandoned. Casa has succeeded in finding sixteen families to adopt HIV-positive children.

It takes a tenacious person to do this kind of intervention. Pediatric nurse Mary McDonnell says, "We hold babies and rock them while they scream for hours because they are withdrawing from the drugs their mothers have been taking during pregnancy. . . . Young men and women, and often retired teaching nuns who are older and know nothing about caring for sick kids, come to Casa and give the kids the one-on-one respect and love they need. Kids that are called terminally ill—one was green because her liver and gall bladder were shutting down—learn what it is to be loved, and they live and eventually they thrive. These women are tenacious and stubborn in that they won't give up on a child."[10]

Kathy Foster is that kind of woman. Once she had founded Casa de Esperanza, she became so convicted by the mission that she left her religious order to become a full-time mom to the children she adopted herself. Having adopted six, she has done double duty, running the organization and mothering her adopted kids. On any given day, she's juggling appointments, cell-phone calls, and pickup schedules for the children, like any other mother. One of the children she adopted was a little girl who had been left alone and was severely burned in a fire. The girl got AIDS from the blood transfusion she received. For the time that this girl lived as Kathy's adopted daughter, she was loved with a tenacious love.

Best Practices: Casa de Esperanza

- Family-based care programs stabilize abused children with intensive intervention.
- Specialized medical, educational, psychological, and developmental assistance on site nurtures recovery and development.
- Stabilization progresses through placing children into loving foster or adoptive homes.
- Residential care for HIV-positive children meets an acute need seldom addressed.

Results

- Stabilization of more than two thousand abused or neglected children
- One hundred fifty-three placed for adoption, including sixteen HIV-positive children

Kids Hope USA: One Mentor, One Child, One Hour

Virgil Gulker looked at all the possible needs in our country to see where the faith community could intervene to make a real difference. He had a long history of mobilizing people to act on their faith while revitalizing their churches. For a full year, he consulted with professionals in education, health services, religion, law enforcement, and volunteer services who worked with children. What he discovered was appalling: "American children are more likely to be murdered, poor, pregnant, drug dependent or incarcerated than the children of any other industrialized nation."[11] Virgil asked police officers and others to explain the causes of this violent behavior. Their answer seemed too simple to be true, says Virgil. "They told me that these children and young people were searching for one person who would love and affirm them."

Kids Hope USA is a church-based mentoring program founded by Virgil Gulker in response to the needs he discovered. The program originated in Spring Lake, Michigan, in 1995.[12] Kids Hope USA links one-on-one: one church to one school, and one adult to one child. Each adult is required to commit to a relationship with one child for one hour each week for at least a year. The school selects at-risk elementary school children, and their volunteer mentors meet them at school with the cooperation of the principal and the teacher. While the mentors are there to help with schoolwork, their main mission is to let the children know that they are valuable and that they are loved. Their presence has had a profound effect in stabilizing lives of at-risk youngsters.

The program has now successfully replicated in 217 partnerships in twenty-six states across the country, providing a mentor and a prayer partner for 3,800 public elementary school children. Kids Hope USA has been recognized by three presidents, received a Daily Presidential Points of Light Award, and has been named the "premier paradigm of faith-based mentoring" by the Points of Light Foundation.

A solid infrastructure makes this a strong program. To maximize the impact, the youngest children are chosen, most often beginning in the first or second grade. Participating churches are required to hire a part-time paid program director who coordinates the effort with the principal, the teachers, the mentors, and the children. Mentors are screened and trained, and the children's progress is tracked by weekly evaluations by both the teacher and the mentor. Ninety-four percent of the programs established since 1995 are still operational.

School principals like Carmen Hannah, who heads the Van Raalte Elementary School in Holland, Michigan, love the program. "Currently, 74 of the 380 students at our school are with a Kids Hope USA mentor. Each student has significantly improved his or her reading level," she says. "But the greatest evidence of help is in our students' behavior. The pride they show in their work and increased motivation for learning gives them so much confidence they no longer need to fool around or be belligerent to get their needed attention fulfilled. In fact, by the time our mentored students reach fifth grade, their teachers ask me, 'Why do these kids have a mentor? They don't need one.' Well, they should have seen them as first graders!" Dan Takens, principal of Brookwood Elementary in Grand Rapids, Michigan, says, "The Kids Hope USA program has had the largest impact on the students of any program I have ever worked with. It does not throw money at a problem, but rather caring people." School principals are stepping up in droves to ask Kids Hope USA to come into their schools.

While there is an explicit partnership between churches and the public schools where volunteers mentor, Kids Hope makes it very clear that no proselytizing or evangelization may occur on school property. Mentors are warned that infractions may result in their being expelled from the program. However, the children and their parents may be invited to events at the church, where mentors are free to talk about their faith. This clear separation has prevented any difficulties with church-state issues anywhere in the country. Nancy Johnson, assistant principal of Ben Franklin Elementary School in Rochester, Minnesota, says:

> They have very clear guidelines which are explicit. We have never had a breach. The volunteers understand that it is not evangelistic—it's love in action. They're here for the right reasons. It's obvious they have the love of Jesus. Because it's in a public setting, they don't say so. But they have the capacity to carry it, and the power of that love is overwhelming. It's the only power that can change people's lives. If you can tap into this power, it's beyond me why you wouldn't want to.

Tangible Results

When Virgil Gulker began research to devise a model for a mentor-tutor program, he assumed that academic needs would be at the forefront of school principals' concerns. He was surprised when they told him that the children's emotional needs were even more pressing. As one principal put it, "I want you to see these children as emotional checkbooks who are completely overdrawn. What they need is a deposit of love in their hearts." As the emotional and psychological needs of the children are met, their academic performance begins to improve as well, usually taking a leap in the second year.

Teachers' Perceptions of Achievement by Kids Hope USA Students

	Beginning of school year	End of school year	Percent of change
Positive behavior, self-regulation, and control			
Rated excellent or good	34%	52%	+53%
Academic skills			
Rated excellent or good	21%	41%	+95%
Motivation for school work			
Rated excellent or good	26%	52%	+100%

While anecdotal evidence of the success of Kids Hope USA abounded, the first systematic study of its results was completed in 2003. A study done by the Carl Frost Center for Social Science Research of Hope College surveyed the progress of students as assessed by their teachers.[13] Ninety-nine percent of the teachers indicated that the program was beneficial to the students. The study found a significant increase in content achievement—including reading level, math, and writing—as well as general achievement, including self-regulation, motivation for schoolwork, and general academic skills. Noting that the influence of the program extended deeper than academic performance, the teachers commented on the importance of the stability of the relationships offered through Kids Hope USA as anchors in otherwise unstable lives.

School personnel at Sunset Lake Elementary School in Vicksburg, Michigan, monitored the progress of at-risk students in Kids Hope. They reported:

• Detentions dropped from an average of seven to fourteen per year to half that, and in some cases, to zero.
• Reading comprehension increased. Children focused on the text with greater accuracy, and performed better on standardized tests.

- Mathematical skills improved. Students demonstrated a greater willingness to tackle problems with critical thinking.
- Confidence on tests increased, followed by improvement in grades.
- Writing skills improved, particularly journal writing, length, and quality.

Janis Hughes, principal of Burlington Elementary, Longmont, Colorado, reports:

- All students working with Kids Hope USA mentors made academic gains.
- Fifty percent of these students are now reading at grade level.
- All of the students, specifically the students that have English as their second language, have made significant gains in the ability to communicate through speaking.

Some teachers reported that the interaction with a Kids Hope mentor had a significant effect on children, sometimes after only one or two visits. How can this be? Recent research on the activity of the brainstem offers an explanation. Children who live in unstable environments are emotionally unbalanced, and are operating near the base of the brainstem area of their brain. Memory storage or processing is very difficult for these children. There are only two responses physiologically possible: fight or flight. Deb Feenstra, retired principal of Longfellow Elementary, Holland, Michigan, explains:

The reason we are seeing this success with the Kids Hope USA program and not with other similar programs is this: Our only hope for a student at that point is to give him/her enough emotional support to move up their brain function from the stem area to the middle of the brain so that processing and memory can begin to take place. The consistent emotional support provided by the Kids Hope USA mentors allows this movement in brain function to happen.[14]

Kids Hope Serves Families by Mobilizing the Church

Sharon had been a Kids Hope mentor for a boy named Sam for three years, beginning in the third grade. Sam's mother, Rachel, was a single mother in need of a job. So the mentor's husband helped her find employment where he works and drove her to work, becoming her friend and advisor. Recognizing the mother's desire for economic stability, the church enrolled her in an Individual Development Account, matching her contributions to a savings account. This program also provided classes in home buying, insurance, and maintenance. The church had a rental home available for families in mentoring relationships with their members, so Sam and his mom and sister moved in. The church put 80 percent of Rachel's rent into an escrow account to be applied to purchase of a home, and a Realtor at the church will donate his assistance to help her choose one, when that time comes.

The male members of the church took Sam under their wing to do "guy" things like attending hockey games, swimming, and playing basketball. The mentor's husband took Sam on a camping trip, and the mentor's son tutors him in math. When Rachel was in an accident, the mentor's husband and a mechanic from the church helped her find another car. Rachel, Sam, and his little sister Laura have become regular attendees at the church. And they have become part of a much bigger family because one person was willing to develop a relationship with a third-grade boy.[15]

Building Up Churches

Part of the power of Virgil Gulker's vision is to breathe life back into the church by giving its members the opportunity to put their faith into action. The church is a logical pool of potential mentors. But most churches today have proven unwilling or unable to initiate relationships with troubled kids. Churches are almost always ready to provide things— holiday food baskets, food, coats, boots, and rides to the doctor. As one wag put it, "They pay, they pray, and they give stuff away." But they have not been good at building relationships. The problem is not that people in America don't care about at-risk kids. The problem is that "at-risk kids in general" are a diffuse target. But almost anyone can find one hour a week to show up at a school to meet with one child.

Unlike many programs that sputter to a halt when the first blush of enthusiasm wears off, the Kids Hope model has grown in the churches where it has been planted. Serving as a church-mobilization strategy, Kids

Hope USA engages prayer partners who pray at home for each adult-child relationship, giving shut-ins and the elderly a way to participate actively. The experience not only changes the kids; it changes the mentors, the prayer partners, and their churches.

The program also provides a point of entry into the community that has changed both the hearts of the parishioners and the chemistry of the neighborhood. The result has been transformational. Some churches are now utilizing Kids Hope USA as their primary outreach strategy. Michael Mulder, who is the pastor at Servants' Community, a church of seventy-five members in a needy Grand Rapids, Michigan, neighborhood, says, "This is by far the most exciting thing that has happened since I've been at this church. Attendance at children's programs has exploded since launching this ministry. . . . We have a new passion and vision for reaching the youngest members of our community. More and more members want to participate."

Kids Hope USA appeals to a wide variety of volunteers. "The cross-section of people is phenomenal," says Dave Deters, pastor of Alger Park Christian Reformed Church in Grand Rapids, Michigan. On a recent afternoon, tutors from his church crossing the threshold of the school included a middle-aged businessman, a high school student, a retired registered nurse, and a senior citizen, all on their way to mentor a child. "It's rare to have something cross-generational that unites us," observes Deters. In St. Luke's Methodist in Houston, mentors include a retired jazz band director, a medical research scientist, a pediatrician, a professional businesswoman, a computer consultant, an ICU nurse, an accountant, a retired insurance salesman, and a district judge.

Best Practices: Kids Hope USA

- *One-on-one relational approach.* One mentor for each child, meeting weekly for at least one year.
- *Organization.* One professional staff person administers each team of mentors, assisted by a support team provided by each church.
- *Training.* Directors are trained by national Kids Hope USA staff; mentors are screened, trained, and supervised. All are held accountable to written standards.

- **Sustainability.** Partnerships link one school and one church. Ninety-four percent of all programs since 1995 are still operational.
- **Cost-effectiveness.** Effectively mobilizes and retains volunteer talent, while using one part-time administrator in each church to guarantee professional standards.
- **Strengthens families.** Participating churches provide social, emotional, and spiritual support for families of at-risk children.
- **Builds up churches.** Provides a vehicle for engagement in the community, while bringing the energy and relationships back into the church.

Results

- Successfully replicated in 217 partnerships in twenty-six states, now providing 3,800 children with a mentor
- Documented improvement in children's behavior, academic skills, and motivation for school work

Urban Ventures: Transforming the Kids' Neighborhood

As a veteran youth pastor, Art Erickson might have been satisfied bringing together thousands of youngsters for music and evangelistic outreaches he organized in Minneapolis. But he wasn't. He realized that whatever positive changes might come about in kids' lives were quickly undone when they were re-immersed in troubled neighborhoods and families. He is convinced that "There is a big difference between saved souls and changed lives."[16] He wanted to find a way to get at the systemic issues that were perpetuating poverty and crime where at-risk kids lived. When he walked down Crack Alley into an old potato chip factory at 4th and 31st Street in south Minneapolis, he dared to dream big. He envisioned a center that would offer kids a chance for a different life in a transformed neighborhood.

Eleven years later, much of that vision has become reality. Urban Ventures began in 1993 when Art Erickson joined forces with Ralph Bruins, a former banker, to empower youngsters and their families in Minneapolis's poorest neighborhoods. Their goal was to "raise up a generation of urban youth leaders that is excellent educationally, vocationally, technically and morally."[17] They launched Urban Stars, a sports program that includes leadership and life skills, which now provides eight hundred inner-city youth with a better alternative than gang activities. They created the Learning Lab to provide tutoring, classes in computer programming and Web design, and to take aspiring youth on visits to businesses and colleges. Public school students are shuttled to the Learning Lab, where last year nearly 350 received hands-on academic intervention from a cadre of thirty-two tutors.

The absence of a father is one of the clearest high-risk factors for youth: 85 percent of all prisoners come from fatherless homes, 82 percent of pregnant teens, and 78 percent of high school dropouts.[18] So Urban Ventures launched the Center for Fathering in 1995. Men take sixteen-week classes in parenting, and can participate in drug and alcohol recovery groups. Because the center has taught fathers how to take an active role in their children's lives, 82 percent of the men have implemented new parenting skills; 36 percent spend more time with their children. Al Hawkins is one of the fathers who relies on the Center for Fathering for support as a dad. A social worker told him, "You can't raise four kids alone." He replied, "You don't know me or my God." He goes on to say, "She certainly didn't know my friends. Men at the Center for Fathering have supported me over potlucks weekly since 1999. We've learned how to be loving and nurturing as dads, how to discipline, for example, by taking away privileges rather than getting tough. I'm proud of my kids. They're turning out great." A platoon of participating fathers has been mobilized to patrol streets through M.A.D.D.A.D.S., which has resolved 225 street incidents. This past year, 260 men participated in the Center for Fathering, which also provides job and housing placement to stabilize families. In partnership with life coaches, mentors are paired with boys who do not have an active father.

Urban Ventures has grappled with the root causes of urban distress. One of the most intractable problems is that of unemployment and underemployment. To bridge the gap into meaningful work opportunities, Urban Ventures did a $1.3 million renovation of 3,000 square feet of its headquarters to create the Kitchen of Opportunities. This facility provides training in food handling for people who can't afford culinary school, while giving them the opportunity to produce meals for the poor from food donated through Second Harvest Heartland. A partnership with Kids Café is in the works to teach children nutrition and cooking skills.

Urban Ventures has claimed a ten-block area where it is rolling back crime and sparking renewal for kids and their families using a holistic strategy. The broad and deep intervention is changing the neighborhood dramatically. The pimps who used to cruise "the Ave." no longer do. People who drive by Lake Street and Fourth Avenue wouldn't know that it was until recently a favorite hangout for drug dealers and ladies of the night. But the scars are still on the hearts of the people who live there. Rose Delaney still mourns her son Tony's untimely death. But she's determined to change the odds for kids in the neighborhood now. She patrols the streets and calls the cops if prostitutes are on the prowl. Ann Heron joined her to help clean up the rat-infested building for the Learning Lab when it was started. "It was nasty," Ann says, "with condoms, needles and drug paraphernalia."[19] But it's now a haven of hope for aspiring kids. Rose has become an agent of change, working at People's Exchange, an Urban Ventures project that provides food, clothing, job referrals, or counseling for 4,500 neighbors annually. The rising tide is lifting many boats.

Urban Ventures is now poised to take its work to the next level with the planned Colin Powell Youth Leadership Center. The $18.7 million facility will bring together the comprehensive resources of a dozen agencies, hundreds of mentors, and a continuum of services to empower youth and their families. Forty-six thousand people live within a one-mile radius of the center; eighteen thousand of them youngsters under eighteen. When Colin Powell spoke in the Twin Cities at the kickoff for the center's campaign, he said, "We must get into the life of any child who believes that hope is not there for them. We owe them nothing less. We must not fail them."

Best Practices: Urban Ventures

- Focused ten-block area targeted with comprehensive resources
- Holistic renewal serves physical, educational, and spiritual needs of kids and their parents
- Education and job creation dig at root causes of poverty

Results

- 800 kids in Urban Stars Sports
- 350 kids tutored in Learning Lab
- Eighty-seven percent of 260 fathers implement new parenting skills
- People's Exchange provides food, clothing, job referrals for 4,500

Cornerstone Schools: Raising the Bar for Performance

In what is increasingly becoming an hourglass economy, it is no longer possible to enter the labor market at the bottom and assume that you can work your way up. It's not a ladder anymore. While there are lots of low-paying jobs at the bottom and high-paying jobs at the top, the middle is thin. The only way to access knowledge-industry jobs at the top is to get an education. Kids from poor neighborhoods seldom have access to good schools, which locks them into multigenerational systems of poverty, unless educational opportunity gives them a chance to break the cycle. Some street saints are giving urban kids that opportunity.

Education Is the Ticket

Not content with the lackluster performance of most inner-city schools, the founders of the Cornerstone Schools in Detroit set out to prove that, given an opportunity to achieve, kids from low-income environments can excel. What began in response to a challenge from Archbishop Adam Maida to the Detroit Economic Club in 1990 "to make all things new again" produced less than a year later a school that opened its doors to 167 children. Today, the Cornerstone Schools serve 821 children, almost all African American, on four campuses in Detroit in a model that has raised the bar for performance for all other schools in the nation serving the inner city. It has also defined a new paradigm for partnership, engaging individuals, corporations, and families in this award-winning school.

The schools, which are headed by Ernestine Sanders, are committed to academic excellence and require their pupils, from pre-kindergarten through the eighth grade, to attend school eleven months a year. While the youngsters entering perform below the national norms on standardized tests, their achievements soar with each year of instruction. Youngsters in preschool read by the end of their first year. By the end of the fifth grade, they are performing at the grade equivalency of 7.43 years, as measured by the Stanford Achievement Test.[20] This is a marked contrast to performance elsewhere: 58 percent of low-income fourth graders in the United States cannot read. Sixty-seven percent of the eighth graders from the inner city cannot meet the basic math requirements. Inner-city blacks and Latinos are most affected by this dismal failure of education.[21]

While a surge of performance for individual kids is not unheard of in elite private schools, it's rare in schools where virtually all the youngsters come from the inner city. The few who have broken through have been highlighted in the "No Excuses" project of the Heritage Foundation, which has profiled their successes. Another one of the winners, charter school KIPP Academy in Houston, has taken poor Hispanic kids, many them with parents having only a grade-school education, and transformed them into high achievers winning scholarships to the most prestigious prep schools across the nation.[22] Cornerstone and KIPP Academy have several strategies in common: longer hours, a nearly year-round program, a contract for parental involvement, and high expectations. "The biggest thing in inner-city education is a transformation of attitude," says Ernestine Sanders, explaining Cornerstone's success. "Urban settings have low expectations, dilapidated buildings, and deflated children. Here we ask: What high expectations do you have for your own child? What are you willing to do to achieve those expectations? Cornerstone can help to make them a reality."[23]

Partners Make It Possible

One of the most striking aspects of the Cornerstone Schools has been the development of partnerships that make them flourish. Far from a hollow term in glossy publicity material, these schools really rely on their partners. Individuals sponsor a particular child, paying $2,000 or more a year toward the cost of his or her education. But their involvement doesn't end with writing a check. These partners meet with the child they sponsor four times a year for hands-on interaction in a project with the child at school. They write notes of encouragement during the year. The children develop a relationship with their partners, updating them with notes on their progress and talking to them when they come to the school. By making the participation personal as well as monetary, a remarkable energy has been unleashed that has engendered enthusiastic participation: the sponsoring partners have a 91 percent renewal rate. Some partners who backed a child from kindergarten through graduation from the eighth grade have come back to sponsor another one. Others have embraced as many as ten youngsters at a time.[24] Some corporate partners sponsor an entire class.

Gifts from partners make it possible to take in the children who want an education, but whose parents couldn't begin to pay its cost. The actual cost is $5,800 a year, although the school charges only a fraction of that to the parents. Some parents pay as little as $300, others as much as $2,700, and the rest is covered by the partners. But it's no free lunch: everybody pays something, and the participation of families is crucial. Parents are asked to sign a covenant of support and are expected to be on board to nurture their offspring in their education. There's homework every night, even for the youngest pupils, and parents are expected to monitor it. Parents also agree to volunteer at least ten hours a year and to attend all conferences with teachers.

The curriculum includes a strong dose of classical education: reading, writing, math, and science, integrated with moral and character development. Cornerstone Schools are not affiliated with any particular denomination, but they are explicitly Christ-centered. Ernestine Sanders, the president and chief executive officer of Cornerstone Schools, says plainly, "We want to deliver an education that is founded on the teachings of God and Jesus Christ."[25] That orientation is reflected in the curriculum and in the culture of the school. The school teaches "gospel values, the teachings of Christ, loving one's neighbor, and knowing Christ in daily life."[26]

While the corporate world has historically been skittish about funding organizations with a religious aura, corporate executives have stepped up by the droves to support Cornerstone. Automobile executives, general contractors, and auto suppliers have all ponied up, and they are going into the classrooms to mix it up with the kids they are sponsoring. "Cornerstone is *built* on business participation," said the *Wall Street Journal*, with backers that include everyone from GM, Chrysler, and Ford to DTE Energy, Penske, TRW, Comerica, NASCAR and Kmart.[27] Clark Durant, who was the prime mover behind the schools' founding and has continued to serve as chairman of the board since 1991, is not shy about encouraging his contacts to step up. Once they get involved, they keep coming back.

"It's not all about money, but dedication," says Wayne Webber, who has sponsored an entire class of twenty-four kids since 1999, and donated $1 million to the initial campaign. "You can see it. These teachers are dedicated, second to none, and I think that dedication . . . is a recipe for success. This is what can be done."[28] The proof is in the success of the kids who have come through Cornerstone Schools. The high school graduation rate for Cornerstone alumni is 83 percent, compared to less than 50 percent for most urban schools. Because the partners are asked to do more than write a check, it's possible that the changes have been as meaningful for them as they have been for the kids. Cornerstone's winning approach builds community and relationships, as well as delivering sterling quality academics. Much of Ernestine Sanders's success has been in changing the climate for urban education. "We have high expectations for every child who comes through our doors," she says. "Expectations are often made, and if we model high expectations, we'll get that."[29] Ernestine Sanders was awarded the Salvatori Prize for American Citizenship in 1999 for her leadership.

A steady stream of visitors has come to the Cornerstone Schools to see what they can learn from their success. Sanders says:

> One of the defining differences is the broad community that's wrapping its arms around the children we serve. It's a larger stake of involvement. We have parents who care, teachers who go the extra mile, a board that's engaged, and a broad and beloved, committed community. What's so different about Cornerstone schools is the people who come here and work with the kids take on a responsibility within the community, not only as mom or dad, but as friends, who through teaching of Jesus, see their work as an extension of his love.[30]

Best Practices: Cornerstone Schools

Cornerstone Schools have been recognized nationally for excellence in urban education. Among their hallmarks:

- Christ-centered curriculum and school culture
- Parental covenant of support
- Eleven-month school year
- Individualized learning labs
- Standardized testing of all students annually
- Partner program that engenders financial and personal involvement of community supporters with pupils

Results

- Documented academic progress moving well beyond grade level
- High school graduation rate of 83 percent

The Oaks Academy: Wraparound Renewal

In Indianapolis in 1997, the Martindale Brightwood neighborhood had the highest syphilis rate in the state, and the lowest number of tax returns filed in the country. Neighbors called it "Dodge City" because of the bullets that flew around. The local elementary school had shut down. Any kids in the neighborhood who wanted a good education were flat out of luck.

Six Indianapolis families had a heart for this neighborhood, and they wanted to do something together. They pooled money to buy a house and renovate it, and one family moved into the neighborhood. As they got to know the kids there, they saw how few of them could read at grade level and concluded that a new school would be a real godsend. The local elementary school, which had been closed for two years, was put on the auction block. This group of six Presbyterian families discovered that they were bidding against the local St. Vincent Catholic Hospital, and decided to see if they could make a common cause. What resulted from that venture is one of the more remarkable developments in holistic renewal: the Jubilee Center.

This innovative partnership provides wraparound services for the entire neighborhood. The Shalom Health Care Center serves the indigent with primary and preventive care on a sliding fee scale, offering screenings, immunizations, parenting and nutrition classes, and referrals for substance abuse and domestic violence. A group of lawyers from several churches and synagogues offers pro bono legal services in the Neighborhood Christian Legal Clinic. The St. Vincent Unity Development Center offers GED preparation, computer training, job readiness and interview training, counseling, and assistance with tax preparation. Kids with a Mission runs an after-school program and a summer program for youth. The local families have access to useful services in one convenient location in a dynamic center that is changing the neighborhood.

Rich Classical Education

The Oaks Academy, a Christ-centered pre-K through eighth grade school founded in 1997 that now occupies two-thirds of the Jubilee Center, offers a curriculum of classical education that is rare in America altogether, but almost unheard of in an urban setting like this one. On a given afternoon, you might discover second graders learning about Egypt, eager to tell you about mummies and pyramids. They would also tell you about Joseph in the Bible and his time in Egypt. Linking the biblical plagues to their science instruction, the class is studying grasshoppers and locusts.

When they reach the third grade, they will start learning Latin, and will study the Romans. Sixth graders might tell you about their study of *Hamlet* or *Animal Farm,* or perhaps the texts of slave narratives they are reading as they learn about the Civil War, or the books of the Bible from Hebrews to Revelation they are studying. Middle school students learn logic, read *Gilgamesh, Beowulf,* and Shakespeare, and grapple with material many young people don't touch until college, if at all.[31]

The school offers an academically rigorous and comprehensive classical education that draws heavily from Western Civilization and does not shy away from challenging its pupils from the moment they arrive in prekindergarten. Youngsters receive a rich immersion in subjects including math, science, language, history, art, philosophy, and literature, based on the classical *trivium* approach, which teaches the grammar, the logic, and the rhetoric of each subject. As unusual as that is today, it's altogether surprising in a school that has set out in its charter to always have at least 40 percent of its pupils from low-income families. Although nondenominational, it is an explicitly Christ-centered school that recognizes the "firm foundation and boundary of God's truth expressed through the Scripture, through nature, and through the person of Jesus Christ."[32] The school attracts families from more affluent areas of town, but more than a third of the youngsters currently enrolled come from within a one-mile radius of the school. Forty percent of the children qualify for free school lunches because of their parents' income. They are flourishing. All of The Oaks Academy students are reading at least one year above grade level, and are performing two years above their grade level, according to the national IOWA standardized test. The seventh graders are reading at an eleventh-grade level and are performing at a tenth-grade level in math.

The Oaks Academy "offers rich academics and fosters the character development of students to become mature spiritually and socially," explains Head of School Andrew Hart, who left a career at Lilly to come here. The classes are small, about fifteen students. The ratio of students to teachers is eight to one, with a total of 220 students attending. By design the school is half black, half white; 75 percent of the families receive some financial assistance. It costs $6,850 per year to educate each pupil, but the school charges $4,850 in tuition and actually receives on average only $2,400, based on a sliding scale for financial aid. The rest is made up by contributions from individuals and corporations, some of whom are beginning to sponsor a particular child or a whole classroom—and build relationships with them.

As strong as the school is, "We believe strongly that the parents are primarily responsible for the education of the children," says Hart. Parents are woven into the classroom as volunteers and are asked to sign a contract solidifying their involvement of at least two hours a month at the school. They also agree to read to their children every night for at least twenty minutes, and to monitor their homework. Parents are enthusiastic about the school. Faith Wilhite, whose son Stanton began in the first class here in 1998, says, "It's valuable to bring the different cultures, socio-economic and ethnic groups together." She has been taking college classes recently and, as she reached World Civilizations, she discovered her young son already knew a great deal about the things she was just learning. "I love this school," she says. "He's getting something here he wouldn't get anywhere else."

Troy Mulder has two daughters at The Oaks Academy. He is struck by the way it fosters inquisitiveness and expands their horizons. The fourth grader was discussing with the first grader her assignment to pick three places she would like to go. "When I had that assignment in first grade, I picked Disney, Florida, and New York," said the older sister, whose understanding of both geography and culture has improved since then. "But now that I've studied them, I would pick Egypt, Rome, and Greece," she told her younger sister.

Part of the problem in the public schools is the rootlessness of the children. When Laura Grammer, one of the award-winning Oaks Academy teachers, taught in the public school system, only half the youngsters entering her class were performing at grade level. In a classroom of twenty-five children, only five from the class with which she began in September would still be there in May, and twenty new ones would have come during the year. With that kind of turnover, it's not surprising that their academic achievement was lackluster. The Oaks Academy has managed to change that pattern by providing stability. This school is helping these youngsters put down roots to become the "oaks of righteousness"[33] they are capable of becoming.

Best Practices: The Oaks Academy

- Challenging classical curriculum
- Class size no larger than fifteen
- Chartered to include low-income students and have a 50/50 racial mix
- Wraparound services for families in Jubilee Center: health care, legal services, job training, after-school programs

Results

- All students performing one to two years above grade level
- Seventh graders performing three to four years above grade level

Religion and At-Risk Youth: The Research

The success of faith-based programs like the ones discussed in this chapter is significant. According to sociological research, faith serves a very important role in insulating at-risk kids from the ill effects of their neighborhoods.[34] Faith apparently has a more profound effect on inner-city youngsters than on their suburban counterparts in better surroundings. The Center for Research on Religion and Urban Civil Society did a series of sociological studies to examine the effects of the "faith factor" as it affects behavior in urban and suburban settings. John DiIulio, Byron Johnson, and their colleagues led many of the probes. Their research on juvenile crime, drug use, teen pregnancy, and academic achievement indicates that faith-based intervention can transform individuals at the decision-making level and change their behavior. The results document conclusive evidence of faith in decreasing juvenile delinquency, drug use, and other high-risk behavior.

A study by Mark Regnerus examined whether churches in poor neighborhoods play any role in helping kids stay in school and achieve. He concluded, "[C]hurch attendance (and general religious involvement) is *much more likely* to positively contribute to their academic progress than it is among youth in higher-income neighborhoods."[35] There are so few positive influences in the high-risk urban environment that the church's influence is even more pronounced as the one, clear, asset-building institution. Indications point to faith as a potent force that is little understood but that is effective in changing human lives for the better, particularly those of at-risk kids.

Medical scientist David Larson joined forces with criminologist Byron Johnson to review four hundred juvenile delinquency studies published in peer-reviewed journals in the United States between 1980 and 1997. They narrowed the field to those forty scientific studies that took religion into account as a quantified variable factor in studying behavior. Three-quarters of the studies, which together scrutinized nearly 93,000 individuals, indicated that religious participation resulted in less delinquency. The more consistent the involvement—as demonstrated in attending church or synagogue, praying, studying scripture, or placing a high importance on faith—the less likely is juvenile delinquency.[36]

In their study on "Religiosity and At-Risk Urban Youth," Larson and Johnson analyzed data collected on inner-city black youth and concluded that church attendance has a direct impact in reducing delinquency, drug use, and alcohol use. Church attendance "indirectly reduces delinquency involvement by fostering stronger social bonds, good peer relationships, and high involvement in productive social activities." They concluded that "religiosity, as measured by church attendance, appears to be a strong protective factor in insulating at-risk youth from the crime and delinquency" of the inner city.[37]

In a 2003 study, Byron Johnson and Marc Siegel looked at the effect of religion on delinquent behavior of high-risk youth. They surveyed 2,358 young black males from poor neighborhoods in Boston, Chicago, and Philadelphia. They found that youth who attend church more than once a week were 46 percent less likely to use drugs, 57 percent less likely to deal drugs, and 39 percent less likely to commit non-drug-related crimes.[38] Johnson and Siegel conclude that "religiosity may be a strong protective factor in keeping young black males distant from the various forms of deviance so often associated with inner-city poverty tracts."[39]

Drug use by teens, which has declined slightly in recent years, is much less prevalent in youngsters who take their faith seriously.[40] Byron Johnson examined usage among poor urban teens and discovered that greater religiosity reduces the likelihood of using drugs. He looked at several factors to assess linkages and their effect on disadvantaged youth. Disorder in rundown neighborhoods corresponds with drug use, especially marijuana. But youth with a strong religious commitment are 27 percent less likely to use marijuana and 33 percent less likely to use hard drugs, despite the neighborhood factor.[41] The effect of faith seems to be cumulative: the older a religious teenager becomes, the less likely he or she is to be a user. Attachments matter, according to the report, and they can overcome the ill effects of dysfunctional neighborhoods. Youth who have positive relationships with their family and school are less likely to use illicit drugs.[42] But negative peer influence is a significant factor: those who have friends who use drugs are much more likely to join them.[43]

Apparently the neighborhood is not the critical issue in predicting drug use. Convictions are. Johnson discovered that "highly religious youth living in poor urban neighborhoods are less likely to use illicit drugs than non-religious youth living in middle-class suburban neighborhoods."[44] Put another way, middle-class kids without faith are more at risk for drug use than inner-city youth with faith.[45] In fact, the "faith factor" was most pronounced in youth in "bad neighborhoods," where there were fewer other stabilizing influences. The more rundown the community, the more likely faith is to have a profound influence.[46]

Although much more remains to be investigated, accumulating sociological evidence indicates faith-based programs are having a measurable impact in improving the lives of at-risk youth.

chapter 5

Transforming Offenders and Victims

More than two million Americans are in prison. A total of 6.6 million are under some kind of correctional supervision including probation or parole.[1] This year some 650,000 prisoners are going to be released, and the likelihood is that when they get their bus fare the day they get out, they will go back to the same life they had before.[2] As one ex-offender explained it, "There's two kinds of guys in prison. There's the kind that keeps his mouth shut and his head down and does his time waiting to get out and get back, and there's the kind that's in there doing business, becoming a more effective criminal learning from the other guys. Sad thing is, both kinds are coming back."

The likelihood is high that an ex-offender will commit new crimes that send him back to jail. A Justice Department study released in 2002 found that 67 percent of inmates released from state prisons committed at least one serious crime within three years. Two-thirds of these inmates who were apprehended were rearrested within a year of their release.[3] The grim bottom line is that about 48 percent of the prisoners released will return to prison within three years.[4] And the odds are worse for those with drug and alcohol problems. The overall rate of recidivism may be as high as 70 percent.[5]

It shouldn't be all that surprising. If released inmates are dropped off at a bus stop with a few dollars, with no understanding of the conse-

quences for the victims of their crimes, no new job skills or education, and
no change in their hearts, why should their behavior be any different? If
they are not motivated to change and lack a support network to help, odds
are they will derail. Even someone with good intentions who finds himself
in the old neighborhood can be easily sucked back into the old ways of life
that landed him in jail in the first place.

Building more prisons has not solved the problem. In the absence of
intensive intervention, the same people who have committed crimes are
very likely to do so again. There is a direct correlation between the number of previous arrests and the likelihood of repeat offenses. Prisoners
who have three prior arrests have a 55 percent recidivism rate. With each
prior arrest, the rate climbs, reaching a rate of 82 percent for offenders
with more than fifteen arrests.[6]

The problem of repeat offenders and the damage they leave behind
has been a stubborn one, resisting almost all attempts to cure it. Several
million lives are damaged in the wake of the incarcerated—the victims of
their crimes, the wives left in isolation, and an estimated 2 to 2.5 million
children who have one or both parents in federal or state prisons, or in
jail.[7] Some 93 percent of prisoners are men, and 55 percent of them have
school-age children. The average age of these kids is eight.[8] Even before
incarceration, two-thirds of the fathers weren't living at home, married to
the mothers of their children, and their absence has serious consequences
for the kids, who have been called the most at-risk population of all at-risk
youth.[9] In the absence of intervention, there is a 60 percent chance that
the children who have been plunged into a dysfunctional spiral will end
up in jail themselves.[10] Rehabilitation programs have been axed in many
prisons due to cost-cutting measures. For the sake of all concerned—the
offenders themselves, their children, and the victims of crime—the need
for intervention is acute, particularly in light of the recent findings on recidivism. What's needed is a different kind of approach that gets to the
heart of the matter: the human heart.

Recent years have seen the birth of several bold initiatives that go deep
into the hearts and minds of inmates, touching deep dysfunctionalities,

unlocking rage, and bringing criminals face-to-face with victims of crime. These innovative programs have offered a total immersion in a different way of thinking, challenging offenders to accept responsibility for their actions and to make restitution to the people who have been hurt by their crimes. And they have offered prisoners the chance for a fresh start through faith. The first results are in, and they are encouraging: several of these faith-based programs have succeeded in reducing recidivism while healing the hearts of the victims of crime as well.

InnerChange Freedom Initiative: Total Immersion Transforming Inmates

InnerChange Freedom Initiative (IFI) is a pioneer program in the United States, first launched in Texas by Prison Fellowship International. Patterned after a successful approach in Brazil, the model has been adapted and replicated in Iowa, Kansas, and most recently, in Minnesota. Together, these programs are reaching nearly seven hundred U.S. prisoners, and the idea is growing. The program at the Carol Vance Unit in Richmond, Texas, was the first to launch in 1997, when then-governor George W. Bush agreed to give Chuck Colson's bold idea a try. In a public-private joint venture, the Texas Department of Criminal Justice agreed to provide the space and to be responsible for security and custody, and IFI agreed to provide the inmate programs and their personnel and materials.

The first major study tracking IFI participants two years after their graduation, completed by Byron Johnson, documented that recidivism was effectively reduced. For those who completed the program, 17.3 percent were rearrested within two years, compared to 35 percent of the comparison group. Even fewer of the graduates went back to prison: only 8 percent compared to 20.3 percent of the matched comparison group.[11] Now that the documented results on IFI's success in reducing recidivism are in, other governors are queuing up to see how they can get the same salutary effects for their prison populations.

InnerChange Freedom Initiative is total immersion in a radically different way of thinking and living. The mission is to "create and maintain a prison environment that fosters respect for God's law and rights of others, and to encourage the spiritual and moral regeneration of prisoners."[12] The intention is nothing short of remaking the man. Inmates apply voluntarily for admission, entering at least eighteen months before they will be released. Those who are accepted enter a "prison-within-a-prison," a life totally different from that of the other inmates, with a twenty-four-hour, seven-day-a-week program that encompasses them. From the moment they rise at 5:00 a.m., these men are immersed in a life of scripture study, mentoring, academic studies, life skills training, and reconciliation.[13] The program is holistic—addressing multiple aspects of each man to change his mind and heart before release—while providing both vocational and personal skills to reenter the outside world successfully. The comprehensive approach is demanding. Applicants must complete a thirty-day self-study before applying. A thirty-day orientation follows once prisoners enter the unit. They then enter a three-phase program involving sixteen to twenty-four months of biblically based programming while they are in prison, and six to twelve months of aftercare.

Changing the Mindset

Phase one immerses each man in biblical education to transform his mindset from that of a criminal to that of a disciple. This phase effectively changes the prison climate that so often perpetuates criminality and violence. Instead of watching television, the inmates have daily interaction with trained volunteers from the community's churches, who come in to mentor them and to offer spiritual guidance and counseling. Teachers impart reading skills or help them with high school equivalency classes. Seminary graduates serve as biblical counselors, introducing the men to a book few of them know much about. The program is explicitly Christ-centered, offering teaching on topics like Growing in Jesus. However, Muslims and people of other faiths are welcome, and a number have participated. Christian men from local churches meet with the inmates for one-on-one mentoring for at least two hours every week. In addition to receiving GED preparation and tutoring, the inmates take classes in substance abuse prevention and life skills. Evening programs to deepen personal faith include Survival Kit, Heart of the Problem, Experiencing God, Masterlife, and Community Bible Study. The seminars and Bible studies teach concepts such as "surviving the prison environment, beginning a relationship with God in prison, overcoming obstacles, building better families, sharing the Gospel behind bars, and preparing for life on the outside."[14] Prisoners are challenged to set goals for themselves, to prepare themselves for release.

There's a deep difference at the philosophical level between the Inner-Change Freedom Initiative approach and most contemporary methods, which are usually based on the therapeutic model. Instead, IFI is based on the transformation model. As Dr. Henry Brandt and Kerry Skinner explain, "Therapeutic communities seek to equip prisoners for life after prison by learning to manage behavior. . . . The therapeutic model seeks first to reconcile the relationship of a prisoner to other human beings."[15] The IFI approach stands that logic on its ear.

> The IFI model, in contrast, seeks to reconcile people through changing their relationship with God. . . . The IFI model seeks to "cure" prisoners by identifying sin as the root of their problems. Inmates learn how God can heal them permanently, if they turn from their sinful past, are willing to see the world through God's eyes, and surrender themselves to God's will. IFI relies on and directs members to God as the source of love and inner healing. Members then build on this new relationship to recast human relationships based on Biblical insights.[16]

A few examples may suffice to point out the differences between the two approaches:

Founder Chuck Colson tirelessly asserts that inmates must be transformed by the power of God, and that they must willingly turn away from a sinful past and be "born again." Colson says they must recognize that "sin is not simply the wrong we do our neighbor when we cheat him, or the wrong we do ourselves when we abuse our bodies. Sin, all sin, is a root rebellion and offense against God."[17] If sin is the problem, repentance and a new relationship with God is the solution.

If you grapple with sin, you have to get past the excuses to the root.
And you have to look at the consequences. In the Sycamore Tree Project,
for several hours each week, mediators put prisoners face-to-face with victims of crime like those they have committed to work through reconciliation issues of guilt and forgiveness. The inmates are asked to find a way of
restitution. If the changes are going to last, the family has to be part of the
process as well, so throughout the IFI program, inmates' families are
brought in to be reunited with the men who have been absent from their
lives, and to walk with them through the transformation. It's all part of a
process that is slowly penetrating into the deepest recesses of the men's
hearts and minds. Brandt explains, "Repentance and reconciliation are an
ongoing state of mind and do not simply exist in one moment of time. IFI
emphasizes this realization, and fosters humility and a teachable attitude,
that in turn, creates opportunities for prisoners to break free from old
habits. They learn new life skills, rooted in biblical principles and God
turns their lives around."[18]

Transformation	vs.	Therapeutic Model[19]
All problems in life arise from a condition of sin.		Problems in life may arise from past inability to have one's needs met.
Transformed persons seek to appropriate God's ways as revealed through biblical truth.		Therapy seeks to manage symptoms according to human understanding.
Criminal behavior is a manifestation of an alienation between the self and God.		Criminal behavior is a result of an alienation of self from society.
Transformation enables prisoners to see the world and others as God sees them.		Therapy seeks to help prisoners see how the world can meet their needs.

Putting Progress to the Test

Phase two takes the newly reconstituted character of the participants
and puts it to the test. These inmates, who are nearer to being released, are

given opportunities to serve the community in projects like building a house with Habitat for Humanity, leaving the prison grounds for part of the day. These six hours off-site are when the rubber hits the road in proving responsibility. Back behind the prison walls, the men continue to interact with their mentors and support groups, while working on leadership skills. Their characters are still being solidified in Bible study and Christian education as they prepare for freedom. In Kansas, Iowa, and Minnesota, inmates have the option of a phase-three option, where they can enter a halfway house or work-release program.

Inmates in InnerChange Freedom Initiative say it revolutionizes their lives. One inmate turned down his parole so he could stay in prison to complete the program. Another says:

> The program has awakened me. It has birthed a new me. It has made me who I am. I'm learning to get along with others and to understand why people do what they do. I am learning more by listening. IFI has made me feel like I am somebody and that I have potential. I have a whole lot more discipline and self-control than before.... And I'm learning to control my anger.... Change is not overnight and it's not easy to change, but God is changing me.[20]

It is moving to see these men gathered for prayer in their white prison uniforms, hands stretched in the air, singing. Thieves, murderers, and drug dealers emerge with a changed heart and the desire to lead a sober, productive life. It is evident they are getting the spiritual, educational, and relational tools to succeed. One of the most potent means of their transformation is the modeling of biblical principles.[21] The inmates absorb them through daily immersion in a life-changing climate of spiritual authenticity. IFI is a community of individuals, including both staff and volunteers, who are committed to living out Christ-like behavior. Their example and their commitment have a palpable, powerful effect.

Release Is Not the End

Once an inmate is released, he is not through with the program. Since the most acute danger period is right after release, in the final phase, a mentor is assigned to each participant who will meet with the man regularly when he leaves the prison. (In practice, it has proven hard to mobilize enough mentors, so not all men so far have been matched with one when they leave.) Aftercare managers assist parolees in securing housing and employment, help them to find a halfway house if necessary, and assist them for another six to twelve months. If they don't have a church home of their own, churches are mobilized to extend open arms to the men. Before an ex-offender is considered a graduate of the InnerChange Freedom Initiative program, he must complete sixteen months in the in-house program, six or more months in aftercare, hold a job, be an active member in a church for the past three months, and have verification from the people overseeing him: parole officer, mentor, sponsor, community coordinator, and the IFI staff. If anybody manages to slip through the cracks, he has to really want to.

The results of InnerChange Freedom Initiative were compiled in a 2003 study. Dr. Byron Johnson of the University of Pennsylvania's Center for Research on Religion and Urban Civil Society (CRRUCS) identified 177 IFI graduates and scrutinized their performance in comparison with a matched comparison group of 1,754 other ex-offenders.[22] This was the first intensive, multi-year field study that quantified the results of the innovative program. Johnson tracked the prisoners for two years after their release and found that prisoners who completed all three phases of IFI were significantly less likely to be arrested or incarcerated. Of the IFI graduates, seventy-five of whom completed all phases of the program, 17.3 percent were rearrested, roughly half the rate of the matched group, which was 35 percent. Even more striking was the difference between the rates of re-incarceration. Only 8 percent of the IFI graduates returned to prison, compared to 20.3 percent of the matched group. It's interesting to note that prisoners who entered the program but did not complete it were just as likely to be rearrested or re-incarcerated as those who were not in the program at all. Apparently, the full immersion over time, plus mentoring after release, is necessary for genuine transformation that lasts.

Johnson concludes that several elements combine to give this program its potency. One is the full-immersion approach, which includes Bible training, academic work, life skills, personal planning, spiritual transformation, and mentoring. The IFI "environment . . . fosters rehabilitation"; it is "extremely open, supportive, upbeat, friendly, and nurturing."[23] The sincerity and engagement of the volunteers has a profound effect on the inmates. Mentoring is a crucial component, especially in the post-release period, and is linked to lowering recidivism. Johnson concludes, "The current study contributes preliminary but important evidence that a faith-based program combining education, work, life-skills, mentoring, and aftercare has the potential to influence in a beneficial way the prisoner reentry process."[24] Considering the fact that 650,000 prisoners are being released every year throughout the United States, the implications are significant. While IFI is now up and running in Texas, Iowa, Kansas, and Minnesota, other states are already considering replicating the innovative program.

The day the study was released in June 2003, President George W. Bush made national news by hugging a convicted murderer in the Roosevelt Room in the White House.[25] He had become a friend of sorts. This was the same man Bush put his arm around in 1997, when he visited the new InnerChange Freedom Initiative program in Texas he had helped to initiate as governor. George W. Bush and this convicted murderer were photographed together singing "Amazing Grace." Now the evidence of that grace is in.

Best Practices: InnerChange Freedom Initiative

- 24/7 immersion in faith-saturated Christian program for volunteer prisoners
- Comprehensive approach fosters spiritual transformation
- Long-term intervention: Inmates enter sixteen to twenty-four months before their release, continue six to twelve months after release
- Multi-faceted program: job skills, life skills, continued education, Bible study, reconciliation with victims, anger management, substance abuse counseling
- One-on-one mentoring while in prison and after release
- Post-release assistance: help finding housing, employment, connection to local congregations

Results: Decreased Recidivism

• 17.3 percent rearrested in two years, compared to 35 percent in matched group
• 8 percent returned to prison vs. 20.3 percent in matched comparison group[26]

Bridges to Life: Reconciling Victims and Criminals

The last thing John Sage thought he would ever want to do would be to go into prisons and spend hours talking to convicts. When his sister Marilyn was murdered by two nineteen-year-olds in 1993, investigators said it was one of the most brutal killings they had ever seen. The attractive forty-three-year-old mother of two had been attacked in her Houston apartment by two thieves, who bludgeoned her with a statue, stabbed her with three different knives, and suffocated her with a plastic bag. John went ballistic. He had been very close to Marilyn since their childhood, and they were just eighteen months apart in age. They had attended the same college, and he had married her close friend. This incomprehensible murder of someone close to him was devastating. First came rage, followed by depression. At the trial, he envisioned himself putting his hands around the neck of the murderer. "I would have felt good about killing him," John admits. It was a cold consolation to have both the murderers receive the death penalty.[27]

The painful journey out of clinical depression and years of sleepless nights took John to the writings of Henri Nouwen and Scott Peck, and into study of the Bible. In his utter despair, John cried out, "Just tell me what to do, God." *Give it to me, John,* was the answer.[28] When he did, he discovered the ultimate source of healing. When a journalist called John four years after Marilyn's death to ask whether he was looking forward to the day of the second murderers' execution, John was surprised to find himself mildly answering no. There had been a slow transformation of his attitude through his search for God, and an inner healing had resulted. The former CEO and college football hero decided to reapply his energy and determination to launch a ministry that would serve both prisoners and the victims of crime, and attempt to heal both.

Bridges to Life was founded in 1998 as a restorative justice ministry; its primary mission is to reduce crime by reducing the recidivism rate of released inmates. Its spiritual mission is to "minister to victims of crime and to inmates to show them the transforming power of God's love and forgiveness."[29] Based on his initial experience in reconciliation work at the Carol Vance Unit in Texas with InnerChange Freedom Initiative, John decided to take the restorative justice approach modeled in the Sycamore Tree program and expand it into a stand-alone ministry.

Bridges to Life now reaches into eight prisons throughout Texas. More than 1,000 prisoners have graduated from the program, which has mobilized some 250 volunteers, most of whom are victims of crime. The results have been impressive: a recidivism rate of only 8 percent. The Texas Corrections Association chose Bridges to Life as an exemplary program in 2000, and John Sage received the Texas Governor's Criminal Justice Volunteer Award for Restorative Justice in 2001. Bridges to Life was chosen as the 2003 Program of the Year by the Texas Department of Criminal Justice Victim Services Clearinghouse Conference. Now people in other states are looking into replicating the successful model.

Face-to-Face with Murderers

Inmates who are usually within eighteen months of release from prison can volunteer for the program. A trained facilitator coordinates a small group of two or three victims and five inmates for face-to-face encounters for two hours every week for twelve weeks. A woman whose husband was murdered may find herself seated across the table from a convicted murderer. A father whose child died of a drug overdose may be seated across from a drug dealer. The victims and the criminals agree to be open in telling their stories to each other. The victims are brutally frank about how they felt when their family members were killed, or when they were robbed or raped. The inmates are asked to share their stories, truthfully and with no excuses. The sessions can be pretty raw.

Gilda Muskwinsky tells them about her seventeen-year-old daughter, Raynell. The beautiful girl with chestnut hair was murdered with her fiancé on an August night in 1984. The bodies were found in the car the next morning, riddled by bullets fired by teenagers. After the funeral, the mother "got into a truck and started beating the dashboard with her fists." She said, "I couldn't stop myself. I kept screaming."[30] She had so much rage that she "scared herself and her family. 'I did not just hate those two boys, I hated their families; I hated everything about them. I would have hurt any one of them, if I thought it was going to make them hurt like I did.'"[31]

Connie Hilton tells them about the three men who broke into her home and murdered her husband with a shotgun as she screamed in the hallway. They beat her until she couldn't move, then tied her up and raped her. They cleaned out her possessions and killed her dog. That was twelve years ago, and she has gone through acute post-traumatic stress disorder. But she has come back from the depths of despair and overcame her fear to meet with inmates. She has become the regional coordinator for Bridges to Life and received the Texas Governor's Criminal Justice Volunteer Award for Restorative Justice in 2002. Every time she tells prisoners her story, her healing becomes more complete. She hopes that the convicts will hear the depth of what she has to say, and not commit offenses again. Some of them weep when they hear her.[32]

Stories Are Raw, Tears Are Real

Weekly sessions with the inmates are structured around a curriculum that moves through topics including responsibility, accountability, confession, repentance, forgiveness, reconciliation, and restitution. Small-group facilitators pose questions from the Bridges to Life curriculum for discussion each evening. The focal point of the small-group meeting is each victim and each inmate telling his or her story some time during the twelve-week project. The participants focus on active listening. No preaching is allowed. When victims tell their stories, it is often the first time the criminals have heard what effect their crimes had on other human beings. Even though these victims are not the actual victims of these inmates' crimes, the effect is much the same—their stories connect real faces and real people to the crimes. Their tears are real. Even perpetrators of so-called victimless crimes like drug dealing wake up to the fact that the drugs endangered someone's child who used them. All the participants pose tough questions and ask for full disclosure. Hardened criminals who have kept up a ruse of innocence for many years have broken down and admitted their guilt. And once they have admitted guilt, the process of restoration can begin.

As part of the process, each inmate is asked to write two letters, which he reads to the small group. One letter is to the direct victim of his crime, asking for forgiveness. The other letter is to a member of his family who was affected by the crime or imprisonment. The first letter is not mailed, although the act of writing it and reading it aloud has a profound effect. The letter to a family member is often sent. Facing up to the unintended consequences for a wife or children left behind is sobering.

Both the inmates and the victims are skittish about getting together in the first place. There's good reason. It's pretty daunting to go to a prison if you've never been in one before. The nervousness sets in when the highway signs warn you not to pick up hitchhikers. As you stand outside looking at the tall metal gates topped with razor wire while you're waiting to have your identification checked, your apprehension increases. When the armed guards take away your identification, you feel like you've lost both your identity and your autonomy. When you're herded into a holding pen and double-locked between two metal gates, the steely, unbending reality of force is evident. By the time the guards take you through the third metal door that clangs shut behind you and you walk down an echoing hall where you hear prisoners' voices, anxiety notches up your blood pressure even higher. You try not to think about what the men did to land them there, and what they would be capable of now. Then you wonder what you're going to say to the tattooed and scarred inmates you meet that will be honest but not unleash an outburst of rage from them.

The inmates who volunteer for the program aren't exactly at ease either. The last thing a prisoner wants is to have angry and vengeful victims come in and fry him for what he's done. There are few things worse than justified anger. As one inmate put it, "When this cat said I should go to Bridges to Life, I said 'you crazy, man. This ain't gonna work for me.'" A prisoner named Chris said, "I was skeptical at first. I didn't want to be someone they beat up on, meet victims who get on my butt." But they both took the risk, and toughed it out to come back every week. Chris was surprised to find "the only thing I've experienced in twelve weeks is love. It's given me a safe haven, something I'll never forget. They helped me deal with a lot of things in my life I never dealt with. The greatest thing I learned is that I have another chance."[33]

"You People Fascinate Me. Why Do You Do It?"

The change in the inmates is nothing short of astonishing. Oscar is serving time for murder. He ran a gang with fifty men at his beck and call, and was no stranger to violence. He lost twenty family members to killings. Oscar has served ten years, and has a twelve-year-old daughter he has hardly seen as she has grown up. But since he's been through Bridges to Life, he's decided to use his remaining months in prison to work with kids on parole and teach them a better way to live. What has changed in him? "My heart, my character. God spoke to me and told me: *See what you're doing, hurting innocent people.* I didn't feel God could forgive me. But through John Sage and the group I realized God could cast sins as far as the East is from the West."

Bridges to Life was founded on Christ-centered principles, but is open to people of all faiths. A number of Muslims and several Jews have participated, as have inmates of other faiths or no faith. While the volunteers make no overt attempt to convert participants, spiritual awakening sometimes takes place through their mere presence. "You people fascinate me," one inmate admitted. "You keep coming back here week after week, and you're not getting paid to do this. I don't get it. Why do you do it?" When a victim volunteer explains what he or she has lived through and credits the source of his or her forgiveness, the spark jumps. As one prisoner from the LeBlanc prison put it, "You have planted the seed. Now I have to water it with obedience to God."

At a recent graduation in the Sugar Land prison in Texas, inmates got up one by one and told friends, family, and other prisoners what had transpired over the past three months. A prisoner named Brian said, "When I first met the victim volunteers, I was blown away by the compassion and love they showed for us." Another named Gregory said, "As the volunteers began to tell their stories, that's when my life began to change. The life I was living was illusions, it wasn't real. I never faced reality until I was in prison—sin hit me. This is not the life I want to live."

With the assistance of the Texas Department of Justice, Bridges to Life has meticulously tracked the behavior of the inmates who have come through the program and have been released from prison. So far, only 8 percent of them have returned. That's a remarkable result in light of the fact that 67 percent of prisoners throughout the nation are arrested again within three years of their release.[34] On average, 50 percent of the prisoners released end up going back to prison. The cost is vast: first, there's the direct cost of the crime itself, the damage to persons and property. Add the cost of incarceration, which for one person for twenty years is $360,000.[35] Then add the cost of lost labor from what would have been a working citizen, and the taxes he would have paid. The total cost to the public, both direct and indirect, for one criminal, could be more than half a million dollars. But the damage to the human souls—to the families of prisoners and to the victims of crime—is incalculable.

"I Don't Want to See You Here Again"

The victims want the inmates to understand that they have to make an irrevocable commitment never to come back to prison, and to leave violence behind. Jan Brown told a recent Bridges to Life graduating class, "The reason I do this is that each of you will get out of here. You may meet one of my family members. Please hug them, don't hurt them." The message is sometimes tart. A victim volunteer, Gina Schaefer, gave a bracing farewell:

> My entire way up here I pray for the right words. Unfortunately those words have pissed you off many times. But that's better than walking out of here unchanged. You certainly don't want the things to go on that have. Every moment of your life you have the chance to make a good difference or a bad difference. So decide and do it. You have my admiration and trust. Just remember I don't ever want to see you here again.

Although the program was founded to reach prisoners, Sage was surprised by the intensity of the effect on the victims who participate. The healing that takes place at the deepest levels is profound. The fact that the victims are extending good will, even though it's hard, is a potent spiritual act of reconciliation. A wellspring of healing grace follows. Mary Brown, whose husband was murdered, has volunteered in the Bridges to Life program five times. She says, "In the telling comes the healing, and I've gotten a lot of healing out of this." Jan Brown has done fourteen programs in six different prisons with this ministry, and she keeps coming back. Her nine-year-old daughter was kidnapped, was missing for two weeks, and was then found face down under a pile of rubble, almost completely deteriorated. She was unrecognizable. Her abductor and murderer was a middle-aged alcoholic junk dealer. For fourteen years, her murder was slowly killing her mother. But no longer, affirms Jan. "Bridges to Life helped me heal my life in ways I never expected."

The spiritual value of this work goes to a deep level, taking the participants face-to-face with the ultimate source of reconciliation and restitution. Tim Mattingly has been a friend of John Sage since high school. As the survivor of a drug gang attack, Tim had no interest in going into prisons to talk to criminals. But John persisted, reminding him of the words of Christ: "When you visit prisons, you visit me." Tim finally agreed. And since then, he hasn't stopped coming behind the razor wire to be with the inmates in white prison uniforms. He has discovered what Mother Teresa discovered when she said she touched the body of Jesus as she bathed and fed the poorest of the poor. Tim told recent Bridges to Life graduates in prison, "I'm here because Christ said to come. I see the face of Jesus Christ here, dressed in white. You can now go into the free world and be a peacemaker. This can become a victory if you wrap Christ around it."

Best Practices: Bridges to Life

- Pairs victims of crime with perpetrators of crime face-to-face
- Twelve-week encounters in small groups work deeply, relationally
- Inmates are required to write letters to victims and their own families asking forgiveness

- Curriculum covers responsibility, repentance, reconciliation, and restitution
- Victims demonstrate unconditional love

Results

- Eight percent recidivism rate among graduates, compared to above 50 percent national average
- Award-winning program rapidly replicating to reach new prisons; more than 1,000 graduates

No More Victims: Tough Teens Stand Up

When Marilyn Gambrell was a parole officer in Houston, one day she was seared by a scene as a woman was arrested and shoved into a police car, screaming. A barefoot two-year-old toddler clung to the officer's leg, howling that her mother was being taken away. The grandmother who was taking care of the child smacked the little girl with such vehemence that she knocked her down. "Shut up," she yelled. "I have enough problems without you screaming." She dragged the toddler by the arm up the steps to the house, hitting the steps with her ribs, and slammed the door. *What did the grandmother do to the baby girl when she got her inside the apartment where no one could see?* Marilyn wanted to know. "It haunted me," she says.[36]

For Marilyn, this scene drove home concern for the needs of a child left behind when a mother or father is taken to jail. Marilyn wanted to do something to help the kids left behind. She knew the community well, having served as a parole officer with a successful track record building relationships with the parolees she oversaw. With the core support of these locals, she launched No More Victims, a program to reach the children of prisoners.[37] At Smiley High School, in the tough northeast section of Houston, 70 percent of the students are economically disadvantaged, and at least 40 percent have one or both parents in jail. Marilyn offers a class to them, a refuge where they can come for help.

These are kids with lousy odds for success. According to the Bureau of Justice, nearly three-quarters of the kids who end up in state reform institutions grew up with at least one parent behind bars. The likelihood that they will follow a parent into trouble with the law is high: estimates are that at least six out of ten will end up in jail. They are more than twice as likely as other kids to be abused or neglected, suffer behavior disorders, become suicidal, get kicked out of school, or drop out. These are kids out on the street where the gangs and the drugs are, and most of them aren't just spectators.

Twenty-four kids came to Marilyn's class the first day. Gang leaders came with hoods over their heads, sullen and skeptical at first. But she had enough experience in the 'hood not to be intimidated. One gang member later told her, "We figure if you've got the guts to come in with kids like us, you're probably pretty cool. We're going to get down for you." More than three hundred kids have enrolled in the program at Smiley High School since its inception in 2000.

These are angry kids, raised with abuse and violence as the norm. They have bruises. Some have scars on their faces and their bodies. Many of the girls have been sexually assaulted. Some of the boys have been too, but find it harder to talk about being sexually abused. When these kids start opening up to talk about what has been done to them, they cry so hard that some of them vomit. One we'll call Lakisha was tied up and raped repeatedly by her mom's live-in boyfriend. "How could she leave me like that?" she wails with anguish. "How can I love her now?"

In the classes, Marilyn facilitates an exchange that gives kids a safe place to vent and she offers unconditional love. Her classroom has become a safe haven, a place of mutual healing, where the shame and the stigma of having a parent in jail are lifted because all the kids are in the same dilemma. Marilyn gives them something most of them have never experienced at home—consistent love and availability. "She tells us we are precious," says Dequlah Woods. "Nobody ever told us that." This love has tangible effects on even the toughest of kids. Gang violence declined 70 percent at Smiley High School in the first two years after No More Victims began. Six kids out of every ten in the program have raised their academic performance by at least half a letter grade and aren't skipping school. Arrests on campus have dropped by 75 percent.

Marilyn Gambrell is also going into the prisons to give the parents there some straight talk. She drives home the plight of the kids they have abandoned. And she works with the parents to get them ready to reenter society and let them know how the children feel who have been left behind. In an eye-opening exchange, the kids in No More Victims are given a chance to tell their side of the story to inmates who are doing time. Marilyn takes groups of the older kids into several of Houston's correctional facilities, where they tell the inmates face-to-face what it's like to be left behind. Although they are not speaking to their own parents, the therapeutic value of surrogates benefits all. "I hate him when he breaks all his promises," one boy shouts. A girl sounds off against the abuse she receives. "I don't care if your momma and daddy done that to you. You gotta stop." Another boy voices what many would like to, when he chokes, "All I ever want to hear is he love me, but he never tell me." When asked how many of them have been raped, a wave of most of their hands goes up. The prisoners put their heads in their hands and sink down into their chairs, realizing that their own children may have suffered the same horrific experiences. Some sob quietly.

The fact that somebody takes an interest in these kids is life giving. Brandon O'Neal's father was taken to jail one Christmas Eve and drifted in and out of his life all the years afterward. Anger flashes as he says, "My father was nothing but a sperm donor." Brandon tried to commit suicide several times. He has a scar on his chest where he put a knife in and ran against a wall. "I was so mad I wanted to get rid of myself. If it wasn't for this program, I'd be dead." But he pulled through to make the honor roll at high school, and graduated with his new friends in No More Victims.

It is too late to save some kids. The No More Victims class brought a stone to put on the unmarked grave of baby Traci. She was taken out to a state facility for babies born in prison when she was two days old. She died when she was ten days old, having been severely sexually abused as a newborn. The kids took her tragic plight to heart. They said, "Nobody cares about children of incarcerated parents, even newborns, especially babies born in prison." They raised the money to buy the marker, which says,

They stuck pink and red roses in the ground and said, "Somebody's going to know you're here now."

Amachi: Mobilizing Mentors for Prisoners' Children

When Wilson Goode was twelve years old, his father was sent to jail for being abusive to his wife and family. This sharecropper family left North Carolina and moved to Philadelphia for safety's sake, before Wilson's father was released. Young Wilson joined the First Baptist Church of Paschall, where the minister and his wife took an interest in him and mentored him. When others had given up on him, including his counselor at school, this couple had confidence in him and encouraged him. They succeeded in raising his aspirations, and eventually sent him off to college. From the good that was sowed in his soul, he went on to become Rev. Dr. Wilson W. Goode Sr., and to serve as the mayor of Philadelphia for eight years.[38]

Because he knows personally how much it matters for a kid with a parent in prison to have a mentor, Wilson Goode is passionate about Amachi. The program he founded in Philadelphia bears the name of a West African word that means "who knows but what God has brought us through this child." Amachi was founded to reach the 2.5 million children of the incarcerated, a population that includes prisoners in federal and state prisons as well as in local jails.[39] These children are nearly invisible, yet they are the most acutely at-risk of all youth. As Wilson Goode explains it:

> The Amachi program is geared to a targeted group of young people I believe are the most at-risk in our society. These young people have one or both parents in jail and are most likely to end up in jail themselves. In fact, the U.S. Senate says 70 percent of these children will follow in their [parents'] footsteps. The Amachi program is an intervention to redirect the negative energies of these young people by placing in their lives a loving, caring adult.[40]

When the police car pulls up at the door and a parent is arrested, children are sent into a maelstrom of trauma. They are terrified and ashamed. They face taunts and cruelty at school. Many children are plucked out of their homes and shipped off to relatives, where they are often abused, malnourished, and poorly educated. They feel abandoned and depressed. They suffer fits of anger, often get into fights at school, skip classes, and drop out. Some join gangs as a substitute for family. Delinquency and drug abuse often follow. The path to destruction opens wide to swallow them. Even when the parents get out of jail, their children most often live in poverty and lack positive role models. Without intervention, the children of prisoners have bleak prospects, most tinged with violence.

Passionate about Recruiting

The Amachi program has set out to reverse that downward spiral, pairing children of the incarcerated with mentors drawn from local churches. A partnership launched this ambitious effort, including Public/Private Ventures, Big Brother Big Sister of Southeastern Pennsylvania, the Center for Research on Religion in Urban Civil Society at the University of Pennsylvania, and local congregations. The partnership takes the expertise of the oldest successful mentoring agency in the country[41] and couples it with one of the most effective research organizations tracking the progress of faith-based initiatives. A certain amount of the meteoric success of Amachi's launch came from Goode's personal credibility and his deep engagement with the project. Drawing on his extensive knowledge of the Philadelphia community, Goode personally visited nearly fifty churches throughout the city to recruit participating teams. He gave presentations in cellblocks of the prisons. He contacted prison chaplains and social workers to gain their support.

Wilson Goode says:

> I am personally passionate about this program because I believe that bringing together local congregations with the private sector offers a new vehicle for attacking an age-old problem. The marriage between the private sector and the faith sector is one which I believe can yield huge dividends in the future. In-

deed, if the past three years is any indication of what can be done, there will be successful programs all over the country to assist children of incarcerated parents.

Nick Barbetta, the prison's head chaplain who helps coordinate the program, points out, "This has always been a weak link in the chain of prison ministry."[42] Criminal justice officials in Philadelphia welcome the presence of people of faith in addressing the needs of prisoners and their families. Alan Appel, director of inmate services at the Philadelphia Prison System, observes, "I'm not a person of faith, but I'm very practical. And from a practical standpoint, what's missing in the lives of many of these children is the development of a value system. . . . So the fact that these mentors come from a faith-based values system, to me, is terrific."[43]

Amachi has succeeded in mobilizing more than 800 volunteers from forty-two congregations, who in turn are screened and matched with youngsters from their neighborhoods. Each participating church receives a stipend to hire a coordinator for its team. So far, 542 mentoring matches have been made, and 400 are currently active, as the children rotate through the program. The results are being monitored. Mentors are asked to commit at least an hour a week. In practice, they are spending more than nine hours a month, not counting at least four phone calls, which are sometimes a lifeline for the kids. A mentor might spend time taking a child to a park, playing baseball, swimming, helping with homework, or just getting a hamburger. He or she might invite the youngster to come over for the weekend and join the mentor's family. Mostly they are there to listen. "It's keeping promises to them," says Larry Watson, mentor of eleven-year-old Andrew, whose father is now in jail and whose mother has also been imprisoned. "It's filling a gap of loneliness. It's being there for them."[44] Watson fills that gap with particular understanding, as he had a childhood of abuse and violence.

Mentoring Matters

As research on the effects of Big Brothers Big Sisters demonstrates, having a mentor "significantly reduces a young person's initiation of drug and alcohol use, improves their school performance and attendance, and reduces incidences of violence."[45] Big Brothers Big Sisters had never focused specifically on the children of prisoners until this initiative, but they have embraced the challenge. This group of kids is more likely to suffer high rates of child abuse and neglect, illiteracy, drug and alcohol abuse, crime, violence, incarceration, and premature death.[46] But with the intervention of one caring adult, a remarkable turnaround can take place. Based on internal evaluations done by Public/Private Ventures and Big Brothers Big Sisters, the children participating in Amachi have shown improvements in their academic performance, in relationships, and in building trust with others. These children attend school more regularly, present fewer behavioral problems, and show a better attitude toward their peers.

While there was some concern that parents might resent the intervention, most are grateful for the assistance. Lakisha Gray, whose husband has been in prison for most of her eight-year-old daughter's life, is relieved to have the help of mentor Nikeeta Warren. Lakisha concluded that holding down three jobs wasn't leaving her much time to spend with her daughter. She's grateful for the presence of a mentor in her Secola's life. "Nikeeta's there when we need her," she said. "It feels like I've known her all my life and she helps me, too."[47]

Amachi has made quite a splash. Because it is effectively meeting the needs of one of the target groups the White House has singled out for intervention, President George W. Bush has visited the program in Philadelphia. The Executive Session at Harvard University has adopted it for study the next two years. The FASTEN (Faith and Service Technical Education Network) project of Pew Charitable Trusts has adopted Amachi as one of its vehicles to enter additional cities. One thing that sets Amachi apart from most faith-based programs is that it was designed with a sophisticated evaluation component built in. Launched with a grant from the Pew Charitable Trusts, along with funding from the William Simon Foundation, Amachi originated in partnership with CRRUCS and Public/Private Ventures, organizations skilled in tracking results and evaluating outcomes. So at every step of the way, data is being entered on the incoming children, the mentors, the amount of time they spend together, the performance of the participating churches, and the response of the kids. This overview will reveal the value of the program, and its founders are confident it will justify its replication in other cities.

The current mayor of Philadelphia, John Street, has made Amachi one of six priorities of the city in dealing with children. What Amachi is now doing for five hundred children in Philadelphia is what Wilson Goode would like to do for two million children nationwide. "These children are the most at-risk in our society," Goode says. "By mentoring these children, we can alter their behavior."[48] He's passionate about giving these children of promise a chance for fulfillment. And he wants every single one of them to have a mentor. Preferably, today.

Best Practices: Amachi

• Provides intervention for acutely endangered at-risk children
• Effectively mobilizes mentors from local churches
• Provides an infrastructure for administering partnerships
• Couples solid research and evaluation to the strategy

Results

• Four hundred active matches between children and mentors, mobilized from forty-two congregations.
• Replication under way in other cities

Craine House: Keeping Mothers and Babies Together

Young children whose mothers are taken away from them to prison are traumatized. The experience can lead to depression, aggression, and learning disorders,[49] and the likelihood that they will follow into law-breaking activity later is five to seven times higher than for other children. Between 70 and 80 percent of women in prison are mothers of children under eighteen.[50] If the children witness their mother's arrest, they may suffer post-traumatic syndrome.[51] Since the effect is so catastrophic, it is somewhat surprising that there is not a concerted effort to keep the families together, particularly mothers with babies and preschoolers. In fact, four innovative facilities in the country allow mothers and their young children to live in an alternative sentencing house. The Craine House in Indianapolis is one of them. What has been a home for female offenders since 1978 redefined its program in 1993 to keep newborns and toddlers with their mothers while they serve their sentences.

Recognizing the need for young children to keep the bond with their mothers, the founders of the Craine House program set out to provide an alternative that would stabilize the women while giving their children a chance to break the cycle of abuse and dysfunctionality. Nonviolent offenders can receive a sentence to the Craine House rather than to the county jail. The women are expected to get a job, pay partial rent, and care for their children. The Craine House staff provides rooms equipped with cribs and toys, meals, counseling, encouragement, and a framework of accountability, including daily Breathalyzer tests and random drug testing.[52]

The turn-of-the-century house in Indianapolis, which can accommodate up to eight adult residents, is cheerful and inviting, with a porch, comfortable sofas in the living room, a piano, a backyard for children to play in, and private rooms for each of the women with their children. A well-equipped playroom in the basement painted in bright pastels is decorated with big pictures of Babar, Winnie the Pooh, and Big Bird above the playhouses and little tables. The women's rooms are furnished with respectable donated furniture, which they can take with them when they leave if it is needed. Photos of the children are tucked into the mirror frames, and baby shoes, cribs, and toys give a nursery touch to each woman's personal quarters. The garden gives residents a chance to see that you reap what you sow.

For the women who come here, this may be their last chance. Most of them have been sentenced for drugs, forgery, or prostitution. Getting an alternative sentence like this is rare, and if they break the rules, they go straight to jail, losing daily contact with their children. Vanessa Bell has six children, ages nine months to fourteen years. The youngest three live with her at Craine House. She was convicted of prostitution and drug use, was in and out of jail for a number of years, and lost custody of one of her children, who was placed for adoption. "I was disgusted with myself back then," she admits. Now she is working on her GED and has a job. "I look at my kids and I keep going because I know they are proud of me," Vanessa can say now. "I love my babies, and I want them to see me grow and know that I'm not that person I used to be and I'm going to be even better in time."[53]

"I'm Social, She's Justice"

Substance abuse is a problem for 60–70 percent of the women who are arrested, so Craine House refers its residents to local programs to help them. The program also offers job and parenting skills as well as vocational training. The staff does intensive one-on-one counseling and mentoring. All of the staff members are believers, and they attempt to model a Christ-like life. A total of nine to twelve women on the staff provide round-the-clock supervision. Several of them have a background in criminal justice. The executive director is Suzanne Milner, a former deputy sheriff with a no-nonsense attitude. Her slightly more laid-back colleague, Kathy Mance O'Brian, says only partly in jest, "I'm social, she's justice."

The combination of tough boundaries and nurture has an effect. The women who live here have to stick to the rules, report where they are going, and not deviate from their plan. It's one strike and you're out. But while the offenders live in the house, they have the opportunity to learn a different way to live, modeled by the staff and practiced with the other women and children. More than half of all women in prison have been abused. They come from dysfunctional backgrounds, and the opportunity to live in a wholesome environment can have a deep healing effect. If they stay at Craine House a full year, the effect can be transformational. A study was done through the Indiana University School of Social Work to track the results of Craine House. An analysis of the participants between 1993 and 1999 found that of the women who successfully completed the program and left Craine House, only 21 percent of them returned to prison.[54] This is a significant improvement compared to overall national recidivism rates of 50 percent or higher.

Craine House receives slightly more than half its funding from Marion County Community Corrections, which pays a portion of the costs for each woman who utilizes this alternative to incarceration. The rest of the $350,000 budget is raised from private sources, including the local Episcopal diocese, which founded the house in 1978 as a living memorial to Bishop John P. Craine, who had a particular interest in prison ministry. The model holds promise for halting the multigenerational damage of incarceration by protecting the most vulnerable victims of crime: prisoners' young children.

Best Practices: Craine House

- Provides an innovative alternative sentencing option for mothers of small children
- Lessens traumatic separation of infants and toddlers, decreasing their likelihood of future damage
- Challenges mothers with keen oversight, drug testing, and a one-strike policy on infractions
- Provides discipline, encouragement, and character formation through classes and mentoring

Results

- Decreases recidivism to 20.8 percent, compared to national average of 50 percent

chapter 6

Faith, Health, and Holistic Change

Human beings are complex, and any efforts attempting to make a shattered life whole have to take into account a host of variables. While it's tempting to think in terms of single causes for social maladies, the reality is often multicausal. The most successful faith-based groups have healed hurting people by addressing both body and soul together. For example, homelessness, drug addiction, and unemployment are often overlapping lassos on a life, and until they can be untied simultaneously, one or another of their knots will hold a person down. Faith-based practitioners insist that each of these issues has a physical and a spiritual dimension. A holistic approach looks at them in the broader context of the whole person, who consists of more than the hunger for a fix, or the absence of a job or a place to live. Until individuals get to the root cause of their misery, they cannot be free or whole. Until they can cope with the multifaceted demands of life, they cannot remain stable. Holistic ministry helps them do that.

If a homeless or unemployed person is addicted, the best intentions in helping them find employment or an apartment will end in failure until the addiction is mastered. But there are other needs as well. A person who has relinquished responsibility needs to nurture character and inner strength. He or she may need to learn marketable job skills and practical life skills like parenting, resolving conflicts, or managing a family budget. The habits of the heart determine how people solve problems, withstand temptations, and plan for the future. A holistic approach integrates faith into the approach, and addresses the complete person: body and soul, mind and will. Ron Sider and Heidi Unruh have defined holistic outreach as that which "combine[s] techniques from the medical and social sciences with inherently religious components such as prayer, worship, and the study of sacred texts."[1] Caregivers who embrace all these concerns, fusing faith with an understanding of medical and social science, are having greater success in changing lives for the better.

Holistic Welfare-to-Work

Many of the faith-based programs assisting in the transition from welfare-to-work have embraced the holistic approach. In fact, this is one characteristic difference they have had from secular programs, which focused more on job readiness alone. When the first flurry of activity followed the Welfare Reform Act in 1996, there were many efforts to help single mothers with the job search. But it became clear that women making the transition had a whole complex of issues that needed to be addressed before they could become stable in the workplace. For many individuals, getting a job proved easier than keeping it. Unless a single mother had a childcare system nailed down, including a backup plan if her child was sick, she was likely to miss work and lose her job. Or if her transportation was unreliable, she would be chronically late and risk being fired. If she had never prepared a family budget and learned how to live within it, the paycheck wouldn't cover the utility bills at the end of the month. If she had never learned to shop comparing prices or to prepare nutritious homemade meals, the money would evaporate into fast food.

Holistic care groups sprang up in churches all over the country to make mentors available to provide assistance in each of these areas, to impart life skills as well as offering Bible study and personal encouragement to solidify character and motivation.[2] Care circles clustered around these single mothers, meeting with them every week, encouraging and admonishing them, praying with them, and helping them acquire the internal fortification they needed to succeed. Neither job-search coaching, resume assistance, childcare, transportation, nor Bible study alone would have guaranteed success. But the combination had a profound effect.

Good Samaritan Ministries in Michigan was one of the pioneers in the field, developing a church-based mentoring curriculum. Under the initial leadership of Bill Raymond and later Janet DeYoung, the organization trained small teams from local churches to assist low-income families with budgeting, goal setting, developing self-esteem, and managing day-to-day problems. The organization collaborated with Ottawa County and was the first in the country to successfully transition "every able-bodied welfare recipient into a job."[3] New Focus, under Jenny Forner's direction, established effective Compassion Circles to surround impoverished individuals to help them move toward financial independence. Participants completed a twelve-week financial freedom class, and were then placed with a team of volunteers who worked with them to devise a long-term plan. The mentor circles offered both advice and friendship in a relationship of accountability. The effects on transitioning families have been profound.

Transitional Living: New Hope Serving the Homeless

So often, well-intended efforts have perpetuated a state of dependency, rather than getting down to the origin of the problem. It may give volunteers a good feeling to hand out sandwiches to the homeless under the bridge. But the truly loving thing would be to discover the reasons for their homelessness, and to help them no longer be homeless. But it is much harder.

Open Door Mission

For fifty years, the Open Door Mission has been serving the homeless in Houston. The traditional "soup, soap, and salvation" approach that many Christian shelters have had for years goes deeper here. Not content to merely deliver a prayer before meals and an optional sermon in the chapel, this mission is out to break the cycle of homelessness. In a holistic approach, the Open Door Mission offers not only food, shelter, and showers, but also transition out of homelessness into jobs, housing, and a new life.

Drug and alcohol abuse are frequently factors in homelessness. The DoorWay Recovery Program at the Open Door Mission offers addicts a chance to leave addiction. About a third of the 214 men who can stay at the shelter at any given time are enrolled in the program, which lasts nine months. It's no cakewalk: the first ninety days are spent totally cut off from the outside world. Classroom instruction points participants toward faith in God in a program much like a twelve-step program, while their bodies are being weaned from drugs or alcohol. Discipleship classes, prayer, Bible study, and work are all part of the routine, which remolds habits and character. Participants assist in preparing food, doing laundry, or handling registration for the shelter, gradually taking on more responsibility as they prepare to enter the workforce. Graduates of the program are tracked for one year after its completion to see if they are still drug and alcohol free, employed, in permanent housing, and not in trouble with the law. Seventy-two percent of them have been successful.[4]

In fact, the "faith factor" is a potent influence in treating drug addiction. "If ever the sum were greater than the parts, it is in combining the power of God, religion and spirituality with the power of science and professional medicine to prevent and treat substance abuse and addiction," according to Joseph A. Califano Jr., former U.S. Secretary of Health, Education and Welfare and president of the National Center on Addiction and Substance Abuse at Columbia University. "Too often, clergy and physicians, religion and science are ships passing in the night. When we separate the worlds of medicine and spirituality, we deny effective help to a host of individuals with substance abuse problems," says Califano.[5]

One of the most intriguing approaches the Open Door Mission utilizes is the technique of EEG-biofeedback, fused with the faith-based approach.[6] Many of the men have been addicted to crack cocaine. Because of repeated use of drugs or alcohol, an addict has a pattern of brain waves that is measurably different from those of a healthy person. The disorder affects the addict's ability to focus, disturbs sleep patterns, and is linked to impulsive behavior. When electrodes are connected to the head and both ear lobes, brainwaves are translated into a visual image. A person can learn to control his mental responses to bring the visual representation of brainwaves into a pattern of concentric circles, responding to the visual images on the computer screen or to audio cues. The participants do three sessions of biofeedback each week, for a total of thirty sessions. Through repetition, the brainwave patterns can be altered, which results in less sleep disturbance, less uncontrollable anger, and more focus. Participants who have used the technique say it has helped them learn better in the other areas of the program because it has removed some of the obstacles. The length of stay at the mission tripled for those who were involved in the therapy, according to Dr. John Cummins.

Results were compiled on 178 crack-addicted men who remained in the program to complete all thirty biofeedback sessions. Of these, eighty-seven could be located for a one-year follow-up. Before the study, four out of five of these men had been imprisoned for drug-related offenses, and all of them had been addicted for at least twelve years. One year after the treatment ended, 49 percent of them had not used crack at all, and only 10 percent had relapsed to full-blown addiction. Forty percent of them had used it fewer than ten times during a relapse, but were clean at the time of the follow-up.[7] Ninety percent of the men reported they had not used alcohol or marijuana, which are common fallback drugs to replace crack use.

The biofeedback approach is a fascinating technique with challenging implications. Southwest Health Technology has been working in partnership with the Open Door Mission since 1999 to administer the process and study the results. The study done on its efficacy concludes, "The addition of EEG biofeedback to crack-cocaine treatment regimens offers promise as an effective intervention for treating crack-cocaine abuse."[8] Secular homeless shelters have tried the biofeedback technique alone but were disappointed in the results.[9] But the Open Door Mission has found that in combination with its faith-saturated DoorWay Recovery Program, biofeedback has boosted its success rate from 60 percent to 72 percent. A participant is considered a success if, after one year, he is drug free, employed, not in trouble with the law, and has permanent housing. When the faith-centered approach of the DoorWay Recovery Program is coupled with the EEG-biofeedback technique, the results seem to foster holistic recovery.[10]

The Open Door Mission also has a Healing Dorm, the only facility of its kind in the region, which provides beds for up to forty-four men who leave the hospital after surgery. Amputees and men in wheelchairs, who would be otherwise out on the street after an operation, can stay there to recover. The men sometimes arrive in a cab sent by the hospital, still in their hospital gowns, with no possessions and nowhere to go. Most of them stay for several months, during which time the Open Door staff helps them get benefits while seeking permanent housing for them.

A work-study program at the Open Door Mission allows residents who have completed drug recovery to continue to live at the mission while they are pursuing education or embarking on a first job. In collaboration with the local Houston Community College, Open Door Mission makes it possible for its residents to enter programs to learn culinary arts, heating repair, or welding, with the opportunity at the end of the process to transition into a job that pays well. Random drug testing and a zero-tolerance policy reinforce recovery while participants solidify their skills for a productive future.

Wheeler Mission Ministries

Wheeler Mission Ministries in Indianapolis has embarked on an innovative path to move its homeless into self-sufficiency. In their two shelters, which sleep 160, about 10 percent of their clientele have been willing to enter their "Life with a Purpose" program, which is a biblically based program to leave drug or alcohol addiction, similar to the twelve-step approach. "You have to get to the core of the problem, which is addiction," says Rick Alvis, president of Wheeler Mission Ministries. Of the men who have entered the program, 50 percent have successfully left addiction. Once they have taken this step, they can go to a learning center, which provides an individualized computer-based tutorial to help them complete a GED or teach them new subjects they need. Classes in life skills teach them how to balance a checkbook and set up a budget. Other neighborhood ministries help to round out a full curriculum of possibilities for individual development. Men at this stage who land a job can continue to live at the shelter while they save money to launch out on their own.

The organization offers a radical change in environment to give recovering addicts a fresh start: a program called Hebron. Wheeler Mission owns a 280-acre camp adjacent to a 12,000-acre park. Men who have only known urban environments who come to stay are shocked by the absence of gunshots and traffic noise. No newspapers, television, or telephones disturb the pristine experience of nature. Some come and stay for a year, slowly putting their lives back together. Families have been reunited here, reweaving the fabric that had been torn through addiction. Some participants have been so captivated that they have come back to stay another year as servant leadership volunteers.

Wheeler Mission Ministries and the Open Door Mission are members of the Association of Gospel Rescue Missions, an umbrella organization for three hundred member ministries in the United States and Canada, serving 35 million meals and providing shelter for 13 million nights of lodging. As admirable as their track record of providing food and shelter for the homeless is, the even more impressive achievement is that together they returned 15,131 people to the community as productive citizens in 2002. These were homeless people who took part in transitioning programs from three to twelve months long who now have made it back into sobriety and a residence. While this number is still a small proportion of the total these shelters serve, it represents a giant step forward in dealing effectively with the root causes of homelessness and in rehabilitating the whole person.

Interfaith Housing Coalition

The Interfaith Housing Coalition in Dallas, founded by Ben Beltzer, has taken on the task of transitioning homeless women into employment

This prisoner begins a new life with a changed heart. InnerChange Freedom Initiative is immersing prisoners in Scripture, mentoring, and life skills classes to form men who will not return to prison. This pioneer program in Texas, Iowa, Minnesota, and Kansas is reaching nearly 700 U.S. prisoners to effect moral and spiritual regeneration. It has cut recidivism by half.

LEFT: Cordelia Taylor transplanted her family to Milwaukee's inner city to found Family House, a residence for the elderly poor. She has reclaimed an entire city block from drug dealers, while providing food and basic medical care to several thousand neighbors.

BELOW: Brian King (left) was a Gangster Disciple in Chicago who didn't expect to survive his addiction or the shootouts of his drug dealing days. A changed man, he now reaches at-risk youth and their families with the credibility that comes from experience.

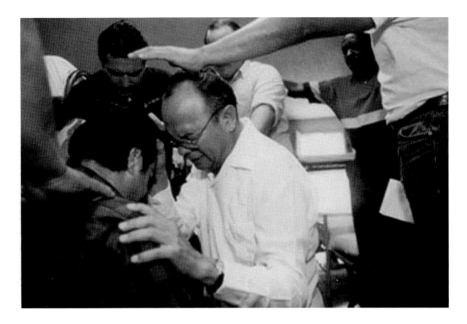

Freddie Garcia prays for a drug addict that just walked into Victory Home in San Antonio. Prayer, Scripture, and discipline have been the beginning of a new life for more than 13,000 addicts his ministry has helped leave drugs.

John K. Sage (*left*) and Chris Dearnley (*right*) put their Harvard business skills to work in founding Pura Vida Coffee, a social entrepreneurial enterprise that harnesses the market to support ministry with its profits. Sage runs the coffee growing industry, marketing gourmet beans on the Internet while Dearnley serves street children and drug addicts in Costa Rica with soup kitchens.

Having spent a lifetime in community renewal, John Perkins invites high school and college students to join him in Mississippi, where he equips them with the skills to serve as street saints.

BELOW LEFT: Open Door Mission's combination of EEG-biofeedback and its faith-saturated DoorWay Recovery Program has boosted drug rehabilitation success rates to seventy-two percent in this homeless shelter in Houston.

BELOW RIGHT: Dismayed by black-on-black violence in Boston, Eugene Rivers gathered pastors and police to form the Ten Point Coalition against juvenile bloodshed. In less than a decade, the crime rate dropped seventy-seven percent.

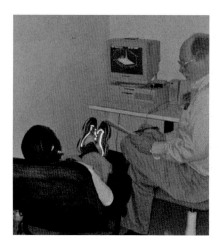

Social entrepreneur Bob Cote' covers fifty-five percent of the costs of Step 13, his homeless shelter in Denver, by putting the resident men to work in jobs where they can learn marketable skills while leaving drugs and alcohol. He accepts no government funds.

Economic Opportunities provide jobs for men coming out of prison or drug rehab, pairing character and spiritual development with real labor, so they can establish a good work record and keep their next job.

Kids Hope USA takes a one-on-one approach, linking one adult to one child, and one church to one school. The result is transforming not only at-risk children, but the mentors' churches in 217 partnerships nationwide.

The Oaks Academy provides a challenging, classical, Christ-centered education for children in an inner city neighborhood of Indianapolis. In partnership with the Jubilee Center, they offer wrap-around services to families.

In Detroit, Cornerstone School third graders learn to play the violin as part of the overall instrumental music program introduced to build a passion for the arts in all students.

The changing ethnicity of America is making city-wide renewal increasingly colorful, as these Hmong dancers illustrate.

There are 18,000 kids under the age of eighteen in a one-mile radius of Urban Ventures in Minneapolis. To serve them, Urban Ventures is building the Colin Powell Youth Center to house a dozen agencies offering a continuum of mentoring, leadership and life skills, fathering classes, and entrepreneurial businesses.

ABOVE: Prisoners in InnerChange Freedom Initiative who are willing to enter into this intensive faith-based program are given eighteen months of round-the-clock training before being released into the care of a mentor. George W. Bush initiated this program as governor, and later welcomed graduates into the White House.

LEFT: In an innovative alternative to prison, Vanessa Bell was able to serve her sentence at the Craine House in Indianapolis, and keep her baby and two young children with her. Children of prisoners left behind are six times more likely to follow their parents into jail.

and housing. Women may live there in furnished rooms for three months, during which time they are expected to find a job, save $1,200, and transition into permanent housing. Mentors who volunteer from more than thirty Dallas congregations surround them, with some addressing spiritual growth in Bible study while others assist in budgeting and yet others coach the job search. Finding a job is the women's first responsibility, and keeping it is the next one. With such comprehensive mentoring, it's virtually impossible for these women to fall through the cracks. "The greatest gift we have to give is love," says Beltzer. "Unconditionally."

It's a tough-love approach. If residents are caught using drugs or alcohol, the staff ejects them. Some have come back to thank the staff for holding them accountable. A program like this requires a comprehensive plan to address many issues at one time, and a large group of committed volunteers, but this one is doing it successfully. An independent study confirms that more than two-thirds of the participants make the transition into employment and self-sufficiency, and that two years later they are still off the streets and on the job.

Star of Hope Transitional Living Center

The Star of Hope has three emergency shelters for women, men, and families in Houston, Texas, which together served nearly eight thousand individuals in 2003. The Transitional Living Center is a cutting-edge approach that provides quarters for parents with children who want to make a transition into a stable life. While they live here, the building blocks for self-sufficiency are laid. If drug addiction is the issue, which it often is, an in-house treatment center is the first stop. If there's a need for literacy training or GED, there are educational courses available. Computer labs are on-site. Childcare manages the little ones while Mom or Dad is in classes or looking for a job. Classes in parenting skills are part of the package. The Baylor College of Medicine provides therapists, a psychologist, and psychiatrist to help in cases of depression or schizophrenia and so on. A marriage and family counselor is available, as are classes in anger management. Each one of the educational units concludes with a graduation ceremony with robes, and participants walk across a stage with a new-found pride in accomplishment. "I've never finished anything before," one woman tearfully admitted at a recent graduation, probably speaking for many others.

The City of Refuge Church provides mentors for the graduates, working with them in their transition into self-sufficiency through Bible-based character development. A circle of mentors surrounds each woman, meeting with her every week to provide coaching in how to get and keep a job, time and money management, parenting, and encouragement in spiritual growth. Then graduates move into apartments, where they receive follow-up contact. Some families are transitioning into houses built by Habitat for Humanity.

The Transitional Living Center was launched in 1988, a concept that was ahead of the national curve in serving the homeless. Residents stay for a full year, then go out on their own, as forty participants did successfully last year. Star of Hope began a similar recovery program in its men's shelter in 2001, which is helping male residents get their lives back on track.

Leaving Addiction: Teen Challenge

One of the best-documented success rates among faith-based efforts is that of Teen Challenge, which combats drug addiction. Teen Challenge began in 1958 in Brooklyn, New York, when David Wilkerson, a Pennsylvania pastor, read about a violent gang murder. He decided to intervene on the streets of New York, and discovered that the young people he met were confronted with a host of problems, including drug addiction and prostitution to support their habit. Today there are 130 Teen Challenge centers in 43 states and Puerto Rico, and 250 more in 67 nations throughout the world. Teen Challenge provides 3,400 beds for residential treatment in the United States. The organization is privately funded. It is a faith-based, self-accrediting ministry with ninety-eight accreditation standards its affiliates must fulfill. Its staff members have training in theology rather than in social work or medicine, because the approach is that of a ministry.

Residential faith-based programs like Teen Challenge offer holistic healing as well. Even after a teen's decision to leave drugs, a wide range of issues have to be addressed to heal the whole person. That's why this program focuses not only on faith—which is central—but also on family relations, anger, depression, attitudes toward authority, and work. Living in an environment with people who model Christ-like lives is another crucial part of the process. Intensive work in all these areas over time is necessary to accomplish lasting character transformation. If the participants stay for a full year, the change is profound.

When Teen Challenge claimed a 70 percent cure rate for addiction, it was challenged by the U.S. Department of Health, Education and Welfare, which funded a study by the National Institute of Mental Health in 1975. Critics were skeptical of Teen Challenge's claims. To the surprise of the investigators, the study published in 1976 showed that 86 percent of Teen Challenge graduates were living drug-free lives.[11]

A 1994 follow-up study conducted in Chattanooga, Tennessee, surveyed alumni of Teen Challenge over a twelve-year period. Although 72 percent of the respondents had failed in other drug treatment programs before entering Teen Challenge, 67 percent of those who graduated still abstained from illegal drugs and alcohol. Evidence indicates they had gotten their lives back on track.

- Eighty-eight percent of the graduates did not require additional drug treatment after leaving Teen Challenge.
- Sixty percent of the respondents continued their education after graduating from Teen Challenge.
- Seventy-two percent of the respondents were employed.
- Sixty percent of the respondents indicated that their relationship with family was good.[12]

A further study tracked participants in the Teen Challenge program in Rehrersburg, Pennsylvania. The study showed that those who stayed in the program a full year until graduation were more likely to remain drug

free, hold a job, continue their education, and not be arrested. Of those
who remained until completion:

- Sixty-seven percent were verified drug free by urinalysis.
- Seventy-two percent continued their educations, including GED or college.
- Seventy-five percent were employed, more than half at their present job longer than
  one year.
- Although ninety percent of the graduates had been arrested before entering the program,
  only thirty percent had been rearrested in the seven years following graduation.[13]

A fourth study was released in June 1999, by Northwestern University
in Illinois. It showed that 86 percent of those who complete the Teen
Challenge program have remained drug free. They were more likely to escape the "revolving door phenomenon" of substance abuse, lead a stable
life, and hold down jobs. Apparently, the faith involvement had staying
power: 84 percent of the graduates were found to attend church weekly.
The study also revealed that while only 41 percent of the graduates of
other drug treatment programs were employed two years later, 90 percent
of the Teen Challenge graduates were gainfully employed.[14]

The difference between Teen Challenge and secular drug and alcohol
programs is the belief that an addict must find a "personal relationship with
Jesus Christ" if he or she wants to find permanent freedom from addiction.
Teen Challenge does not believe drugs are the root of the problem, but a
symptom of a deeper internal problem, which is at its root spiritual. Addicts often use drugs to mask pain from broken family relationships, sexual
abuse, anger, and interpersonal conflicts, and these issues are dealt with.
Daily classes address life issues in a structured curriculum, with a focus on
personal application.

The Teen Challenge staff teaches students to assume responsibility, to
become productive, to become good parents and spouses, and to deal
with failure and depression. As the students begin to apply these teachings in their daily lives, they develop new life skills, attitudes, and behavior. Students are also immersed in the disciplines of work activity, preparing them for self-sufficiency.

Experience indicates that it takes a full year to establish new habits and patterns of thinking that will enable participants to continue to live drug-free lives once they leave. Those who leave earlier have a markedly lower rate of success, again indicating that transformation is more a process than an event.

Because faith is at the center of its methodology, Teen Challenge has been dubbed a "faith-saturated" approach. The method has been emulated by other ministries that have not had the benefit of studies to validate their success. But the track record of Victory Fellowship, for example, is comparable according to its internal reporting—which makes sense, since its founder, Freddie Garcia, is a graduate of a Teen Challenge program. Both Teen Challenge and Victory Fellowship immerse addicts in a twenty-four-hour program centered on instruction in faith, which produces sobriety in 70–80 percent of the participants if they stay for one year.

Where Faith, Health, and Human Behavior Intersect

Programs like these that deal with faith and drug addiction operate at an intriguing intersection. A number of recent studies have examined the relationship between the practice of faith and health-related and social outcomes. While for years science found the possibility of a relationship between faith and wellness implausible, a small but significant number of researchers have begun to probe this field. While more research is needed, many of the results give empirical evidence of the beneficial influence of faith.

Dr. David Larson called the power of faith "the forgotten factor," which has been neglected by scientists because of their attitude toward religion.[15] But as the research continues on the intersection of faith, health, and human behavior, studies have concluded that the "faith factor" has a verifiable influence. Dr. Byron Johnson compiled the results of a review of eight hundred studies in "Objective Hope: Assessing the Effectiveness of Faith-based Organizations."[16] Johnson found that people regularly involved in religious activity are less likely to abuse drugs and alcohol. They are less likely to commit suicide. Ninety-seven percent of the studies indicated that religiously involved people were less likely to engage in promiscuous sexual behavior. Those who worship regularly are less likely to physically abuse others. Eighty-one percent of the studies reported that religious involvement corresponded with greater "happiness, life satisfaction, morale, positive affect or some other measure of well-being." While the number of such studies is steadily increasing, much more remains to be done to accurately assess the efficacy of the "faith factor."

Johnson makes a distinction between what he calls "organic religion" and "intentional religion." Organic religion is the kind practiced by people who grow up in a family with faith, believe in God, go to worship services regularly, pray, and demonstrate some everyday evidence of faith in their lives. Intentional religion is the sort that a drug addict or a convict in prison might experience when he or she seeks a faith-based program and finds God. Intentional religion, Johnson tells us, "is the exposure to religion one receives at a particular time in life for a particular purpose." More research has been conducted on organic religion than on intentional religion. In fact, of the eight hundred studies Johnson reviewed, only twenty-five dealt specifically with the "efficacy of faith-based interventions."

Johnson says, "Theoretically, organic religion is interesting because if a relationship can be established between religious practice and overall health and well-being, then there may be additional justification for assuming that intentional religion via faith-based organizations may yield similar outcomes as to those among organic studies."[17] In other words, if the everyday variety kind of religion ordinary people practice has a measurable impact on their health, it is conceivable that the "intentional religion" that a recovering drug addict, homeless person, or convict experiences in a faith-based program may also have corresponding tangible health and behavioral outcomes that can be validated.

Documenting the Faith Factor

Although the tendency of the modern mind is to deny that faith could have any tangible influence on physical health, a growing body of studies is probing the relationship between religion and medical science. Drs. Harold Koenig, David Larson, and Michael McCullough have directed a number of studies validating that faith and health have a great deal to do with each other. A 1999 study tracked nearly four thousand older adults for six years to see if there was a correlation between their religious involvement and their rate of mortality. Koenig, Larson, McCullough, and others concluded "the relative hazard of dying for frequent church attenders was 46 percent less than for infrequent attenders . . . The effect on survival was equivalent to that of wearing vs. not wearing seat belts in auto accidents." Or put another way, the "effect on survival was equivalent to that of not smoking vs. smoking."[18] Another study by McCullough tracked nearly 126,000 people and concluded that those individuals who regularly attend a church, synagogue, or mosque have 29 percent higher odds of survival.[19]

Apparently, the faith factor gives aging patients better odds for living without some ailments as well as increasing their likelihood of longevity. A 2002 study examined 196 patients fifty-five or older with congestive heart failure or chronic pulmonary disease. The researchers concluded that the patients who were religiously involved on a regular basis had correspondingly less severe illness or functional disability, and fewer psychiatric problems, hospitalizations for depression, or drinking problems.[20]

Why might this be the case? Dr. Koenig set out to investigate a substance present in the bloodstream called plasma interleukin-6, which affects the immune system, and other factors associated with aging. IL-6 levels are higher in older people with lymphoma, osteoporosis, Alzheimer's, some kinds of diabetes, AIDS/HIV, and other immune disorders. A study of four thousand people sixty-five or older revealed that regular churchgoers were half as likely to have high levels of IL-6.[21] While this is certainly not the only factor affecting longevity, it may be one.

Koenig documents that people who practice their faith regularly seem to be less likely to engage in destructive lifestyles, such as drug or alcohol abuse. A study on nearly three thousand individuals ages 18–97 concluded that those who participated in religious services at least weekly were 71 percent less likely to have alcoholism in the past six months and 52 percent less likely to have it in their lifetime.[22] Comparable studies have validated a clear correspondence between religious involvement and decreased use of alcohol and drugs among inner-city youth, who are otherwise at risk for such behavior.

But the "faith factor" goes into zones that surprisingly have nothing to do with the volitional behavior of the subject. The effects of prayer have been validated in studies of heart patients. Cardiologists William Harris and James O'Keefe directed a study at the Mid-America Heart Institute in Kansas City. In a group of one thousand heart patients, unbeknownst to them, half the group was being prayed for by volunteers and the other half was not. Patients who were prayed for had "11 percent fewer heart attacks, strokes, and life-threatening complications than those not prayed for."[23] In another study, 150 acute cardiac patients were offered various therapies, including stress relaxation, imagery, touch therapy, and distant intercessory prayer. Patients who received off-site intercessory prayer had the lowest complication rates.[24]

Apparently, religious involvement has an effect in speeding the recovery of patients from conditions including clinical depression. In a 1998 study, ninety-four hospitalized older patients diagnosed with a depressive disorder were studied. Those who participated in worship regularly had "70 percent more rapid remissions than patients with lower scores."[25] A Canadian study produced similar conclusions. Among one hundred clinically depressed patients, those who regularly attended church and prayed recovered faster than their counterparts who did not.[26]

Together, studies like these present the possibility that faith does in fact have a tangible effect on wellness, healing, and recovery in a way that pushes the borders of understanding for both religion and medical science. Dr. John Templeton Jr., a retired pediatric surgeon who heads the John Templeton Foundation, lamented that in the early '90s "you couldn't take a course on spirituality in medical school if you wanted to. Now these courses are required in many schools."[27] By 2003, classes on spirituality and healing had entered the curriculum in 65 percent of the medical schools in the United States.[28] The field is expanding in light of encouraging studies examining effects of the metaphysical on the physical, pushing the outer boundaries of the unknown.

The evidence amassed by doctors including Koenig and McCullough has significant implications for faith-based organizations. If the power of prayer really can affect the rate of recovery of cardiac patients who do not know they are being prayed for, why could it not enhance the recovery of drug addicts in a faith-based program where they learn to pray for themselves? If the practice of religion speeds recovery from serious conditions like clinical depression, why could it not be a factor in psychological recovery from abuse or abandonment? The implications for further investigation of the faith factor, particularly as it applies to the healing of human beings broken in body and spirit, are intriguing.

Chapter 7

Social Entrepreneurs

Social entrepreneurs are people who approach social problems with the mindset of an entrepreneur in the business sector. These creative people have one leg firmly planted in the entrepreneurial marketplace and the other firmly planted in ministry. They have come up with some innovative ways to harness the energy of both worlds. Social entrepreneurs are results-oriented, innovative, cost-effective, nimble in responding to changing situations, and can demonstrate a successful track record. They use the principles of business to produce good in the social sector. Some provide jobs to the people they are serving, generating spiritual growth as well as a boost from business to support the ministry. It's an inspired mix.

It is also a whole different mindset. Think soup kitchens that, instead of just ladling out soup, employ the people who serve there. Instead of computer games to keep kids off the street, think teaching at-risk teens programming to build Web sites for corporate clients. Instead of therapy for the handicapped, think micro-enterprises where they can work. It's where money meets ministry in a way that lifts people up.

- Homeboyz Interactive in Milwaukee takes at-risk young people from the inner city and teaches them computer skills, giving them client projects doing programming and building Web sites. They encourage youngsters to return to school, get an internship in information technology, or start their own businesses.
- Golden Gate Community Inc. in San Francisco has spawned three enterprises with a creative twist to employ at-risk youth and young adults, some of whom have been homeless or drug

addicts. Ashbury Images produces artsy T-shirts, while Einstein's Café serves up sumptuous salads and sandwiches. The Pedal Revolution is another such enterprise, a bicycle shop now sought out by San Francisco's bike messengers.[1]

- Pastor Jim Ortiz in Whittier, California, snaps up homes in need of repairs from HUD and deploys a team of recovering addicts and men released from prison to spiff them up. The men learn to show up for work on time and acquire marketable skills as carpenters or electricians. My Friend's House turns a profit of about $10,000 on each house, which is reinvested in the ministry. And the neighborhood improves with the addition of attractive, affordable housing.
- Pastor Rufus Smith at the City of Refuge Church in Houston teaches entrepreneurship to inner-city kids, ten to fifteen years old, in Vocation Beginner's School. Their curriculum teaches the vocabulary of capitalism, the content of the U.S. Constitution, Bible-based character traits, and work ethics. After the study segment, teams go out to power-wash driveways and do mobile car washes in office parking lots. Their summer earnings are paid out in vouchers for school clothes and supplies, and kids pay their own way on mission trips to places like Mexico or the Appalachians.
- In Aurora, Colorado, donated goods stock shops for people in transition. Men leaving drug treatment or prison can work in Bud's Warehouse, where they sell recycled building materials, receive a mentor, and take classes in life skills, while getting job experience. Single mothers can learn and earn at Baby Bud's, a thrift store for baby items, which offers classes for these inner-city moms to acquire job and life skills while they work. The profits finance the programs.

Social entrepreneurship has spawned a new kind of philanthropy as well, which works like venture capital funding. The Roberts Enterprise Development Fund in San Francisco invests in nonprofits to allow them to earn as well as serve. REDF has concluded that hybrid approaches like these "social purpose enterprises" have multiple advantages. They can provide jobs for the hard-to-employ. They can provide financial stability in a volatile philanthropic climate or generate money to support new programs. And they can bring some of the discipline of business to the ministry mindset.[2]

Another aspect of social entrepreneurship is financial literacy. In Chicago, Goodcity encourages low-income residents to enter the mainstream economy through financial education and matched savings accounts. Individual Development Accounts must be used for education or business capitalization to qualify for matching funds dollar-for-dollar. These accounts are a ticket out of poverty and into entrepreneurship for the low-income folks who have discovered them. Goodcity is currently coaching one hundred sixty individuals with their accounts. Participants are required to complete a twelve-part course in financial literacy that covers topics including stewardship, capitalism, family financial security, credit and debt management, insurance, home purchase and maintenance, and investing.

Participants in IDAs agree to save at least $25 a month, many of them for the first time in their lives. Some use their savings to launch micro-enterprises. For example, Sindanny Pizzinni withdrew $609 of her savings and was matched with $1,827 to help capitalize her business. Other participants acquire assets that would have been unthinkable before. Colleen Lane, a single mother, joined forces with her sister, leveraging $3,400 in IDA savings to purchase a $169,000 two-flat building in Garfield Park. To give low-income residents even more of a leg up, Goodcity links its IDA participants to an employment clearinghouse and business opportunities. The result is self-sufficiency.

These and the following examples of the nation's cutting-edge strategies show what may be the future face of the faith-based community.

Pura Vida: Coffee with a Cause

Coffee, Christianity, and capitalism. It sounds like an unlikely brew. But it's precisely the blend that John K. Sage and Chris Dearnley came up with to use Web technology to feed street urchins and to give a hand up to recovering crack addicts in Costa Rica. Two Harvard Business School graduates came up with the concept for Pura Vida Coffee, which grows and packages gourmet coffee beans from Costa Rica. John Sage runs the marketing end from Seattle on the Internet. The profits finance the ministry Chris Dearnley runs in Concepcio de Alajuelita, a rough neighborhood of Costa Rica's capital, San Jose. It's a brilliant example of social entrepreneurship that harnesses the energy of the market to support a faith-based ministry that is helping the poor.

"Pura Vida" means "pure life" in Spanish. In Costa Rica on the streets, it's more like "way cool" or "awesome." It's an apt label for the "coffee with a cause." Sage and Dearnley forged a friendship at the Harvard Business School as they learned finance and world economics together. When they graduated in 1989, their paths diverged. Sage went to Microsoft, where he spent five years, often putting in an eighty-hour workweek. He quit, took a short breather, and went to work for an early Web company, Starwave, which was later acquired by Disney. His friend Chris Dearnley headed to Costa Rica to work with a company training business executives, and ended up becoming a pastor in the charismatic Vineyard Church. As a student at Wheaton College, Dearnley had taken as many courses in religion as he did in business. After getting his MBA at Harvard, the call to serve took the upper hand, and Dearnley committed his $250,000 family inheritance to the ministry, which included an outreach and drug rehabilitation center, a job-training program, a carpentry shop, and health checkups for street kids.

Sage and Dearnley got together again at the Harvard reunion in San Diego in 1997. Dearnley had started the ministry in Costa Rica to rescue street children and addicts from disease, drugs, and death. But once his inheritance was gone, which it nearly was, the ministry would be too. He was long on vision, but short on cash. Sage, at thirty-eight, had enough money that he would never need to work again. What he needed was a purpose.

After a round of golf and a margarita by the poolside, inspiration struck. Dearnley had brought a pound of coffee beans from Costa Rica as a gift. Sage had recently consulted on a charity project for Starbucks. It occurred to both of them that these coffee beans from Costa Rica could be marketed for less than a pound from Starbucks, and the profits could be used to finance the ministry. The idea was born on the back of a cocktail napkin. Within a week of returning to Costa Rica, Chris Dearnley had convinced a local coffee producer to sell him five hundred pounds of beans and to store them in a Miami warehouse. John K. Sage agreed to put up the capital and market the gourmet coffee beans from his office in Seattle, via the Internet. With a Web site, they could bypass the expense of mailing photos and letters to explain their cause.

Bone-Grinding Poverty, Neglected Children

Sage went to Costa Rica to firm up the business plan with Dearnley, to order more beans, and to immerse himself in Alajuelita. The stench of the river that doubles as a sewer assaulted his senses. What he saw there overwhelmed him even more: addiction, brutality, and neglected children with scabby faces and fungus infections, bone-grinding poverty, ox carts groaning with the weight of firewood on streets pocked with holes, and concrete-block houses with teenagers outside smoking crack.

Pura Vida's mission is to combine the efforts of business and philanthropy to help the lives of at-risk children. The Web site, www.puravidacoffee.com, includes photos and stories of the families served in Costa Rica. "For people drinking a cup of coffee in a law firm in Miami or in a church in Milwaukee, who in some way are committed to this ministry, this is how they can participate," says Sage. "The money is nice, but what this is about is stirring the passions of people devoted to Jesus Christ."

It's not exactly usual corporate practice to give money away, or to hire the homeless. But Sage and Dearnley like being iconoclasts. Their brand of social entrepreneurship is garnering attention. They both are invited back every year to the Harvard Business School, where a case study on Pura Vida was written for its class on Entrepreneurship in the Social Sector. Recent years have added another dimension to Pura Vida: social justice. The company is committed to buying the coffee at a price that guarantees a living wage to the farmers that produce it. Pura Vida is moving toward producing all its coffee under certified fair trade. Because coffee prices are now at a one-hundred-year low, that means Pura Vida is paying roughly double the commodity price. They have joined a co-op so they can buy from family farmers; as Sage explains, they are "refocusing on the ministry aspect upstream," as they benefit the farmers as well as the street children. Most of the coffee is also organic, so there is an environmental commitment on the part of the company as well. "From bean to cup we are extracting every bit of value," says Sage. They're producing coffee for other nonprofits, giving them their own label: Habitat for Humanity has its House Blend; World Relief has the Mission Blend; and the Episcopal Relief and Development markets its Bishop's Blend.

"I love the challenge of running a business," Sage says. "It lets me keep score." The score is $2.8 million in revenue this past year, and the company is growing. More than $400,000 has gone back into the ministry in Costa Rica, including donations. Capital requirements are growing, and raising money from investors is a tricky business for a nonprofit. Pura Vida invented a new financial instrument, which obtains funds in a standard five- to seven-year note at six percent, but with a new twist. When the note is paid off, the lender can become a shareholder in the company, and designate a favorite charity to receive the proceeds. It's an imaginative approach, blending finance and philanthropy.

What really keeps Sage hustling in his two-story brick building in Seattle is the harsh reality of homes with rusted corrugated roofs that leak and the dirty faces of dark-eyed children in need in Costa Rica. Every pound of coffee Sage can sell helps serve kids in need. Karina Matamoros Gutierez wasn't responding like other children, so Dearnley's church members took her to a doctor, who concluded she couldn't hear. The profits of Pura Vida bought her a hearing aid. In the doctor's office after Karina had been fitted with the hearing devices, the girl's mother, who was standing behind her, called her name. The little girl turned immediately and embraced her. The opportunity to help children like Karina keeps Dearnley on the streets of Costa Rica and keeps Sage plugged into his computer. "We can't just wash our hands in situations like that and say God will provide," claims Sage. "We have to do it."[3]

Best Practices: Pura Vida Coffee

- Harnesses entrepreneurial skills to support ministry in a cost-effective way, utilizing the Internet for marketing coffee
- Utilizes local produce to support local ministry serving the needy
- Improves living standard of not only ministry recipients, but also coffee producers through fair wages
- Gives consumers and investors a way to participate in the ministry
- Utilizes forces of the free market to produce social, economic, and spiritual good

Results

- $2.8 million company generates $300,000 to support ministry in coffee-growing countries
- Street children, single mothers, and recovering drug addicts are beneficiaries of after-school programs, life skills classes, and computer centers
- Three soup kitchens feed 30,000 people each year

Resources: Turning Immigrants into Entrepreneurs

Much of the debate on immigrants centers on the fear that they will end up on welfare or never be assimilated into America. A job-training program called Resources, founded by a Roman Catholic priest in Brooklyn, shows how private programs can take English-illiterate immigrants from China, El Salvador, and the former Soviet republics, as well as refugees from Haiti and Vietnam, and turn them into successful, English-speaking chefs, professional cleaners, and graphic designers. The program's success in training and placing immigrants in jobs that pay well—all without government assistance—could help shift the immigration debate from the language of exclusion to that of empowerment.[4]

It all started with a wrong turn. Monsignor Ronald T. Marino worked for fifteen years at the Roman Catholic Migration Office in New York, but had never confronted the problem of immigrant employment. On a sweltering day in July 1994, however, he found he couldn't avoid it. While scouting for a used office furniture store in a building on Brooklyn's 65th

Street, Marino stumbled upon a sweaty room overflowing with perhaps 150 women and children, most of them Chinese. They were sewing, and all the windows were painted over to hide their existence from outsiders.

Marino demanded an explanation from the manager, who was seated in his air-conditioned office. "Why are there children working at the sewing machines? Isn't that illegal?" asked Marino. "Don't you feel any compunction about the morality of this whole thing?" He was promptly escorted to the door. Marino realized he had stumbled upon a nest of illegal immigrants working in a sweatshop: something he thought no longer existed. "The church has to do something about this," the Catholic priest fumed. "At that moment, I started to get obsessed with the work issue for immigrants." Marino decided to found Resources, which has become one of the country's most successful job-training programs for immigrants. The program he directs in Brooklyn has helped more than six hundred men and women—many with little work experience and limited English— to become literate in English and to qualify for good jobs. If the passport to economic independence is effective job training, Marino is the sort of man you want stamping the papers. He trains immigrants in one of four nonprofit businesses owned by Resources. About 98 percent of his graduates are employed and have avoided the welfare rolls.

Finding the right training formula took some undercover work. Marino posed as a man in search of a career change to see how government job-training programs worked. He found they were both costly and ineffective. Vocational schools taught some skills, but the participants were still virtually unemployable. The programs were rewarded with subsidies for keeping large numbers of participants in training, but not for placing them in jobs. Neither were they penalized for failing to make the trainees marketable. Marino told the *Washington Times:* "The people running the programs would say to me, off the record, that I as an American who could speak the language so well stood a pretty good chance of getting a job, but that these immigrants basically had no hope." Marino launched Resources in 1994 with $50,000 in seed money, and has received no funds from the government. The successful training program owns the businesses where its trainees work, and their work helps fund the program. It is now self-supporting, grossing about $1 million during each of the past three years.

Trainees are tested in their English ability and are required to take remedial English until they demonstrate proficiency. As Marino explains, "If you're serious about living and working here, you have to be able to understand a supervisor's instructions in English." Trainees attend one of thirty English schools run by the Catholic Migration offices in Brooklyn and Queens. Once they learn enough English, immigrants get professional training in one of the four businesses run by Resources: commercial cleaning, computer graphics, culinary arts, or construction and carpentry. If they pick professional cleaning, they receive 120 hours of instruction. For graphics and culinary arts, students take three semesters of instruction totaling 300 hours. Then they receive on-the-job training through an apprenticeship. Participants pay $400 per semester, either in advance or over time from their salaries. The price is a steal of a deal: a comparable course from the Culinary Institute of America costs $20,000 for a year.

Resources is distinguished from other programs by its underlying philosophy: "The aim of work is not the work itself, but rather it is man." The words are those of Pope John Paul II, from the encyclical "On Human Work" (1980), and they hang on the wall at Resources as a reminder. They reflect the modern Roman Catholic understanding that honest work—whatever it may be—has an ennobling effect on the human spirit. This is because work encourages the virtues of discipline, cooperation, honesty—all essential to fostering the dignity of the worker. "I try to communicate an attitude toward work to the participants," says Michael A. Campo, a job trainer and manager with Resources. "The attitude is very important. Some think work is what you do for a wage, but it is far more. The feeling in the heart comes first before the technical procedures. If you put your heart into your work, and do whatever you do well, it's contagious."

When Dave Ali arrived in America from Trinidad, he did not know how to turn on a computer. After two years in the program, he became a full-time assistant in computer graphics at Resources. "I'm very excited about it," he says. "I never knew I had any artistic talent, but they put a lot of effort into teaching me. Now I help other people discover their own ideas." The clients of Resources Graphic Design have included Italian fashion designer Max Mara and Telesoft USA, a global telecommunications company. Much of its business has come from the Catholic diocese, for which they have produced pastoral letters, the bishop's Christmas cards, posters, and parish letterhead.

Professional Cleaning did more than $130,000 worth of business in its first year alone, and since then has grown to produce more than $850,000 each year in revenue. Marino seeks clients in the faith community, like Catholic schools and church buildings. Trained apprentices get a company uniform and join a supervised team at a work site, earning wages starting at $10 an hour. After a year they can be trained as supervisors, managing a crew, ordering supplies, handling customers, and earning upwards of $13 an hour. Supervisors can then be trained as managers, who bid on new contracts, ascertain the needs of customers, obtain machinery and chemicals, and dispense work crews. Competent managers can form their own small businesses, and Resources gives them two contracts to get started if they wish to go independent.

Students of culinary arts receive 300 hours of instruction; then they are ready to apprentice in a restaurant. Restaurateurs are each asked to contribute $1,000 toward a scholarship for a student. Each student learns on-site from a professional chef. Many are offered a permanent position with their sponsors after graduation, as they have become valuable to the chefs who have personally trained them. All of the students who have graduated from the culinary arts program are now gainfully employed.

After several years' experience with Resources, Marino discovered that he had missed an opportunity. "So many of these immigrants come from countries where they have to use their hands. They are skilled carpenters, plumbers, and painters. And I was trying to turn them into something else," he admits. Capitalizing on their existing skills, he founded Resources Building Services, which takes these masters who have the skills of a "jack of all trades" and hires them out to do repairs, construction, and carpentry. It's a perfect fit. The new line of business grossed $350,000 in its first year.

The Resources program effectively combines job training with job creation. It offers an occupational training program that can train immigrants while legally paying them a stipend as long as they are in training. After intensive training, some qualify for specific jobs only they can fill, and can obtain documentation if they do not already have it. Most of the program's graduates work in businesses owned by Resources, and the local business community and Catholic parishes and schools in the diocese are regular clients for cleaning and graphics services. Local businesses and printing shops that cannot afford in-house graphics staff also contract with Resources, as do parishes and schools. The basic strengths of the model—teaching not only marketable skills but also the inherent value of work and vocation—are in urgent demand.

Marino likes to reflect on the purpose of work—and of life—and on how his program helps to strengthen the character of immigrants and those who are working with them. He believes those who empower the needy to live in dignity and provide for their families reap spiritual fruits for themselves. "We are made in the image of Christ," Marino says. "In order for me to find my dignity, I need to help you find yours. If you serve Christ, you see Him in the person you serve. You discover your own dignity in seeing Him in others."

Best Practices: Resources

- Requires proficiency in English and provides instruction to those trainees who need it
- Teaches trades through both hands-on training and classroom instruction
- Strengthens the character of participants; teaches the dignity of excellence in work
- Creates companies to employ the trainees
- Assists trainees in obtaining documentation for permanent employment
- Helps graduates gain clients, launches them in their own business, makes them self-sufficient

Results

- More than six hundred immigrants trained in trades; 98 percent of them are employed

Step 13: Putting Recovering Alcoholics and Addicts to Work

When Bob Coté started drinking a fifth of vodka for lunch every day and landed on skid row in Denver, he looked at his drunk friends passed out around him and realized he was just as doomed as they were unless he made a radical change. He poured out the bottle and created a new program for men like himself to get a grip on their lives. Step 13 takes the twelve steps to recovery and takes it to the next level. It's a faith-based program coupled with work.[5]

The former Golden Gloves boxer stands 6´3˝ and doesn't take any guff from anybody. And he's not overly sentimental about the homeless population he is serving. "Yeah, there are women and children out there down on their luck," he says, "but half of these guys are psychopathic maniacs." If they get too rowdy, he has a baseball bat behind his desk as an enforcer. "You have to set the tone," he explains with a chuckle, but it's clear he would use it if he needed to. Fights are not unusual, and he's not intimidated when they break out.

Men who come to Step 13 go cold turkey with drugs and alcohol, and Bob gives them Antabuse® and random drug tests to make sure they don't cheat. It's one strike and you're out. Learning discipline is part of the process, so the men are expected to hit the decks early and be out the door by 7:30 a.m. on their way to work. If they don't make their beds, he says, "I nail the door to their room shut." His philosophy is "work works," and he sends the residents out on various jobs run through Step 13, like power washing trucks and moving furniture. When there are games at the nearby Coors Stadium, his men do auto detailing for sports fans who park in the nearby lots. His men print logos on everything from baseball caps to coffee mugs and mouse pads for companies that hire them. Bob's clientele includes twenty-six companies throughout Denver who are willing to give these men a shot at taking on responsibility to earn an honest wage. Altogether, the business activity generates about half the program's $435,000 budget.

Work experience is an important part of the process of getting the lives of the recovering men back on track, as well as the engine for revenue that keeps the doors open. As the residents learn the discipline of showing up on time and getting a job done, they acquire the habits and skills that will allow them to support themselves when they leave. The fact that Step 13 secures the contracts for work gives the men an opportunity they would find tough to merit on their own. It's up to them to sink or swim, but they are given the chance.

As a shrewd observer of human character, Bob has figured out how to use what he calls "constructive envy" as an incentive for his men to become productive. Newcomers to the shelter live in a dorm-style room when they first arrive, with no privacy and an early curfew. But if they perform at work and stay off drugs and alcohol, they can work their way up to the next level, with a separate room and a key with privileges to come and go.

It's not an approach that coddles the men. Some decide to leave rather than comply with the stringent rules. But for those who tough it out, they have the opportunity to get their lives in order and make the transition to sobriety and productivity. They do so with the encouragement of staff members, most of whom are men who came through the program and have succeeded. They also know all the wiles of winos and addicts who are in denial. "It takes a duck to know a duck," says Bob. But he knows as well as anyone what it is to be grateful for beating his addiction. "Every day I don't drink I thank God," he says. "I should have been dead a hundred times."

Best Practices: Step 13

- Getting to the root problem in homelessness, which is often addiction
- Setting tough standards for sobriety and enforcing them
- Offering practical job experience and training
- Creating revenue streams in social purpose enterprises
- Creating a community of responsibility that changes character

Results

- Thirty-five percent of the men who walk through the door end up living in sobriety

Jobs Partnership

It all started with a parking lot that needed paving. When inner-city pastor Donald McCoy called Chris Mangum's company in Raleigh, North
Carolina, and was unexpectedly put through to the boss, a conversation
began that tapped into the needs of both. The black pastor and the white
businessman met weekly to talk over lunch, probing the nudge that had
brought their very different worlds into intersection. Six weeks into the relationship that led beyond paving, an almost offhand comment crystallized the reason they had come together. Mangum remarked that ten of his
trucks were parked because they had no driver. McCoy responded that at
least that many of his able-bodied parishioners were "parked" because
they needed a job. An idea was born.

McCoy and Mangum challenged each other to find a dozen others in
each of their disparate realms to join forces to prepare people willing to
work, and to plug them into opportunities in the business community.
Both were men of faith, and they believed that a biblical basis of character
formation, coupled with hands-on job-skill training, could be successful if
mentors in the local churches could be mobilized to walk with the people
making the transition into productive employment. They convened a
steering committee of eight pastors of different denominations and races
and an equally diverse group of seven businessmen to reflect the city of
Raleigh. Jobs Partnership is the result of what these two men believe was a
divine appointment. The program that began in Raleigh in 1996 has now
been replicated in twenty-seven cities throughout America, and has effectively prepared and placed 1,800 people in jobs that pay well.

Anyone who has worked with the unemployed or underemployed
knows that getting a job is not their biggest problem. Keeping it is. Jobs
Partnership works on two tracks for precisely that reason. The twelve-
week curriculum, which entails two nights of instruction each week, focuses on personal spiritual growth and character development in tandem
with practical job-preparation skills. "Keys to Personal and Professional
Success" uses the Bible as its textbook, and guides its participants to ex-

amine who they are in relationship to God and others, and their attitudes toward work and authority. It also addresses skills in communication, conflict resolution, integrity, and stewardship. The aim is nothing short of reshaping the participants' spirits into a godly model. The second track, "Steps to Personal and Professional Success," focuses on application in a work setting. Participants learn from local human resources experts how to fill out job applications, prepare resumes, and have a successful interview. But the deepest focus is on how to keep the job once they get it, excelling and advancing. The one-two approach over the course of three months is potent. The desirability of the job-willing applicant is honed to produce a more appealing applicant, but more importantly, the skills to keep the job are inculcated. The program instills in its participants the character required to keep showing up for work, to take orders well, to cooperate with others, and to strive to excel—making it more likely that these new employees will stay on the job and thrive.

But the power of the Jobs Partnership goes beyond this. It comes in the partnerships it fosters. Participating churches agree to take responsibility to walk with the participants for two full years, providing mentors and backup in transportation or child care for them, helping them find housing, and providing personal support as needed. "We are connecting disconnected people to lifelong community," explains Rev. Skip Long, who has headed Jobs Partnership in Raleigh since its inception. "These are relationships that turn into friendships, till the Father comes back or they go to be with the Father."[6] Allen, the man he has mentored for the past six years, has become a friend, along with five other men who have met with Allen, prayed with him, helped him find housing, and assisted him in getting a grip on his finances.

Partners from the business community pool their opportunities into a job bank, opening the doors for positions with benefits and prospects for advancement for these trained job applicants. But the support system goes even further. Once a grad has been hired, he or she is given a "buddy" in the workplace, who agrees to look out for the newcomer, answering questions, giving encouragement, and providing an on-ramp into the work environment.

It is a strategy so comprehensive that it has produced a remarkable track record for its graduates, 84 percent of whom are still employed a year after placement. As they see changed lives, the participating churches have found they have an engine of regeneration humming in their ranks. And the businesses that have opened their doors are discovering that graduates of Jobs Partnership are not as likely to leave as other entry-level employees, which brings down their costly turnover rate. It's win-win-win for all involved.

Two of the byproducts of this approach did not come about intentionally. When Skip Long and five other men came around Allen to mentor him, they came from different churches and backgrounds. The genuine friendship they share now has transcended race and denomination in a way no one could have designed—racial reconciliation came about through their co-laboring. The other surprise is the way mentors have sprung into action to meet needs. The eighty-seventh graduate of Jobs Partnership just moved into his first home, although promoting home ownership is not an official part of the program. The mentors have simply seen needs and have put their faith in action to meet them.

Jobs Partnership is now operating in twenty-seven locations throughout the country, in big cities as well as in small municipalities. The phenomenal success of Jobs Partnership depends chiefly on the infrastructure of relationships. This is not a cookie-cutter program you can take out of a box and start tomorrow, although it definitely can be replicated, as twenty-seven cities have demonstrated.[7] Amy Sherman has written a wonderfully practical and comprehensive manual for replication.[8] A Spanish version of the Jobs Partnership curriculum is now available as well as English. Skip Long urges enthusiasts to take the time to get all the players shoulder to shoulder well in advance of the launch, because the trust that's necessary for this model to thrive across denominational and racial lines isn't born overnight. Some cities and congregations need half a year of preparation. But when the stars align, it's like unleashing a juggernaut.

Best Practices: Jobs Partnership

- Provides a curriculum that addresses job readiness as well as character, attitudes toward authority, and stewardship of time and money from a biblical perspective
- Mobilizes the readiness of churches to mentor people in transition and support them in lasting relationships
- Opens the doors of businesses by providing training and accountability for future employees, decreasing their turnover
- Provides people in transition a continuum of training, mentoring, personal support, and a "buddy" in the workplace to stay on track
- Builds bridges across denominational and racial boundaries

Results

- Eighteen hundred graduates placed in jobs
- Eighty-four percent of graduates still employed one year later
- Successfully replicated in twenty-seven cities in seven years

Brookwood Community: Overcoming Handicaps

The Brookwood Community has created a new breed of social entrepreneurship that redefines the parameters of a productive life. Located in Brookshire, Texas, this audacious institution has taken people with a combination of multiple handicaps that require twenty-four-hour care, and has transformed them into an entrepreneurial workforce. Brookwood offers handicapped adults an opportunity to live together in a model community of cheerful residential houses with gardens, and to participate in on-site enterprises that give them the dignity that comes through work. The community is situated on 475 acres west of Houston, where the first resident enrolled in 1985.[9]

The Brookwood Community is an innovative solution to a growing problem facing twenty-eight to thirty million functionally disabled adults in the United States. These people with disabilities are, for the first time in medical history, outliving their parents. The people who come to Brookwood have a combination of serious mental and physical disabilities. Some result from accidents, others from congenital disorders like Down's syndrome. Two Brookwood residents are seriously damaged victims of drunk drivers. Unlike most institutions for the handicapped, Brookwood mixes disabilities. Some residents have cerebral palsy; others are deaf, have mental retardation, or are schizophrenic. Those who can walk without assistance push the wheelchairs of those who need help. When they go back to their homes in the evening, a man with Down's syndrome feeds one who is blind.

Each person contributes whatever skills they have to cottage industries run on the premises. Individuals with multiple disabilities are all engaged in the businesses of producing angel figures, hanging plants, Christmas tree ornaments, vases, and a host of attractive gift items. The residents are carefully assessed to determine what their physical and mental capabilities are, and they are paired with a task they can master through training. Some place pre-mixed clay into molds, while others create designs for handmade cards, or apply the successive layers of color in the silkscreen process. Some plant seedlings in tiny pots of soil or carry flats of flowers to the delivery trucks. The boldest enterprise is the $1.2 million café on the Brookwood campus, where the waitstaff is comprised of a handicapped person paired with a teacher, in a well-organized system designed with the help of leading restaurateurs. The café has proven so popular that it serves seven hundred people a week.

Enterprise is one of the key elements of Brookwood's success. Each of the citizens at Brookwood has the dignity given the human spirit through work. Instead of being given useless physical therapy exercises, like moving balls from one basket to another, the residents have the opportunity to create objects that have a value. The residents receive a paycheck for what they do. They have the double satisfaction of producing a vase or an angel or a blooming plant, knowing that they are earning money through their work and contributing to their own upkeep. There is a spiritual value in a purposeful existence, and being able to work is one way to fulfill this need in the human heart. Whatever they do, they are trained to do well. Yvonne

Streit, Brookwood's founder, calls her philosophy "pragmatic therapy in tandem with life."

"We're All One Accident Away"

As you walk into the orderly workshops, people sit working on clay figures, some painting colorful glaze on angels, while others are putting malleable mass into rubber molds. Another person takes the figures as they come out of the molds, and chips away excess contours. They work as a team. Some are withdrawn, but most give a cheerful response to visitors. Because of their disabilities, most of the residents are at the emotional level of pre-teens. As Yvonne Streit and her colleague Joe Mazzu go through the grounds, they greet the residents by name, stopping to chat with them. The friendly banter shows that they know each of them individually. Visitors glancing through the workshops can experience a confusing moment in trying to ascertain which workers are the instructors and which are the residents. It's not always evident at first or even second glance. With one stroke, the distinction between "us" and "them" falls away. As Joe gently remarks, "There but for the grace of God go I. We're all one accident away."

There are currently just over one hundred full-time citizens, as the staff prefers to call them, living at Brookwood Community, who are joined by an additional thirty who come each day to participate in the enterprises. It takes a staff of two hundred to care for them, including some part time, dividing the round-the-clock care into three shifts, seven days a week. Some staff members are permanently residential, living on the Brookwood property. The annual budget is $9 million: one-third paid in tuition and more than one-third from solicited donations. But the part of the Brookwood story that is astonishing is that so much of the budget is earned through sale of items the residents have produced themselves. Brookwood Community stocks three distribution centers and offers its wares on a Web site: www.brookwoodcommunity.org. Last year's sales totaled $2.2 million.

Everything in the community speaks to excellence. The entry hall is grand, displaying examples of all the citizen-produced ceramics in handsome display cases. A chapel with stunning stained-glass windows was donated. An aquatic wonderland was specially constructed for Brook-wood's unique needs, with a waterslide that is wheelchair accessible through an elevator. Whirlpool-force water creates a circular stream past palm trees and fanciful faux alligators. The beach-like entry slopes into the water for gradual immersion in a solarium enclosed with rising glass panels. Each of the residential homes has its own décor, suiting the residents who each have their individual rooms there. The property is meticulously landscaped.

After burning to the ground in 2001, the on-site shop for Brookwood's wares has risen like a phoenix from the ashes. What has arisen to take its place is a $1.5 million complex adjoining the café, with colorful combinations of pottery, flowers, decorative touches, and enticing wares. A garden outside invites people to linger by the fountain or sculpture garden, or they can walk through the greenhouse filled with blooming plants. It's a real paradigm shift for anyone who has visited programs for the handicapped elsewhere.

Brookwood Community charges $3,600 a month for its residents who can pay full tuition, while others pay on a sliding scale. This is roughly half the fee for government-run facilities. The national average is $6,800 per person to care for the mentally retarded, while some private facilities charge as much as $12,000 per month to care for a schizophrenic. Seventy percent of the residents at Brookwood are on scholarship, totaling $1 million. Brookwood Community receives no government funding. Not accepting funds from the government has given this institution the capacity to respond flexibly to the needs of its residents and to innovate. Brookwood estimates that the facility is saving U.S. taxpayers at least $2 million for each resident over a lifetime.

Yvonne Streit's passion to help the handicapped flourish was precipitated by the experience of her daughter, who was diagnosed with severe brain damage at age one after mumps left her with encephalitis and meningitis. In order to give her daughter and others like her a better life, she wanted to find a practical and life-enhancing way for them to grow. It became clear that there was a need for a residential facility for those beyond school age who needed full-time institutional care. She joined forces with other parents who had the same need, and set out to discover and visit the world's best models in caring for the handicapped and learn their best practices. Now people are coming from all over the world to learn from Brookwood's experience. Five other institutions have been patterned after this one, including one in Mexico, and dozens of others have adapted their best practices, which are being documented by research teams. Baylor University is currently doing a study on the effects of rapid aging of the population Brookwood serves.

There is an important element of the Brookwood experience that defies quantification, but permeates the place. It is not mentioned in any of the publications, nor do the staff members wear it on their sleeves. What is it? Those who lead Brookwood give a consistent answer. "There's a spirit in this place—it's love. The number one difference is God. We practice the presence of God," answers Yvonne Streit. "Nearly everybody who touches the residents cares deeply," she continues. "It's *agape*. We try to live it." Rick DeMunbrun answers, "It's a very God-centered community." Joe Mazzu adds, "But we don't trumpet it—we try to live it out. We love them in a way where they are valued and their dignity is upheld. We engage them in a personal way." That's what makes the difference here. Rather than looking at people with disabilities as either a project to be fixed or a burden to be carried, the people who work with the handicapped at Brookwood do so out of a love for them, and it shows in the way they speak to and touch the people for whom they care.

Best Practices: Brookwood Community

- Creates entrepreneurial enterprises that earn $2.2 million of the $9 million budget
- Utilizes work skills as therapy and learning opportunities: "pragmatic therapy in tandem with life"
- Offers consumers and visitors a way to participate in their work
- Serves as a learning center on entrepreneurial skills, care for the handicapped, and spiritual growth
- Creates a community permeated by *agape*

part iii

THE CITIES

A Vision as Big as the City

Street Saint Strategies

chapter 8

The Nehemiah Strategy

Destruction is visible in America's cities, where the shattered glass mirrors the shattered souls, where the wreckage of the physical and spiritual landscape is devastating. While the houses in the suburbs may be prettier, there are broken human beings inside the elegant houses that do not keep out evil, even in gated communities. The enemy is within. The walls that once kept destruction away have crumbled, and the ruins of broken families, crippling loneliness, and the ravages of drugs and violence are evident everywhere. There is human wreckage throughout the city, rich and poor, white, black, and brown.

Nehemiah's response to the wreckage he encountered was to weep, fast, and pray. Then he took action. He is one of the earliest street saints, and his story bears retelling today as a model for renewing our cities. Nehemiah was a Jew who lived in Persia, where he served the king in his court. When Nehemiah heard of the despair and disrepair in Jerusalem, the king noticed his gloom and asked him what he could do to help. Nehemiah asked the king for permission to go to the city and rebuild the walls, and for timber from the king's forests that he would need to start the work. He also asked the king to clear the political obstacles that would hinder his journey. The king gave him his approval, the raw materials, and protection, equipping Nehemiah to begin what he saw needed to be done. But Nehemiah would have to formulate the plan and find the people to carry it out.

When Nehemiah arrived in Jerusalem, he stole out alone at night to do a personal assessment of the damage. Some portions of the wall were so broken down they were impassable. Nehemiah called together the residents of the city the next day and told them of his plan to rebuild, a plan he had made with God's guidance and with the king's approval. The combination proved persuasive. Instead of hiring construction workers, Nehemiah called on the locals to do the work, who took responsibility for it themselves. Fathers and their sons and daughters, merchants and priests, goldsmiths and metalworkers paired up to make the repairs right in front of where they lived or worked. The people of the city rallied to the cause, and formed teams to repair segments of the wall in a seamless pattern that girdled the entire city.

Mobilizing Teams

Teams took specific pieces of the wall—the sons of Ha-Senaah rebuilt the Fish Gate, Hanun and the people of Zanoah repaired the Valley Gate and the section of wall up to the Dung Gate. Some brought professional skills to the task, like Uzziel, who was a metalworker, while Hananiah the perfume maker worked beside him as an amateur volunteer in construction. The nobles of Tekoa found the work demeaning and refused to pick up tools, but a team from the neighboring country pitched in.

The renewal strategy was a voluntary public-private partnership, mobilizing diverse participants. Families, next-door neighbors, collaborators from other cities, and foreigners took up tools to do the work, along with city officials, district rulers, businessmen, and priests, all of whom got their hands dirty together. Nehemiah moved them into concerted action but did not micromanage their work. He assessed the needs; then they worked together to fill the gaps. The people took responsibility for the repairs in front of their own houses or shops, or they worked alongside somebody who was on the front line. Volunteers who brought their own tools and talents to the task did the heavy lifting at the wall. Most of the necessary resources were already in the city, but the people had not pooled what they had because they were demoralized and in disunity.

The Nehemiahs of today are calling together the people of their cities to repair what has been destroyed and work together to renew them from within. They are rallying the street saints to come together in a strategy that will encircle the city. The wall is down in so many places, and although there are scores of faith-based efforts, many of them are small and operating in isolation. Today's Nehemiahs are mobilizing the action of entrepreneurs, bankers, city officials, clergy, laypeople, and grassroots neighborhood leaders. They understand that renewal takes a whole team of people working shoulder to shoulder throughout the entire city.

But effective workers need tools and materials. Nehemiah had a grant from the king to provide the materials for the construction, and the king's protection to remove political obstacles. Some believe that this is an appropriate role for the kings of today as well. But notice that the king did not direct or finance the rest of the project—he merely provided a seed grant, and the community supplied the rest of the materials and the labor.

Nehemiah saw that the physical devastation of the city's walls had to be addressed first, because the danger was so pressing. But once that had been accomplished, the internal renewal of the heart had to be addressed. The Nehemiahs of today understand that poverty of the spirit is as crippling as economic poverty. The most effective Nehemiah strategy addresses both. We need to meet material needs as well as spiritual needs, both at the same time. If a person is hungry, body and soul both need to be fed. True compassion addresses both. It takes a holistic approach to heal a troubled city, just as it takes a holistic approach to make shattered people whole.

The frontline workers with Nehemiah encountered stiff opposition, just as they do today. Their detractors ridiculed them, saying they would never be able to finish what they intended. But Nehemiah reassured them and armed everyone doing the repairs; they carried a sword as a weapon, while they wielded a tool with the other hand. The sword of the spirit of the Word is the weapon street saints use today, while actively rebuilding the physical ruin of our cities.

He encouraged the people to "remember the great and awe-inspiring Lord and fight for your kinsmen, your sons, your daughters, your wives and your homes." This is what the most significant battles are always about: our faith, our families, our homes, our communities. These things are at stake, and this is what we are called to protect and renew today.

The opponents taunted Nehemiah's workers, saying, "Can they put new life into stones taken from rubbish heaps and even charred?" That is exactly what street saints are doing today. They are building with living stones, with real people, who have been tossed aside as refuse, burned and damaged. These are the least, the last, and the lost, picked up off the streets of the cities by people of faith, who are breathing new life into them. They are loving them into wholeness. They are restoring cities by restoring one person at a time.

To fortify those at work at the wall, Nehemiah organized a system using a trumpeter to summon help at the point needed. Today's Nehemiahs are needed to rally support for street saints who are struggling, and to bring the resources of the community to strengthen them. Nehemiahs can also trumpet their successes. The nobles of our cities can give the resources to get the tools and materials to the street saints working at the front.

Sweat Equity

The builders at the wall worked long days from sunup to starlight, from dawn to darkness, putting in their own "sweat equity." The people with the most at stake invested their own hard labor in renewal. Nehemiah had the buy-in and active participation of the entire community, whose people worked by day and stood guard by night. He was a servant-leader. Nehemiah worked and slept inside the city walls in solidarity with the workers, the street saints of his day. This was servant leadership in the trenches. He had credibility because of his personal participation. The Nehemiahs of today who practice effective servant leadership earn credibility from their proximity to the people they are helping.

Once the wall had been repaired to keep out the external danger, Nehemiah saw that economic empowerment was a crucial part of community renewal. The poverty in the city was so great that some families had sold their children into slavery. Others had gone into severe debt to pay their taxes. So one of his first acts as governor of the city was to cut their taxes. Nehemiah urged the nobles to forgive the debts of those who were destitute, and he did the same himself. He encouraged a private, voluntary transfer of wealth from the wealthy to those in need. With a combination of public and private means, Nehemiah helped move people out of poverty into self-sufficiency.

Nehemiah practiced decentralization, or subsidiarity, and moved the responsibility down to people at the level closest to the streets. The Nehemiahs of today are doing the same, mobilizing people at the neighborhood level and encouraging them to take responsibility for themselves. The grassroots efforts to heal communities are the ones most likely to succeed because their leaders know the neighborhoods and their dynamics. Strengthening the neighborhood renewers activates the health of the community by renewing from the street level up.

Nehemiah then did an assessment to get an accurate picture of the population, and concluded there was a need for repairs of the families and construction of additional houses. So he did a strategic plan and found the venture capital for social entrepreneurs. He gave a lead grant, investing in the strategic plan himself, and turned to the other wealthy citizens to finance the renewal strategy. They came up with a challenge grant of about half, and he turned to the other citizens of the city to raise the remaining funds. Observe that Nehemiah turned to the private sector to do the fundraising for the housing and family renewal project, not to the king. Nehemiah gave the first grant himself. The other well-to-do people followed his lead, and were willing to finance half the work. The rest of the funding came from people who were not wealthy but were willing to give. Nehemiahs today are doing the same, finding funds for street saints out on the front line, persuading the nobles of the city to support good work, and serving as intermediaries to implement the plan.

Ezra's Potent Prayer

At this point, the priest Ezra plays a critical role in the story. With the most pressing external needs met, the focus moves to the internal needs.

When the people assembled and Ezra read the law from the scriptures, the people wept in repentance. It became clear to them that their distance from God was a significant part of their problem. Ezra took the people to the next level of renewal by dealing with their hearts. In the end, it was an outpouring of the Holy Spirit that moved the people, through Ezra as his vessel. Their hearts had been prepared in the work they had begun with Nehemiah. Now God was completing the renewal. When Ezra prayed his magnificent prayer at the feast, he reminded the people of the great deeds God had performed on their behalf, despite their disobedience. Chastened, they promised to dedicate themselves and their families to a life of holiness, to live by the law, to tithe from their income and support their spiritual leaders. The city entered a golden age, which lasted as long as the people kept the covenant.

Like Ezra, the spiritual leaders of today are the individual pastors and priests who are engaged in spiritual renewal, leading prayer movements, exhorting, chastising, encouraging. Nehemiah and Ezra had separate but crucial and complementary roles. It was not Nehemiah who called the people together to repent—it was Ezra. It was Ezra's job to preach, and Nehemiah's job to mobilize the workers at the wall. God worked through both. Only if both functions are effective can community renewal be complete.

There was another crucial dimension to this community renewal project under Nehemiah. He asked for volunteers, every tenth person living outside the city walls, to move in to repopulate the city. This, too, is a movement that has begun to regenerate the shell-pocked inner-city landscapes of America through godly families that have moved with their children to live among the people they serve. It is a tithing of talent, a powerful method of renewing from within. There are urban pioneers today, people like Randy White in Fresno, Rudy Carrasco in Pasadena, Chris Martin in Knoxville, and Bob Muzikowski in Chicago, who are helping the cities bloom again from the inside out. If one out of ten people of faith were to do the same, our cities would look very different today.

The breadth and depth of the Nehemiah strategy make it comprehensive. It is a multidimensional approach to community renewal. It was sparked through one man whose heart was broken by the things that break God's heart. He repented in the name of his people, and in the end, an entire city repented. Nehemiah asked the king for his support, who in turn made resources available and cleared the political obstacles to launch the project. Ezra provided spiritual leadership for the city. The governor did his part in changing the tax code and the interest rates to lighten the economic burden. The institutions of family, church, government, and the economy were all summoned forth in a shared strategy. The local people labored in their own neighborhoods, in teams of unlike people that spanned socioeconomic, geographic, and racial lines. It began in brokenness, and it ended in wholeness, renewing the community both materially and spiritually. It was evident to Nehemiah, to the people of the city, and even to their enemies, that when the work was finished, it had to have been accomplished through God.

Characteristics of the Nehemiah Strategy

- Initiated in prayer, continues in prayer, culminates in prayer
- Political leader gives approval and seed grant, removes obstacles
- Based on firsthand needs assessment
- Rallies the existing resources in the community
- Grassroots participation; sweat equity
- Teams from diverse backgrounds work in unity
- Strategy embraces the entire city
- Workers encounter stiff opposition, but persevere
- People of faith resettle inside the city to renew it from within
- The result is material and spiritual renewal of the city

Today's Nehemiahs

Today's Nehemiahs are the intermediary organizations committed to renewing America's cities. They are groups like the Leadership Foundations of America,[1] the National Center for Neighborhood Enterprise, Ten

Point Coalition, Nueva Esperanza, National Center for Community and Economic Development, and many others who are leading community renewal from the grassroots up. They have brought together the nobles of the city with the workers at the wall, given them tools and encouragement, and mobilized others to go and work with them. In different ways, these intermediary organizations serve as modern-day Nehemiahs. Some groups are focused on affordable housing, entrepreneurial startups, and economic community renewal. Others are focused on building the capacity of faith-based organizations and getting the tools and training to the workers at the wall. Yet others, like Mission America, are focused on bringing the priestly Ezras together to fast and pray, with the intention that from unity, citywide transformation will be spiritually birthed. The goal is renewal of the person in mind, body, and spirit, and of the community, both physically and morally.

Robert Woodson: Empowering Grassroots Leaders

Robert L. Woodson Sr. created the National Center for Neighborhood Enterprise to identify and empower leaders of grassroots organizations working to renew their own communities. Like Nehemiah, he has identified the frontline workers at the wall, encouraged them, and has gotten them the tools and training to do the work in their own neighborhoods. He has orchestrated initiatives that have mobilized people of faith to re-claim entire sections of cities from violence. He has systematically sought out promising people who are already doing grassroots renewal, are rooted in the community, know its problems, and are working toward their solution. The community leaders have these characteristics:[2]

- They were doing the work before there was money for it
- They make a lifetime commitment to the people they serve
- They live in the same zip code as the people they serve
- They believe in the total restoration of people
- They require something in return for giving

As a modern-day Nehemiah, Bob Woodson has crisscrossed the country as a talent scout, searching out and nurturing promising leaders, most of whom are African American or Hispanic. To assist them in building up the wall in their own communities, he offers them leadership training, seminars on "What Works and Why," as well as access to grants and increased visibility. His protégées have garnered more attention and funding than they would have on their own, which has strengthened them. The issues Bob has tackled include revitalizing low-income communities; reducing crime and violence; decreasing substance abuse, homelessness, and teen pregnancy; and creating economic enterprise and employment.

His knowledge comes from firsthand experience dating from the 1960s, when he coordinated national and local community development programs, and the '70s, when he directed the National Urban League's Administration of Justice division. He saw the issues that affected poverty, and sought solutions out in the field. He discovered faith-based groups as allies, although he wasn't seeking them. Woodson says:

> I didn't discover the power of faith-based remedies through any deep religious convictions of my own. I was simply the founder of a policy institute looking for ways to combat poverty. For two years, I hosted town meetings around the country and invited local leaders to show me strategies of personal and community revitalization that have been effective. I still don't entirely understand how faith-based organizations reach into the heart of the most severely damaged individuals and transform them. But overwhelming evidence shows they can do just that.[3]

His book, *The Triumphs of Joseph: How Today's Community Healers Are Reviving Our Streets and Neighborhoods,*[4] chronicles the strengths of these remarkable people, and is one of the classics in the field of community renewal.

Like Nehemiah, Bob Woodson has the ear of the king—regardless of which administration is in power. He has succeeded in clearing some of the political obstacles to the work of street saints, and in getting seed grants for technical assistance to jump-start their work. Woodson has shaped a generation of thinking on solutions to reducing poverty and crime by consistently lending his voice to the debate in Washington and throughout the country on how best to formulate policy. The effect over time has been to shift the paradigm of discourse.

Bob is a rare bird—he has received the Genius Award from the MacArthur Foundation and has worked for a think tank, but he's willing to take his knowledge out onto the streets himself. Benning Terrace, a Washington, D.C., public housing development, was the battleground for two warring gangs who had taken fifty lives. As a modern Nehemiah, Woodson identified six local men, former drug addicts and convicts, who had the respect of local youth, and put them to work in their own neighborhood. With Woodson as coach and catalyst, together they facilitated a truce with sixteen of the young men from both sides. When asked why they had been trying to kill each other, they said, "No one ever asked us to stop fighting. No one ever brought us together like this for us to reason together."[5] Job training and education solidified their turnaround, giving them new options. The result was changed lives for young people otherwise probably destined for failure. Based on this success, Bob has created Violence Free Zones in communities throughout America by equipping and training local leaders who intervene at the street level. Like Nehemiah, he has helped to orchestrate their work by putting together plans for local coalitions to stop violence, building the metaphorical wall of their cities.

Just as Nehemiah knew there was an important spiritual dimension to the work at hand, Bob Woodson is straightforward when he talks about the moral freefall of our nation and the need for spiritual renewal. The moral decay of our society is colorblind and all pervasive, regardless of income. He cites as evidence the affluent Americans in the suburbs who have discovered that their gated communities do not protect them from drug-related deaths of their spouses and children. "Social dysfunction in the midst of affluence should not be surprising," says Woodson.

> All of these tragedies are outcrops of a crisis in our nation that is fundamentally spiritual in nature and has spread across boundaries of race and income level. America's spiritual freefall is not caused by poverty and it won't be alle-

viated by material wealth. Because the root of America's crisis is essentially a matter of values and morals—the choices people make and the chances they take. It is clearly not a function of race or income level. If prosperity were the key to ending the crisis, how is it that the lists of affluent addicts and incidents of self-destruction among the wealthy continue to grow at shocking rates?[6]

Bob takes a page directly from Nehemiah when he grapples with the issues facing black communities today, what he calls "the enemy within." He says:

Nehemiah could not rebuild the wall until he confronted the enemy among his own people. Wealthy Jews were charging poor Jews high interest rates, and as a consequence they had to sell their children into bondage. They appealed to Nehemiah to say "we have to have release from this." . . . He said words to the effect that "you all have got to stop exploiting your own people. Did we escape the oppression of the Babylonians only to be oppressed by our own people?" Black America is in a similar situation today, where one class of blacks profits from the misery and poverty of another. If we continue this practice, we are playing into the hands of the racists, because if we exploit our own people, how can we say to them, you cannot exploit our people?[7]

The issues go beyond race and poverty, says Woodson.

Ten years during the depression—between 1930 and 1940—the country had a 25 percent unemployment rate, and the black community's was 50 percent. We didn't kill ourselves. We could walk safely in our neighborhoods, our old folks weren't mugged, and families were not disintegrating. It's never an economic circumstance that makes you lawless. And the worst thing you can do is provide someone with an exemption from personal responsibility. That's the most lethal thing you can do is to say to someone, "I understand why you're mugging and killing, it's because of racism. I understand why you are killing and raping is because of your mama and your daddy." No, you're doing it because of you.[8]

Bob tirelessly points toward the agents of healing found at the grassroots level, the street saints who have discovered that faith is capable of transforming hearts and lives, releasing captives from addiction, and giving hope where there is none. "If a solution is to be forged for devastating afflictions ranging from alcoholism and drug addiction to youth violence and gang activity, we must be willing to look where the professionals of the social sciences have feared to tread—to faith-based, value-oriented responses." The moral renewal sorely needed in our country has an origin and an application that transcends income or race. Healing is needed all around us, he affirms, and "remedies forged in the crucibles of the inner-city can heal the wounded in the suites as well as the streets."[9]

Luis Cortes: Nueva Esperanza

Some leaders have characteristics of both Ezra and Nehemiah. Rev. Luis Cortes is a pastor who has moved from the pulpit into the forefront of community development with a passion.[10] As a Nehemiah, he assessed the city of Philadelphia to see where the walls were down, and he has plunged in to mobilize the workers to build housing and strengthen families and their children, calling on the king to provide the needed materials. The results of Nueva Esperanza, the community development corporation he founded in 1987, have been spectacular.

Luis looked around at the growing population in the Latino corridor in North Philadelphia, the poverty and inadequate housing, the underperforming schools and high dropout rate, the unemployed and underemployed people eking out an existence, the difficulties faced by impoverished seniors, and decided he had to take action. The determination forged in that fiery discontent has led to affordable new homes and refurbished abandoned ones, a charter school and a center for higher education, incubation for small businesses, and a camp for youth.

It was clear to Luis that in order to make a dent in the problems facing Latinos in his community, renewal would need to be based on self-help and ownership. "If you give a person a fish, you will cure his hunger for a day. If you teach a person to fish, you will feed him and his family," says Luis, as do others. But he takes it one step further. "If the person owns a pond, he will create opportunities for himself and his neighbors." The motivation for this approach is firmly anchored in faith, but it embraces holistic renewal of the community. "Informed by Christian values, our approach to community development is straightforward and effective," Luis says. "We create institutions around which others can build."

Nehemiah concluded that the people needed economic renewal, including housing. Luis Cortes has found the same in the community where he is working. Latino and African American families' net wealth is on average $4,000, compared to $44,000 for their white counterparts. Because 60 percent of that is in home ownership, one way to begin to build a community's assets and the ability to pass them on to children is home ownership. Nueva Esperanza has built new homes, repaired dilapidated ones, and coached new owners through the application process with bilingual mortgage counseling and homebuyer workshops. They converted an abandoned hospital into two- and three-bedroom apartments for mid- to low-income residents. Specially designed kitchens and bathrooms made it easier for the elderly to live independently. Ownership restores personal dignity, and as the neighborhood began to visibly improve, other opportunities opened up. Nueva Esperanza has fostered locally owned businesses, including a construction company and a grocery store. At the request of local residents, the organization put up a full-service Laundromat in a once empty lot to meet the need for a safe and accessible facility in the community. Ahead of the curve, Nueva Esperanza began to offer job training as one of the first welfare-to-work programs in Pennsylvania in 1996. Taking a page from Nehemiah, Luis obtained money for this program from the king, and has used the grant to provide tools to work.

Nehemiah looked at the overall quality of life for the residents of Jerusalem and made changes in several of the institutions. Cortes has done the same, after looking at the plight of Latinos in Philadelphia. Many Latinos have not graduated from high school, thwarting their opportunities in an economy where advancement is often linked to credentials. The census information for Philadelphia indicated that the average literacy rate is between fourth-grade and sixth-grade levels. Because only roughly half the Latinos in the United States graduate, Nueva Esperanza founded a charter high school to improve the odds. Utilizing English, Spanish, and technology, the academy is training kids who have a chance to succeed. In the first graduating class in 2003, sixty-five of seventy-two students received their diplomas. For those who aspire to higher education, the Nueva Esperanza Center for Higher Education was founded to provide postsecondary education for two years after high school, where students receive credits that can be applied toward a bachelor's degree when they transfer to a college or university while they hone their English skills.

Creating a critical mass of resources in a neighborhood is one of the keys to renewal. So Nueva Esperanza acquired a six-acre campus to launch its initiatives from this nerve center. With a budget of $7 million and a staff of nearly one hundred, Nueva Esperanza is one of the largest Latino faith-based organizations in the country. A one-stop approach offers locals access to the academy and junior college, a gymnasium, twelve businesses, as well as state employment offices. To help other faith-based organizations flourish, Nueva Esperanza has offered technical assistance to 140 ministries. Initiatives are being launched to create jobs and housing in Philadelphia and in other cities. In addition, they acquired a 150-acre campground and retreat center to offer swimming, sports, and crafts, along with character education, teamwork, abstinence training, and academic enrichment.

Moving seamlessly from his role as a Nehemiah to that of Ezra, Luis Cortes is one of the prime movers behind the Hispanic Prayer Breakfast, an event that has attracted the president of the United States since it began. The event is coalescing the spiritual leadership of the fastest growing segment of the American population. It is the spiritual sparkplug behind the kind of community renewal Nueva Esperanza is leading, and the combination is both potent and promising.

What Nueva Esperanza is doing is at the cutting edge of a significant movement nationally. Latinos edged ahead in 2001 as the largest minority in the United States. Faith plays an important role in their lives: 74 percent of Latinos say religion provides a "great deal" or "quite a bit" of guidance for them. So mobilizing the strengths of the faithful to help with the transition educationally and economically is a burning issue. "It's about the people who are closest to Hispanics in need—the church—accessing the resources to meet those needs," says Luis.[11] "We need to build institutions in this country as citizens. We have to create institutions for Latino people and move them forward in this culture to become part of mainstream society. And we need to do it in a way that's palpable and understandable in this country's culture." Nueva Esperanza's approach fuses faith with economic development and civic values. But Luis is clear about the ultimate motivation: "We do what we do first of all because Jesus said we should."

Results at a Glance: Nueva Esperanza

- Built or rehabilitated 150 single-family homes for low-income residents
- Helped 650 families obtain their first mortgage
- Attracted $40 million in new financing to the neighborhoods
- Provided bilingual counseling and homebuyer workshops for 2,600 families
- Enrolled 600 people in job-training programs for retail, telemarketing, hospitality, health care, and other positions
- Charter high school graduated sixty-five in first class of 2003
- Center for Higher Education transitions students into universities
- 150-acre campground provides outlet for city-bound youth

Intermediaries as Nehemiahs

A Nehemiah strategy is needed to address the complexity of renewal in America. In cities all across the country, there are thousands of valiant, hardworking street saints doing the work of renewing segments of communities. But their efforts are fragmented. They are often unaware of each other, or view their counterparts as competitors. There is a crying need for all these players to lay down their logos and their egos to embrace the city together. Fragmented efforts cannot accomplish transformation. To renew a city, it takes the cooperation of neighborhood and civic leaders, spiritual leaders, business leaders, educational institutions, local and state government officials, and the media. The Nehemiahs of today often serve as interpreters among these players. Nehemiahs are cultural polyglots, speaking the language of the economy with businessmen, the language of faith with people of the church, the language of the street with grassroots leaders, the language of analysis with researchers, the language of policy with government representatives, and the language of news with the media. It's as remarkable a gifting as the outpouring on Pentecost.

Intermediaries are hard at work building up the capacity of faith-based organizations in their own cities. Some incubate new nonprofits; others provide leadership training. Some attract large grants that they then subgrant to smaller organizations. Some serve as catalysts and conveners for citywide initiatives. They inspire cities across the country with their vision and their seasoned knowledge of what's working in their communities.

There are scores of intermediaries across America today serving a Nehemiah function. A closer look at three cities will illustrate how they work: Pittsburgh, Memphis, and Fresno.

chapter 9

As Famous for God as Steel

Pittsburgh Leadership Foundation

With the silvery light glinting off the serpentine coils of the Mononga-
hela River below, Sam Shoemaker stood on Mount Washington overlook-
ing Pittsburgh and challenged its leaders to imagine what it would take to
make the city as famous for God is it was for steel. Below lay the titans of
industry, Heinz, Westinghouse, U.S. Steel, Alcoa, and the wealth they produced. Also below lay the gritty, blue-collar existence of foundry workers.
And between these disparate worlds were peppered churches of all stripes
and denominations. What kind of Nehemiah strategy could rally these
workers and nobles to rebuild Pittsburgh together?

"Behold your city," Shoemaker said. "The backlog of untapped Christian conviction and belief in this city means more to it than all the coal in
the hills and all the steel in the mills. If these forces can be trained and mobilized, Pittsburgh might become a spiritual pilot plant for America." This
dynamic Episcopal priest, who provided the spiritual underpinnings for
the twelve-step program for Alcoholics Anonymous, was a visionary with
a passion for big concepts. Shoemaker brought together CEOs and other
worldly leaders to launch what he called the Pittsburgh Experiment in the
mid-1950s. He drew together men from the golf club set to talk and pray
with frontline workers doing evangelism, and this unusual mix spawned a
spectrum of strategic initiatives that today embrace Pittsburgh. They were

all birthed with the DNA of ecumenism, para-church participation in the church's mission, racial reconciliation, and a theology of putting faith into action in a particular place. One of the initiatives born in 1978 that grew up to embody all of these genetic traits is the Pittsburgh Leadership Foundation (PLF).

An energetic Young Life leader named Reid Carpenter caught Shoemaker's vision in the early '60s. Reid's raucous sense of humor and straight-shooting candor endeared him to kids, but he could handle himself with tough characters too, having cut his ministry teeth in the Lower East Side of New York. Two charisms melded in Reid, two God-given gifts for Kingdom work. One was the highly relational approach to evangelism of Young Life: you earn the right to be heard by having a relationship. A highly relational approach would be one hallmark of Reid's work, and that of the PLF. The second was the pastoral committment to unleashing the spiritual potential locked away in a slumbering body of lay believers. These two spiritual gifts, when mixed together, exploded as rocket fuel to launch the Pittsburgh Leadership Foundation.

When the PLF was founded, addiction was one of the most troubling issues in Pittsburgh. Reid Carpenter served as a Nehemiah figure, convening public health officials, criminal justice system leaders, and service providers to build a broad initiative to prevent and treat addiction. The PLF drew together the various workers at the wall to hammer out a strategy that involved them all. The Coalition for Leadership, Education and Advocacy for Recovery (CLEAR) was the network born in 1978. Still going strong, it is the oldest coalition on addiction in the country. This advocacy group has spearheaded educational, legal, and medical changes in the community by bringing together clergy, media, doctors, hospitals, schools, and juvenile justice officials for concerted action together. Research on the effects of alcohol was one result, including insights into fetal embolism. CLEAR is a successful example of PLF's role in convening secular and faith-based practitioners, media, and others to tackle a problem together in a coalition that speaks with one consistent voice. Doctors and clergy who are on the front lines encountering addiction are often woefully under-prepared to recognize it as the source of problems they en-counter, so CLEAR has conducted seminars to give them the knowledge they need to recognize addiction. Currently there are one hundred com-munity agencies and individuals involved in this coalition.

Pittsburgh Youth Network

Reid Carpenter's passion for kids, forged in the fires of Young Life, drove several of PLF's earliest creations. This time, the Nehemiah function was to convene and train youth workers from throughout the city. The Pittsburgh Youth Network (PYN) cuts across denominational and racial boundaries, deploying participants as an outreach team. Church staffers and volunteers converge every month to refuel. The Pittsburgh Youth Network (PYN), tallying more than ninety youth workers today, reaches about one-third of the young people in Pittsburgh in a given year.[1] The collaborative effort forges urban-suburban partnerships and links stand-alone faith-based organizations into a strategy shared with church-es. Storefront churches short on resources can link to suburban churches, which send their teens to tutor inner-city youngsters. PYN puts together high-wattage retreats for middle school and high school kids from throughout the city, where 3,000 youngsters immerse themselves in ener-getic fun and games, inspiring speakers, and straight talk about faith. High school kids can chill out in a summer program called Surf City Camp. College students have accepted the challenge to become interns in urban ministry through Cross Trainers: 300 of them have served 1,500 children in urban day camps. Since PYN was founded, 2,000 youth leaders and volunteers have been trained and mentored, and more than 120,000 mid-dle school and high school students have taken part in the retreats, sum-mer programs, and recreational events.[2]

One significant contribution the Pittsburgh Leadership Foundation has made is a curriculum for youth work. It builds on the work of the Search Institute in Minneapolis, which has developed an excellent tool that's the equivalent of the SAT to measure a young person's personal development. Search has compiled a list of forty "developmental assets," traits and experiences that mark a youngster's attitudes and character. The tool gives an accurate assessment of the assets and weaknesses each individual youngster has, reflecting his or her family life, academic aspirations, and behavior with others. The Search Institute works up a full profile of the population tested. If you test an entire class at school, or a youth group, you get an uncannily accurate picture of the inner workings of the kids—their attitudes toward honesty, authority, and high-risk behavior. And you have a diagnostic tool to know what they need.

This highly professional tool, which schools across the country are using enthusiastically, analyzes external and internal assets. External assets include family support, empowerment, boundaries, expectations, and constructive use of time. Internal assets include a commitment to learning, positive values that guide choices, and a strong sense of purpose. National research indicates that no single one of these assets guarantees success; it requires the aggregate of assets. Asset-rich youngsters have a correspondingly high academic and moral performance. Across the board, asset-poor youngsters show correspondingly high-risk behavior and lackluster academic performance.[3] The obvious solution is to build their assets.

The Pittsburgh Leadership Foundation took the forty assets as a starting point and developed a Bible-based curriculum called "Project 40" to address each of the assets, putting together activities and topics for discussion in a week-by-week format for youth work. The combination of a professional tracking instrument for independent analysis, paired with a Christ-centered curriculum youth leaders can use week after week, is a solid contribution to the faith community and an attractive tool for working with youth.

Pittsburgh Community Storehouse

Convening, converging, cooperating. These are three Cs that have emerged as the Pittsburgh Leadership Foundation's modus operandi in its Nehemiah function of mobilizing and equipping workers in the city.

The Pittsburgh Community Storehouse brings together churches and service agencies throughout the city in a cooperative effort that provides material goods and leverages human energy. Some two hundred participating community nonprofits have become partners for a sliding fee of $50 to $250 a year, and they each agree to provide twelve volunteer hours a month. In return, they receive access to in-kind donations, which they can use in their organization's charitable outreach. Everything donated to and distributed by the warehouse is new, ranging from children's winter coats to women's dresses, school and office supplies, shoes, infant car seats, books, eyeglasses, and paper towels. Upwards of $12 million of new products are received and repackaged by volunteers from all over the city, who provide more than 21,000 hours of work. Only one full-time staffer coordinates the volunteers. The goods reach nearly 150,000 low-income children, men, and women throughout Pittsburgh.[4]

"But that's not the real story," says John Stahl-Wert, who is now the president of the Pittsburgh Leadership Foundation.

> Five days a week, dozens of volunteers at a time from several different nonprofit organizations work together at the Storehouse, oftentimes meeting each other for the very first time. Their joyous experience of new acquaintance is revealed in their regular outbursts of riotous laughter and in their testimonies of heart-felt camaraderie. Suburban Episcopal elderly women mix it up with urban construction trainees. Teams of youth serving out the hours of their alternative court sentence box children's Christmas toys beside men from one of our city's "fathering" initiatives. The real story is one of relationship. The true "product" distribution from our Storehouse is partnership and connection.[5]

Local banks have stepped up to support the storehouse, as have foundations, local church members, and the Pittsburgh Steelers. Since its inception, the storehouse has distributed $31.2 million of corporate and government in-kind donations to nonprofits and churches that serve the poor.

Fifteen years ago, World Vision partnered with the PLF to create a global counterpart to the local warehouse, and attracted a former Pittsburgh-based Gulf Oil executive to head up this effort. This center for gift-in-kind products from American-businesses and corporations today distributes more than $100 million in goods to people in need throughout the world. Frontline Christian workers in World Vision field offices use these commodities to serve relationships through which they communicate the Gospel. What began as a joint venture between World Vision and the Pittsburgh Leadership Foundation has been spun out into a separate organization since 2001. An investment of about $275,000 has produced more than $355 million in ministry value. It's an international manifestation of the Nehemiah strategy, equipping workers at other walls all around the world.

East Liberty Family Health Care Center

When a doctor wanted to establish an urban clinic, he needed partners in the city and an investor. Reid Carpenter linked arms with a Christian philanthropist and a pastor in an underserved neighborhood to put together a partnership that established the East Liberty Family Health Care Center in 1982. What began with one physician has expanded to twelve, who provide health care for low-income patients regardless of whether they have health insurance or not. When the clinic reached its capacity of twenty thousand patient visits annually, it expanded to a second site in 1998. As a testimony to the longevity of involvement, Reid Carpenter still serves on the board. Since the founding of the health care center, it has provided $19 million in ministry value.[6]

City as Parish: Equipping the Church as a Body

John Stahl-Wert has labored in Pittsburgh with a theology grounded in St. Paul, "to prepare God's people for works of service, so that the body of Christ may be built up until we all reach unity in the faith and in the knowledge of the Son of God" (Ephesians 4:12–13). They understand the church as a body. A gymnast and a ballet dancer have a trained athleticism, which, when coupled with grace and hours of practice, can result in feats executed with beauty and precision. So it should be with the body of

Christ, the church here on earth. This body, which is the company of all faithful believers, is supposed to respond nimbly to the affairs of the world in a choreography orchestrated by God. But as John Stahl-Wert explains, the parts of the body have been practicing their moves in isolation from each other. Fractious minds and unbending hearts have severed the limbs of what was to be one body. The city-reaching efforts John leads manifest his commitment to building up the body of Christ throughout an entire city.

How many churches does Pittsburgh have? "One" is the answer you get from John Stahl-Wert. One church, with many congregations. John has done thinking and writing about the different charisms, or spiritual gifts, that have been poured out upon the church. St. Paul enumerates them, spelling out their uses in building up the body. Teaching, preaching, apostleship, prayer, faith, hospitality, encouragement, wisdom, administration, and prophecy are among them.[7] Each gift has an intrinsic value, and none can serve the body in isolation or take another's place, just as the eye cannot perform the function of a foot. Over time, different congregations have received and emphasized different spiritual gifts. John contends that one benefit that may have come from the different emphases in congregations is a kind of specialization, a differentiation of functions, which has deepened the understanding and practice of particular spiritual gifts. He is convinced that the moment has come to use them together.

City as Parish (CAP) is a strategy for equipping the church across denominational lines and deploying members throughout the city as one body. It is based on Ephesians 4:16: "From him the whole body, joined and held together by every supporting ligament, grows and builds itself up in love, as each part does its work." Some congregations emphasize evangelism, some care for the poor, some have experience in holistic ministry, others are experienced prayer warriors. Some are storefront churches in the inner city, and others are wealthy suburban churches. But together, they bring a vast reservoir of strength, experience, and resources to Kingdom work. This equipping process allows people from different congregations to discover their gifts, and to move out and serve in unity with other believers throughout their city.

The concept for City as Parish originated with John Stahl-Wert, the Mennonite bishop who wrote his doctoral thesis about it. The goal is to take the whole Gospel to the whole city, using the whole church. This plan sets out to connect the parts of the body to serve the poor in the King- dom at hand. It's all about lay mobilization, a burgeoning movement in both Protestant and Catholic circles that evokes mixed reactions. As John surveyed pastors, one remarked, "This program will remove me from be- ing the cork in the bottle," a realization John says was "alternately greeted with joy or horror."[8]

The idea for implementation was fleshed out in partnership with the Leadership Training Network as a strategy to change the paradigm of the church. Fresno and Pittsburgh are two pilot cities that have embarked on a joint project to train parishioners in churches to move their people into action, out of the pews and onto the streets. The first training was com- pleted in 1999. The Pittsburgh Leadership Foundation and One by One Leadership in Fresno are blazing the trail in a process that changes the culture of the church by mobilizing the strengths of a slumbering giant.

Equipping the laity has seven steps: assimilation, foundation building, discovery, assignment matching, placement, ongoing growth, and celebra- tion.[9] Pastors agree to release their talented parishioners into local com- passion ministries throughout the city, rather than holding them in the confines of one congregation. The leadership teams that have been mobi- lized are equipped to go back into their own congregations and train oth- ers, while returning to CAP for sustenance. Monthly meetings of the equippers are water for the thirsty, a wellspring of encouragement from co-laborers around the city. As they train and work together, they become the connective tissue in the body.

In Pittsburgh, twenty-five congregations have joined the strategy, reaching nine thousand believers who are now seeking to discover their gifts and put them to use. City as Parish provides a launching platform to deploy them in bold strategies like that of Amachi, Wilson Goode's pro- gram to mentor the children of prisoners now effectively running in Philadelphia. With the infrastructure of CAP, it is possible to ramp up participation all over the city with an experienced team to implement Amachi in Pittsburgh. The proposal submitted by PLF won the highest score nationally in its evaluation for federal funding as a demonstration project. Plans are also under way for an aftercare program for prisoners, called Welcome Home Pittsburgh, which will provide a residence, job training, and entrepreneurial opportunities for ex-convicts starting a fresh life.

"Learning and doing, for the Christian disciple," says John, "are simultaneously necessary, like the task of shimmying up the inside of a circular chimney, left hand, then right, needing to alternatively leverage themselves against the progress of the other. Throughout the training cycle, classroom and street, prayer circle and soup line, textbook and boardroom are designed to be the grip points for growth in this new equipping paradigm."

Several things happen in the interaction among equippers. As they get to know each other, they discover redundancies in ministry, and can converge and collaborate to avoid duplication. But more importantly, parishioners are given a meaningful way to put their faith into action. As the frontline workers go out into the community to work, they are discovering the joy that comes in serving. Because they are serving together, they are beginning to function as a single body. As they go in and out of each other's lives and church homes, "the medium is relationship and the message is love," says John. "What's love got to do with it?" he asks. "With vision, that is? We see the ones that we love. Love always makes time, beyond the tyranny of not enough time. Love is not an ephemeral fancy, not a limp Gnostic noodle with no means to stand. Love sustains sight. Sight sustains vision. The vision for CAP is of a citywide body that loves one another and expresses the overflow of that love, as God does for us, in blessing to its common parish."[10]

Since 1978, the Pittsburgh Leadership Foundation has been the midwife for nearly fifty organizations, served as financial intermediary for several dozen more, and built several multi-sector collaborations.[11] But the foundation did not stop after starting these organizations. The PLF has raised more than $80 million for these initiatives, provided capacity building for several hundred nonprofits in the city, served nearly five hundred congregational youth ministries, and assisted more than a thousand congregations. Through the faith-based initiatives it has fostered, nearly half a billion dollars of added ministry value has been leveraged throughout Pittsburgh in a Nehemiah strategy whose embrace can be felt throughout the city.[12]

Results at a Glance: Pittsburgh Leadership Foundation

The Pittsburgh Leadership Foundation over the past twenty-five years has:

- Raised and distributed $82 million to ministries
- Created new organizations, including East Liberty Family Health Care, World Vision International Distribution Center, Garfield Jubilee Association, and Saltworks Theater
- Introduced faith to 120,000 middle school and high school youth
- Trained 2,000 youth leaders for effective outreach
- Served 300,000 low-income residents with $30 million of new school clothes, blankets, winter coats, diapers, eyeglasses, furniture, and other items
- Equipped 6,000 congregational members with community ministry skills
- Created one hundred community-based drug and alcohol task forces

Through ministries it spun off or helped create, PLF has:

- Provided 200,000 doctor-patient visits for low-income people
- Provided mentoring to 30,000 public school students
- Helped pass fifty local ordinances against pornography
- Provided housing counseling for 15,000 families
- Performed plays with Christian values for 2.5 million school children

Through partnerships that it initiated, PLF has:

- Distributed $350 million of material goods around the world
- Provided Internet access to 50,000 Christian congregations
- Trained ninety-five nonprofit organizations in leadership development[13]

Leadership Foundations of America

Reid Carpenter sees American cities full of people in all neighborhoods who thirst for relationship, who are broken in spirit and body, who are desperate for lives with meaning, and whose most basic needs have not been met. He is convinced that the followers of Christ are not doing a sufficient job to mobilize the resources of the church to reach them. "The task is too huge to do it with our own power," he says. "We need all the gifts that have been poured out on the church to equip us to do the work. We need to learn from the experience of those who have gone before us in our holy history. We need all the brothers and sisters in Christ to work alongside each other, because the harvest is ready but the workers are few. If we continue to work in isolation from each other, we will continue to be impotent."[14]

Reid is a man on a mission today. He is crisscrossing the country to identify leaders in America's cities who have a vision as big as their city. Having seen the power of a citywide effort like the Pittsburgh Leadership Foundation, he began to seek out kindred spirits in other cities and bring them together to learn from each other and build relational bridges between their efforts. The result became Leadership Foundations of America, formerly known as the Council of Leadership Foundations. Reid is devoting his time fully to the national organization, having handed over the reins at the Pittsburgh Leadership Foundation to John Stahl-Wert.

Leaders in this movement in a sense are discovered rather than created. It takes a particular kind of person and history in a city to emerge as a credible convener who can cross denominational, racial, and political divides, and speak the multiple languages of business, church, government, and philanthropy, with a mediagenic presence. In the cities where this work flourishes, it was born in a group of people who intentionally bridged these diverse worlds, first in prayer, then in action. What emerges out of unity is clarity of purpose. In some cities, the first charge has been to grapple with affordable housing or children in poverty, while others might tackle health care for the poor, or employment. Whatever the case, it takes an honest broker to convene the players at one table. They build a common cause and a common language, serving as a catalyst for action.

Leaders like H. Spees in Fresno, Bud Ipema in Chicago, Larry Lloyd in Memphis, and Kathy Dudley in Dallas were among the early participants in this national effort, each of whom has handed off the reins to a successor. Leadership Foundations of America has brought together representatives from thirty-two cities, with another thirty queuing up.[15] An accreditation process assesses their capacity, strengths, and weaknesses, offering assistance to help them grow and mature. Each city has its own character, dynamics, possibilities, and problems. What unites their very different kinds of leaders is a passion to unite the church across denominational lines, serve the poor, reconcile the races, and take the whole Gospel to the whole city. What began largely for purposes of fellowship has now expanded to include annual retreats, leadership seminars with practical workshops for practitioners, a shared Web site with model proposals, and ongoing communication and cross-fertilization. Leaders from throughout the country compare models for replication, best practices, tips on funding sources, and stories from the trenches. Bryan Barry of the Wilder Foundation has stepped in as the chief operating officer.

The relationships among leaders and transferal of ideas have proven fertile. The Urban Youth Initiative that began in Memphis was effectively replicated in Seattle, and has now been adopted by World Vision. An abstinence program called the Silver Ring Thing, which began in Pittsburgh, has been successfully implemented in Knoxville. A four-city strategy involving Seattle, Phoenix, Knoxville, and Memphis combined their expertise to win a Compassion Capital Fund grant for capacity building in each of their cities.

Part talent scout, part cheerleader, and part preacher, Reid encourages the leaders when they converge for their annual gatherings. Given a microphone, he's in his element. "We are people with a holy discontent," he cried out to the group when they assembled in Memphis. "We are not triumphalists. We cry, we suffer, and find solidarity with those in recovery groups because in truth, we're all sinners in recovery. All the way through holy history, God has revealed himself to people who have carried out his will through time and space. The pinnacle is Jesus Christ. We have defined ourselves by accepting a piece of the most radical piece of history. It's preposterous." Reid continues, "We've been anointed with a charism of the Holy Spirit. This movement that carries out the vision requires us to remind ourselves that Jesus loves people outside the family, the least, the last, and the lost. We are called to give our cities hope and healing and sustenance."

If an individual ministry is like one stock, a Leadership Foundation is like a mutual fund. It is the bundled energy of live wires all over the city, whose combined efforts light up the cityscape. Leadership Foundations are serving as catalysts, conveners, equippers, and investors in each of their cities. Their message is unity, and they are laboring to bring together leaders across racial and denominational dividing lines to embrace their cities together. The method is ministry that cuts a broad swath through the needs of the community. Responding to the needs of each individual city, its history, demographics, and particular points of pain, the Leadership Foundations are, like Nehemiah, mobilizing teams to build at strategic points in the city. They are doing so with teams to meet specific physical and spiritual needs, based on a Kingdom vision that embraces the city as a whole. Ray Bakke is the theologian who has shaped their thinking powerfully, encapsulated in his book *A Theology as Big as the City*.[16]

"We have the commandment to love each other, and yet we hide behind our Presbyterianism, or whatever 'ism' divides us," Reid proclaims. As a Catholic convert, he leads a largely Protestant team that includes believers from both sides of the Tiber. There's a deliberate effort to unify the church universal.

> We're on a major radical edge of what Jesus was advocating in John 17, when he prayed "Father, may they be one as you and I are one." Jesus said the gates of hell would not prevail against the church, but we've splintered into lots of individual congregational expressions. But let's not use the excuse of divisiveness. We are fundamentally discontented with spiritual brokenness. We are dissatisfied with disunity. The Leadership Foundation movement needs to be

open to the possibility that the 21st century will be known for re-knitting the broken bones of Jesus Christ, and that the unity of the Body of Christ will be revealed fully.[17]

To convey the heart of what a Leadership Foundation does for its city, Reid shares a story. The words are those of Dr. Richard Seltzer, who was a surgeon, as he describes a scene in a hospital room with a patient on whom he has operated:

I stand by the bed where a young woman lies, her face postoperative, her mouth twisted in palsy, clownish. A tiny twig of the facial nerve, the one to the muscles of her mouth, has been severed. She will be thus from now on. The surgeon has followed with religious fervor the curve of her flesh; I promise you that. Nevertheless, to remove the tumor in her cheek, I had to cut the little nerve. Her young husband is in the room. He stands at the opposite side of the bed, and together they seem to dwell in the private lamplight, isolated from me, private. Who are they, I ask myself, he and this wry-mouth I have made, who gaze at and touch each other so generously, greedily? The young woman speaks. "Will my mouth always be like this?" she asks. "Yes," I say, "it will. It is because the nerve was cut.'" She nods and is silent. But the young man smiles. "I like it," he says. "It is kind of cute." All at once, I know who he is. I understand, I lower my gaze. Unmindful he bends to kiss her crooked mouth, and I, so close, can see how he twists his own lips to accommodate to hers, to show her that their kiss still works.[18]

Reid Carpenter picks up the story there, and says, "That's our task. To accommodate the crooked mouths of people we're called upon to kiss. Jesus asked us to be committed to his kingdom, and to let all else be added to that. We're called on to give preferential treatment to the poor, the vulnerable, the broken. We have the command to love each other. This is what we do in our cities. We kiss the crooked mouth, to show that the kiss—the divine kiss—works."

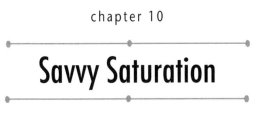

chapter 10

Savvy Saturation

Memphis Leadership Foundation

Larry Lloyd doesn't try to draw attention to himself. But his quiet intensity and his competence flash through his self-deprecating modesty. He has a savvy gift for creating urban ministry, and his work through the Memphis Leadership Foundation has set forces into motion that are changing the city. A strategy he began nearly twenty years ago has been saturating Memphis with innovative outreaches to the disenchanted and the disenfranchised. It has credentialed a generation of new leaders, who are changing their communities from the grassroots up.

Larry's goal was to transition the leadership of the Memphis Leadership Foundation to an African American within ten years, and on schedule in 1997, Larry handed the reins to his vice president, Howard Eddings, whom he had known since Young Life days when Howard was in high school in Memphis. After graduation from college, Howard became a Young Life leader. Since then, Howard and Larry have worked side by side building a strong network of ministries that now saturate the city. The story of what they have done together is a powerful witness to racial reconciliation and the visionary leadership they share.[1] Their strategy has resulted in: a citywide youth program reaching more than ten thousand youngsters; building two hundred new homes for working poor families; helping create two medical clinics for immigrants and the indigent; finding jobs for a thousand hard-to-place adults; creating eighteen ministries throughout Memphis and launching a new foundation to fund them.

Memphis bears the scars of racial tension, which has a long history. It's not a coincidence that the Civil Rights Museum is here. The population is split almost right down the middle—47 percent African American, 47 percent white, and the rest Asian and Hispanic. In a city of one million, 250,000 of its residents live at or below the poverty level, with a concentration in the city itself, which is 60 percent black. There are pockets of affluence, which skew the median income upwards to $57,000 a year. There are an abundance of entry-level, low-paying jobs, and low unemployment, but prospects for increased earning power are dismal. Schools are troubled by high-risk behavior associated with poverty: gangs, dropouts, and violence.

When Larry Lloyd graduated from Fuller Seminary with Urban Young Life experience under his belt, he wanted to launch a citywide ministry that would empower indigenous leaders. With a vision like that of Nehemiah, he saw the need to rally workers to build the wall in their own neighborhoods. He had been influenced significantly by John Perkins and had studied with Bill Pannell, and the combination of theology coupled with a vision of holistic community renewal drove Larry. With a $10,000 grant from World Vision, he started the Memphis Leadership Foundation in 1987 to "seek the welfare of our city by empowering indigenous leaders, strengthening urban churches, building bridges for racial reconciliation and connecting communities of need with communities of resource." The city is full of tangible evidence of the fulfillment of that mission. Today, flying over Memphis, you can look down and see twenty-nine ministry locations throughout the city now pulsing with the life that Larry, Howard, and their team have breathed into them.

Memphis Leadership Foundation, now under Howard Eddings's direction, has a full-time staff of forty-eight and a $1.6 million budget. Together with the affiliate ministries it has spawned, the combined budget is $7 million.

Urban Youth Initiative

It is audacious. The idea of reaching ten thousand or more at-risk kids at once with a trained army of youth workers looks too big to be feasible for one city. But that is what Larry Lloyd has accomplished in this bold initiative. The Urban Youth Initiative (UYI) has trained a cadre of street-smart young people to go into schools in full-time positions funded by the Memphis Leadership Foundation, which deploys them through local urban churches. Nearly all of these frontline workers are minorities between twenty-five and thirty-five who go out onto the front lines among gang members and juvenile delinquents to serve as peacemakers and agents of change. Quite a few of them are reformed troublemakers themselves, so they understand troubled kids. Drawing on his theological training, Larry Lloyd has written a curriculum for study of the Bible that equips these young adults, who receive thirty-three hours of instruction in eleven courses, all accredited through Crichton College, a four-year Christian liberal arts institution. Those who wish can receive college credit. Equipped intellectually and spiritually, then strategically deployed in a citywide sweep, this SWAT team takes the city of Memphis by storm.

"Our goal is nothing less than to see thousands upon thousands of unchurched kids in Memphis come to a saving knowledge of Jesus Christ," says Larry. "I know of no other way to do this than to train up an army of dedicated youth workers who are willing to go where angels fear to tread, armed with the Gospel and power of God's grace, touching young people who are falling through the cracks of our society, filling up our jails or being killed needlessly by yet another drug deal gone bad."

The urban youth workers serve as a volunteer extension of the school staff. They help out in classrooms or in the computer lab, intervening for kids who are on the ropes. They handle students with disciplinary infractions and in-house suspensions. UYI staffer Clauzelle Fisher explains, "They're not bad kids. But they're kids that can't get past their issues. They have violence at home, no parental supervision. They're latchkey kids." If he sees a pattern of abuse, Clauzelle goes and visits the parents.

"You take the risk of getting cussed out," he admits with a shrug. But he offers to help the parent get a job, drug treatment, or transitional housing, if that is what's needed. Part of his job might be to run interference with teachers. "When a kid is acting out in class, he's not necessarily a future gang member that needs to be kicked out," Clauzelle reminds them.

Victoria Noblett handles high-risk youth in the court system, offering clothing, food, and reconnection to their schools and parents. Sometimes she does crisis intervention, like emotional and spiritual care for a youngster whose mother was stabbed twenty-six times. Another UYI staffer, Ken Pendleton, works with kids who have criminal records, some of whom have committed robberies or attempted murder as gang members. Gangster Disciples, Crips, Vice Lords, and Bloods are all actively recruiting kids in the high school to sell drugs or pass counterfeit money. Twenty-six kids in school who have a record with the juvenile justice system are under Ken's watchful eye. As he leafs through their court files, Ken shakes his head. "Not one of these kids has two parents at home," he laments.

A total of 107 youth workers are in training or in the field now, from 146 who have been trained since the program's inception. They are deployed in middle schools and high schools all over Memphis, saturating the schools with the highest concentration of at-risk youth. At least five thousand kids are involved on a regular basis, and ten thousand have some interaction. Fifty-seven churches and nonprofits from throughout the city are collaborating partners. The youth workers receive an annual salary of $25,000 from UYI for three years, and are placed on an urban church staff. At the end of that time, local churches pick up their salaries and keep these experienced workers. The Memphis Leadership Foundation has raised and invested $11 million since the program was launched. A study by the Amherst H. Wilder Foundation validates that the effect on the at-risk youth served has been profound.

Results: Urban Youth Initiative

A 2002 study by the Wilder Foundation verifies that the at-risk kids served in Memphis by UYI increase positive attitudes and behavior significantly, according to the students surveyed, their parents, and school officials.[2]

- **Future orientation** (hopefulness about the future and one's influence over it): increase for 84 percent of participating students
- **Faith and religious practice** (relying on faith as a source of strength, or a guide in making important decisions, interest in knowing more about God, time engaged in religious activities): increase for 81 percent of students
- **Pro-social behavior** (interest in doing things for others, ability to see how actions affect others, ability to get along at home and with adults): increase for 76 percent of students
- **Moral development** (knowing right from wrong, willingness to be honest in relationships, respect for family members and oneself): increase for 75 percent of students
- **Maturity or personal growth (**ability to make good choices, plan ahead and make decisions, finish a project once started, and to see oneself as a role model): increase for 74 percent of students
- **Academic achievement** (grades in school, school attendance, motivation to do well in school): increase for 69 percent of students
- **Conflict prevention or resolution** (self-control when angry, peaceful means to resolve conflicts, willingness to forgive others when they make mistakes): increase for 67 percent of students

Outside the schools, the Urban Youth Initiative workers offer "Club," based on the Young Life model, which is three parts games and healthy hilarity, and one part serious talk about faith and life. The philosophy is that you earn the right to be heard on faith only when you have built a relationship. The youth workers each have on average between fifty and seventy-five kids coming to their weekly activities and twenty-five in discipleship. Jacquetta Cole invites kids to "Club" on Friday night at the church, where she and her husband offer food, prayer, board games, and laughter, modeling a married Christian couple, which is something few of them have experienced. "We give them family," she says. "There's rarely a weekend we don't have a houseful of kids in our house." Many of the UYI workers come from the same background as the kids they are shepherding. Norman Redwing confirms, "This is one place where you can say you were an

addict and got cleaned up, or you were an abused child. I experienced alcohol and drug abuse, sexual abuse. But my whole life has been transformed. I reach kids who have the same experiences I had. I know how
painful it is."

The Urban Youth Initiative workers form a strong net that is cast over
the entire city. This cadre of new leaders now has a solid theological education, valuable work experience, and durable relationships with each
other, despite their different denominational traditions, which range from
Pentecostal to Roman Catholic, Presbyterian, and nondenominational.
Together, they are saturating the city.

Best Practices: Urban Youth Initiative

- Equips young adults from the inner city to reach kids they understand because they share
  their background
- Provides solid theological and job training for youth workers
- Effectively communicates faith to thousands of at-risk youth
- Produces well-documented results in the lives of kids served
- Provides paid positions for youth workers for three years, creating a care network blanketing
  the city
- Strengthens local urban churches by providing a cadre of experienced youth workers who
  join their staffs

Results

- One hundred forty-six youth workers trained; 107 in field now
- Nearly 10,000 kids involved regularly
- $11 million mobilized to create and sustain network

Memphis Athletic Ministries

What happens when you take a Type A successful businessman used
to closing deals, and retread him as the head of a nonprofit? You get
a driven Type A nonprofit leader who ruthlessly overworks the copier,
sends out massive blast faxes, and moves heaven and earth to get things

done. At least that was the experience of Howard Eddings at the Memphis Leadership Foundation as Gib Vestal made the transition from the corporate world to become the head of Memphis Athletic Ministries (MAM). A classic "halftimer"[3] who had a lucrative career for thirty years as an investment banker, Gib wanted to move on in the second half of his life to something that had a deeper meaning. So he traded his business suit for a hardhat. He's now overseeing the final stages of construction for a multi-million-dollar sports complex to serve thousands of kids from the inner city of Memphis.

Situated on a nine-acre site, the impressive facility houses the equivalent of two full-size gymnasiums side-by-side, which can be used for four simultaneous basketball games. Meeting rooms for other activities fill the rest of the facility. Urban churches fielded 485 teams last year, coached by volunteers, and attracted nearly five thousand kids to their activities. When this new $3 million center is finished, they can play each other here. A soccer field is soon to follow. MAM has been teaching the volunteers biblical principles of coaching and how to win kids to Christ by example.

When Gib was seeking a new direction, he did a word test as part of a discernment process, selecting nouns and adjectives that struck him. He came up with "Christian sports administration." He says he had "no idea how that would play out," but was convinced it was right for him. When he had lunch with Larry Lloyd, Gib decided, "This is it." The day after he made the commitment, the company he had been working for was sold. Gib has been working with MAM for three years now and says, "It's like a rebirth." His business acumen equips him well for the entrepreneurial side of this ministry. "It's like God used thirty years of experience to do this. Nothing has been wasted."

Across the street at what was once a military officer's club, MAM has a surprising piece of real estate for inner-city ministry: a nine-hole golf course. Leasing the property from the government, MAM joined with two "faith-friendly" organizations, First Tee of Memphis and the MidSouth Junior Golf Association, who, as strategic partners, bring expertise in course maintenance and golf instruction. MAM provides Christian men who are a blend of driver, mentor, and coach to interact with the kids and practice shots with them. Howard explains, "It's an opportunity for these guys who love golf, but love Christ more, who have never had an experience with inner-city kids." Gib adds, "With golf, you can take a seventy-year-old white dude and connect them with something they feel comfortable with, and they can teach it. They might not be so confident coaching a basketball clinic, because they'd figure they have nothing to teach, but with golf, it's their thing." The program teaches life skills and leadership, emphasizing goal setting, character, honesty, and integrity. This year five hundred kids are expected to take advantage of the program. The coaches hope a future Tiger Woods will be one of them.

Christ Community Health Services

Four idealistic young doctors decided that instead of seeking a comfortable practice in the suburbs, they wanted to serve as domestic missionary doctors in a clinic for the indigent in the inner city. They decided Memphis was an excellent city for their idea, and contacted churches and hospital administrators to garner support for the project. Everyone turned them down. Only when they turned to Larry Lloyd at the Memphis Leadership Foundation did they receive a glimmer of hope. He helped them pull together a team of experienced visionaries and savvy administrators to inaugurate this project. The result is now two cheerful, fully equipped clinics and a medical van serving immigrants and the poor in Memphis.

With a loan of $40,000 and some donated equipment, the doctors set up practice in the heart of the inner city, in one of Memphis's most medically underserved communities. Larry helped them find contractors to spruce up the building they leased for $2 per foot, which had been empty for ten years. He assisted them in obtaining their own 501(c)3 nonprofit status. Howard Eddings introduced the doctors to urban pastors in the area. Larry Lloyd assembled a board for them, drawing on his extensive contacts throughout Memphis, and agreed to serve as chairman. But the team needed a health care administrator as well. Burt Waller had a highly visible track record of high-wattage competence as the CEO of the largest public hospital in Memphis, but his initial response to the idea was less than enthusiastic. He thought the team "looked too young to be doctors." But the prospect left Burt inexplicably restless. He was having breakfast with a friend who is a missionary and confided, "I wish God would tell me what to do." The friend shot back, "He is." Burt decided to join the group and is now the director of the program.

What began with four young doctors and an idea has morphed into a $5.75 million full-service medical care facility with a staff of eighty-five handling more than 48,000 visits annually. Dr. David Pepperman, one of the founders, says with mild astonishment, "This is way past anything we had dreamed of. We never imagined anything more than a small clinic." Ten full-time doctors are augmented by four nurse practitioners, a dentist, a clinical psychologist, nurses, and a clerical staff. Several staff members have been added to do preventive work on abstinence for teenagers and to deal with domestic violence. The failures in these areas end up in the clinics, so the team has concluded it is worth investing in special efforts to intervene early.

Only about ten percent of the patients have private insurance. About 70 percent are on the Tennessee Medicaid program, and another 7 percent on Medicare. Nearly 13 percent are uninsured, but they are not denied service, and pay on a sliding scale. So how do the numbers add up? The answer is, they don't—not in the conventional business sense. These clinics have to raise funds to cover their expenses, just as all nonprofits do. The difference is that this is a market-driven model, so it is largely self-supporting. But they do occasionally sweat making payroll.

These clinics are explicitly Christ-centered. All the doctors and staff are people of faith. The literature in the waiting room tells about Christ in several languages. When patients come in, the doctors or nurses examining them for symptoms will gently offer to pray with them, if they are open to that. But prayer is neither required nor forced on anyone. The atmosphere of *agape* permeates the place. A bigger-than-life mural in the center of the new clinic offers a depiction of the story of the Good Samaritan, set in a contemporary urban context.

The doctors set the tone for the clinics, and their faith inspires their leadership. They make significantly less money than they could in private practice elsewhere, as do most of their staff. Some of the doctors have chosen to live in the neighborhood they serve, bringing their families into daily contact with the poor. They don't view it as a sacrifice. This is their mission field: their neighborhood, their neighbors.

Results: Christ Community Health Services

- Two fully equipped clinics and one mobile unit provide medical services for immigrants and indigents
- Parlayed $40,000 loan into $5.75 million annual budget
- Handles 48,000 visits annually

Neighborhood Housing Opportunities

A lot of people wish they could get out of crime-infested public housing communities and move into a comfortable, new, three-bedroom, two-bath home. Affordable houses on a modest income are tough to come by, and most of them need an appalling array of repairs to be livable. How do generational renters transition from public housing to homes they can afford in desirable neighborhoods?

The Memphis Leadership Foundation devised a plan with three elements: affordable price, clusters of owners, and coaching. They created Neighborhood Housing Opportunities (NHO) to implement the strategy. Architects developed plans for a house they are now selling for $65,000. NHO has purchased groups of lots clustered together to create a critical mass of residents who share a commitment. NHO developed a system to walk potential buyers through the entire process of buying and maintaining a home, sometimes for as long as five years. Since 1988, the organization has built and sold just over two hundred homes at a value of $13 million. To date, they've had only three foreclosures.

When applicants walk through the door of Neighborhood Housing Opportunities, they fill out a credit application and counselors look at their debt-income ratio. Staff members verify employment and income and track down the necessary documentation. They help the family set up a budget so they can stay on track with payments. When the package is ready, the NHO staffer sends it to a lender with an underwriter in the office who knows them, and serves as the advocate for the applicant. Once the family moves in, the staffers counsel them on home maintenance.

Take a driving tour of Memphis with Howard Eddings, and he will proudly point out houses all over the city that Neighborhood Housing Opportunities has built. In Smokey City, a cluster of houses face into a park in the center with a playground where kids play ball. The brick exteriors have variations to individualize them, some with two pillars in front, others with a cozy overhang. The yards are cared for, with landscaping. The cars in front of the houses are not up on blocks, unlike those a few streets away. A neighborhood association keeps a watchful eye on order. In the St. Elmo area, houses illustrate four different designs that new homeowners can choose from. In Calvary Creek, the most recent neighborhood, houses are sprouting up in what will be a sixty-unit community. The city is so enthusiastic about the project that it donated the land.

For more than half of the new owners, this is the first time they are out of public housing. The comfortably designed 1,286-square-foot houses have three bedrooms and two-and-a-half baths. Owners pay on average only $525 a month. If a family doesn't qualify for the full $65,000 mortgage, they can lower the price by providing "sweat equity," helping out with the construction. Local churches provide teams of volunteers to assist them. NHO lends a hand with repairs and maintenance. Howard occasionally gets some unusual calls. "Can you fix my broken window?" a woman inquired. "Sure," he said. "How did it get broken?" "My son was acting up," she said, "and I threw my Bible at him. It was the only thing I had in my hand."

The investment of time, expertise, and coaching makes the transition into home ownership a realistic option for families who have never navigated these waters before. The cost of the staff is not passed along in the price of the houses, meaning NHO has to raise $250,000 every year to cover the gap. But the services they provide are invaluable in qualifying and stabilizing new homeowners.

The benefits accrue in multiple directions. By owning a home, families are building economic value and stability. It has a significant impact on their quality of life, allowing them to live in safe neighborhoods. It imparts dignity through ownership and responsibility. It allows a transfer of wealth to their children. Beyond that, there is a spiritual dimension, Howard Eddings explains: "We exist to holistically empower the urban poor through home ownership. Housing is the platform. The backbone is the opportunity to speak the Gospel into the lives of the people we serve. We do it subtly. If you want to know why we do what we do, we'll tell you."

Best Practices: Neighborhood Housing Opportunities

- Coaches new homeowners through budgeting, purchase, and home maintenance
- Keeps costs for three-bedroom houses to about $65,000; less with "sweat equity"
- Provides clusters of new homeowners to provide a critical mass of renewal in neighborhoods, increasing quality of life and property value
- Builds economic stability for families, allowing transfer of wealth
- Imparts dignity and responsibility through ownership

Results

- Two hundred affordable homes built since 1998
- $13 million value created
- Budget coaching has limited foreclosures to only three

Economic Opportunities

Men coming out of prison or a drug rehab program have a tough time finding employers who are willing to risk hiring them. But if they don't find gainful employment, the likelihood that they will return to illegal activity increases. To break this cycle of recidivism and to create an on-ramp to the job market, the Memphis Leadership Foundation created Economic Opportunities (EcOp), a small business project that pairs character and spiritual development with real labor to give a hand-up to people willing to work. EcOp works with the Barnhart Crane and Rigging Company as a subcontractor, and the men in training learn painting, pallet building, shipping, mechanical work, or maintenance on the company's sprawling property, a former Army depot in the heart of Memphis.

As Howard Eddings drives on the dusty service roads beneath the huge cranes, he explains that the men who have just left prison or a drug and alcohol rehab center "have such negative histories that most employers aren't willing to give them a job. So this is an opportunity for them to establish a positive work history and earn a chance." The Memphis Leadership Foundation staffers, Jim Kennedy and Frank Buchanan, oversee on average eight to twelve men, who become short-term employees of EcOp, fulfilling contract work. The men start the day with thirty-minute devotions to set the spiritual framework for the day. They talk about responsibility, punctuality, attitudes, dealing with authority, and conflict resolution. Then they get to work.

Jim and Frank train the men to be responsible employees so they can keep the next job they get. Participants sign a statement agreeing to the conditions of employment. Bad attitudes, theft, and profanity are not tolerated. Only three excused absences or tardy arrivals are permitted. Drug and alcohol testing are enforced: one strike and you're out. Violators can go to a rehab center. The men earn a paycheck, starting at $5.50 an hour, and can work their way up to $7.50. The participants stay on average eight or nine months, and once they make it that far, EcOp helps them find jobs elsewhere. One quit after he had been there fifteen minutes. "Man, this looks too much like work," he complained. "I thought this was just a program."

Jim and Frank offer counseling throughout the forty-hour workweek on issues like handling conflicts and how to work on a team. They coach the men in establishing a practical plan of action, like paying off tickets that are owed, getting a driver's license, or learning to budget money for living expenses. Frank was an ex-offender who needed a job when he was released. He was astonished when Jim offered him one at EcOp. "Nobody else gave me an opportunity," recalls Frank. "With the spiritual guidance that EcOp offered me, I learned about God and what it means to serve him. I started to get my life together." Because Frank has been in prison and rebounded successfully through this program, he can talk to the men from firsthand experience.

In the eleven years of EcOp, 250 people have been through the program—people like David—who spent twenty-nine years in prison. He comes out of one of the buildings with maroon paint in his hair, on his hands, and up his nostrils. In the year David has been there, he has learned a lot about spray painting since the first disasters. He says, "I had no idea what I'd do when I got out. It's been a lifeline. It has opened my eyes to seeing Christ. And it gave me a positive direction." Now David has a car, he's helping out his daughter financially, and he's becoming a role model for two grandchildren.

When he leaves the program, EcOp will follow up to see if David stays on track. The staff does checkups at thirty, sixty, and ninety days after the men leave training with them for a new job. Three months into their new lives, 75 percent of them are still employed and out of trouble. Without an on-ramp to employment, these men would have a slim chance avoiding recidivism, drugs, or jail. With this opportunity, most of them start a new life.

Mediation and Restitution/Reconciliation Services

Every year, twenty thousand kids in Memphis go through the juvenile court system. Unless something changes, they are likely to end up in worse trouble by the time they are adults. Recognizing the need to intervene, the Memphis Leadership Foundation collaborated with Christ United Methodist Church in 1993 to create Mediation and Restitution/ Reconciliation Services (MARRS). First- or second-time juvenile offenders are given a chance to contact the victims of their crimes, ask their forgiveness, and offer restitution. Having to look the victim in the eye makes enough of an impression that few of the kids break the law again.

The courts keep a lookout for cases like vandalism, burglary, or trespassing, where youngsters have admitted their guilt and there's a clear-cut victim for whom restitution would be feasible. MARRS tracks down the victims and brings them face-to-face with the youngsters, facilitating the conversation. Together they assess the damage and come up with a plan for restitution, which might mean paying the cost of the broken window or taillight from funds the youngster will need to earn. MARRS works with sixty churches and organizations throughout the city to find paying short-term jobs for the young offenders and places for them to absolve sixty to one hundred community service hours assigned as penance.

Most of the kids are intimidated by the process. It's uncomfortable to go to a person whom you have wronged and ask their forgiveness. Precisely because it's hard, the process gets through to the kids. As case coordinator Deteressa Hall says, "It's a turning point when they have to deal with the victims face-to-face, hearing them, seeing their hurt feelings, feeling their anger and disgust. A lot of them are very remorseful." The mediators "try to make it friendly, but we make them understand they have to take responsibility," affirms Adrian Wilson, MARRS director.

The program has an effect. Since its inception in 1993, more than two thousand youthful offenders have been diverted from the court system into MARRS. The normal recidivism rate for juvenile offenders is nearly 40 percent, but MARRS has dropped that rate to 14 percent for the youngsters it handles. The evidence indicates that this approach is effective in putting derailed kids back on track.

Results: Mediation and Restitution/Reconciliation Services

- Two thousand youth offenders referred from juvenile courts
- Reduced recidivism from 38 percent to 14 percent

Urban Plunge

Memphis is like most American cities in that there's an invisible dividing line between the urban and suburban worlds. The people who live in one world seldom interact with the other. It's possible to drive right by for years and never venture into the other realm, because your schools, stores, and friends don't intersect. Many people from the suburbs know little about urban life—not because they are mean-spirited, but because they are oblivious.

If the church is charged to care for the poor, how can it bridge this gap of understanding? Eli Morris has been taking adults into the inner city of Memphis for an "Urban Plunge" since 1991. For three nights and four days, the associate pastor of Hope Presbyterian plucks suburban believers out of their comfort zone and immerses them in a world they do not know, even though they may have lived in the city their entire lives.

The intrepid group of fifteen to twenty-five participants stays at the Streets ministry in one of the poorest areas of the city. The first night Larry Lloyd talks to them about the biblical reasons for caring for the poor, and they see the effects of poverty up close in the neighborhood where they are staying. Howard Eddings does a panel on racism, which cuts to the raw nerve of the issue, and challenges the participants to think about aspects most of them have never considered. The group visits the Civil Rights Museum together. They eat soul food. They celebrate communion together, and they stay up late talking, processing.

To expose the participants to possibilities to plug into later, the group visits a variety of ministries throughout the city that are doing effective work. They do a work project together, like rehab on a house that needs a wheelchair ramp. As they hammer nails that day, they talk for several hours to the man who lives there. Some develop a relationship that draws them back later to build a lattice for him to grow flowers . . . and to continue the conversation.

As Eli explains it, there are three concentric circles in urban ministry. "The outside circle is the user-friendly involvement. It's bringing clothes, or toys for children, or buying books. The next stage is more hands-on, like work on houses. At the center is something relational, a deeper commitment, like mentoring one child every week. Fewer people go deeper, and are willing to go closer to live in relationship." If the participants are willing to go into the urban environment "with the heart of a servant and a student," says Eli, they may have a profound experience.

Oasis of Hope

What grew out of exposure to inner-city ministry through the Urban Plunge was a willingness to engage. Hope Presbyterian, in conjunction with the Memphis Leadership Foundation, purchased a house in the Manassas Caldwell Bickford area directly across the street from the local elementary school to provide a beachhead for ministry into the impoverished community. This little green house, christened Oasis of Hope, is one of the few buildings in the neighborhood with a fresh coat of paint. Small groups from the church have adopted classrooms, providing school supplies, a clothes closet, and tutoring. When the school switched to uniforms, the church helped out parents who couldn't afford them.

In the afternoon, bright-eyed kids race to the door to get a spot at one of the computers. Church members stop by to drop off contributions of food, clothes, and books. For the people who are willing to go deeper and enter a relationship, there are opportunities to teach an adult to read or mentor a child. This project is how one church has built a bridge from suburban believers into an urban neighborhood. It takes some structure, preparation, and experienced partners. But with that combination, a project like this can be a potent source of renewal for the neighborhood, while quickening the spiritual life of people who put their faith into action.

Streets

Streets was founded with Ken Bennett in downtown Memphis as one of the very first projects of the Memphis Leadership Foundation in 1987. His passion for kids took him into the projects, where he adapted the Young Life model for urban application. Now he has a recreation center where 450 kids from one of the poorest neighborhoods in Memphis come to hang out and play basketball, foosball, pool, or ping-pong every week. A staff of six full-time and four part-time workers, some of whom came through the program as kids, help Ken. One of his assistants is an ex-gang leader.

One of the toughest deficits for inner-city kids to overcome is their education. Ken pairs mentor/tutors with middle school youth once a week. He wrote a curriculum to help prepare for the TCAP proficiency test, runs monthly ACT/SAT prep courses, and teaches youth how to write essays for college applications. He also takes promising kids for six weeks in the summer and drills them on English, grammar, vocabulary, and oral communications, challenging them with college-level instruction. He's serious about getting them ready for college: he pays them to do the training. And he mobilizes financial assistance for college tuition and books. "If they can get there, we want to help," he says. In the past year and a half, forty-five kids from his program have gone to college, beating all the odds against their background.

For the Kingdom Camp and Retreat Center

Getting into a new environment is sometimes the best catalyst for change. The Memphis Leadership Foundation just finished converting a green and hilly property outside Memphis into a beautifully equipped camp that accommodates 120. The camp boasts a lake with bobbing boats and fishing, a 7,800-square-foot house, two swimming pools, and a tennis court. The $3.2 million investment also added a ropes course, an outdoor basketball court, and multiple cabins, which are fully heated and air conditioned, and brand-new bunk beds. A combination meeting and dining hall has a state-of-the-art industrial kitchen to feed the hordes of visitors. More than one thousand people visited in the first year. The facility allows kids from the inner city to have a change of environment and leadership training without incurring extensive travel costs. Few inner-city youngsters have been outside their neighborhood, so the opportunity to experience a different setting can have a profound effect.

Multinational Ministries

While Memphis was historically a black and white city, like many throughout America, it has experienced a dramatic influx of refugees and immigrants from all over the world. They have streamed in from El Salvador, China, Vietnam, India, Laos, Cambodia, Mexico, Ethiopia, Somalia, and Bosnia, among many other places. Refugees arriving with anything more than the clothes on their backs are fortunate. And while a number of ministries step up with food, immediate relief, or temporary shelter, the needs of refugees go much deeper. Education and language are obstacles. And the biggest hurdle is getting a job.

In partnership with Associated Catholic Charities and World Vision, the Memphis Leadership Foundation launched Multinational Ministries in 1992 to assist refugees being resettled in Memphis. Local churches have joined in a network to provide job training, placement, relief, education, medical care, and youth ministries. ESL (English as a Second Language) and Read to Succeed programs have eased the transition into a new language. The results have been 500 refugees placed in jobs and 250 mentor matches.

Hope Christian Community Foundation

When Larry Lloyd handed off the Memphis Leadership Foundation to his vice president Howard Eddings in 1997, he started the Hope Christian Community Foundation as a venture capital model for philanthropy in Memphis. Larry's ten-year plan was to empower leaders, to build bridges between communities of resource and need, and then to start a Christian foundation. Once he had built a network of ministries, it was time to mobilize resources to support and expand them. Larry looked at the Christian Community Foundation in Chattanooga as a model, and adapted its approach to assist Christian donors in Memphis in giving wisely.

The goal of the Hope Foundation is to connect resources in the community to groups doing effective, hands-on, faith-based work. Larry's years of experience on the front lines have given him a vast reservoir of knowledge donors can tap into, shortening their learning curve. Some donors a specific interest, serving abused children, for example, and ask his advice on responsible groups doing effective work in this area. Others aren't sure what they want to do, and Larry encourages them to write a mission statement for themselves, coaching them in the discerning process. When they do decide to give, it is because they have formulated specific goals, and they make an informed decision for purposeful giving.

Having spent years on the front lines of ministry himself, Larry then spent much of his time in donor relations, offering his experienced expertise to help them accomplish what they would like to. A donor who prefers to remain anonymous wanted to give a gift to a library for a section of Christian books, but didn't have the time to select them himself. So Larry assembled a team of fifteen people to choose $100,000 worth of high-quality books. Another donor wanted an organization to have a strategic plan. The problem was, he was on the board and didn't want to seem heavy-handed. So Larry devised a plan to allow the organization to apply to the Hope Foundation for a $50,000 grant to hire a consultant. The executive director agreed, applied, and hired the consultant, who was able to discreetly guide the leadership of the group with this strategic gift. Larry's role, until recently, has been to guide donors on their journey of providing Kingdom resources for Kingdom work, and help them discover the joy that follows good gifts. One confided, "Every dollar I make, I give away. Do you know how much fun I have?"

Questions to Ask Before You Give to a Faith-Based Organization

Larry Lloyd, as the founder of the Hope Christian Community Foundation in Memphis, recommends that donors ask a series of questions before they give to faith-based organizations.

- Do they have a clear mission statement?
- Do they have three to four strategic objectives, and specific goals for the year?
- What do they consider success? Can they state results?
- Do they have a board of directors, male and female, beyond family members, that is representative of the community served?
- Are their accounting practices sound?
- What's their proportion of administrative overhead? If it's more than 15 percent for local groups and more than 25 percent for national, that's a red flag.
- Do they get a financial audit? If not, why not?
- Do they have valid 501(c)3 status, and did they file a 990 form?
- Do they have a statement of values and faith?
- What are the credentials of the staff?
- What does a site visit reveal about them?

Since 1998, the Hope Foundation has given away $30 million, 85 percent to Christian ministries and churches. There are 145 donor-advised funds within the foundation, and from the fees that the foundation charges, it has given away about $500,000. To raise the visibility of the frontline efforts and to bridge the gap between the disparate worlds of philanthropy and inner-city ministry, Hope Foundation orchestrates annual banquets to celebrate servant leaders and unsung heroes of the inner city.

The foundation is a key piece in the citywide strategy of renewal that Larry initiated nearly twenty years ago. Taking a page from Nehemiah, he first rallied the workers to repair the wall, encouraging them and teaching them how. Today he can point to twenty-nine locations in the city where his efforts have rallied them to work together, and to one hundred forty indigenous leaders he has personally trained. Then he helped direct the resources of the nobles of the city to the frontline workers, who are living out the vision they share of renewing the soul of the city.

chapter 11

One by One Leadership

Equipping and Connecting in Fresno

Fresno lies in a region so distinctive it is identifiable from outer space: California's Great Central Valley stretches four hundred miles, the breadbasket of the state.[1] The region is economically poor and relatively isolated. In 1983, Fresno placed last in a survey of 273 American cities rated on "livability."[2] Then things got worse.

Fresno experienced a demographic wind shear with an influx of immigration through the mid-1980s and '90s by Latino refugees from Central and South American countries. Waves of Lao, Hmong, Cambodian, and Vietnamese refugees, in addition to the streams of the poorest from Mexico, all flocked to work as service workers and migrant laborers in the harvest. Suddenly, what had been a sleepy agricultural town was popping with a baby boom of prime-crime youngsters.[3] Fresno ballooned to the sixth largest city in the state, with 125 active youth gangs and the highest per capita rate of violent crime in California in every category except murder. Fresno's face is racially diverse today, with roughly 40 percent of the population Latino, 11 percent Asian, 8.5 percent African American, 3 percent multiracial, and 37 percent white. The population in the city today is about 500,000, with nearly a million in the county.

In 1993, Fresno was dubbed the car theft capital of the world, with 13,000 vehicles stolen every year in a city of then 300,000. Poverty was rampant, murder became common, unemployment was in double digits, and teen pregnancy soared. The schools struggled to teach kids who spoke ninety different languages, with many whose parents spoke no English at all. H. Spees, who served as CEO of One by One Leadership until 2003, recalls:

> In the early 1990s, Fresno was losing its soul. I felt it most profoundly as I watched two kids die on two separate occasions, both by gang-related gunshot wounds to the head. Feeling this loss of civic soul deeply in my own soul started me on a journey that has included conversations with literally thousands of people, moving our family residence to one of Fresno's forgotten neighborhoods, and sensing a direct calling to build hope through thoughtful work with others.[4]

The work of One by One Leadership was born in its earliest embryonic form from a multi-ethnic, multidenominational pastors' retreat in the mountains to pray for the city. What emerged from desperation was a conviction that civic leaders from the government, police, business, and faith community needed to join forces to work to renew the city together. One by One Leadership emerged to equip and to relationally connect diverse leaders throughout the city who are committed to civic renewal. It has been a catalyst, sparking multiple new initiatives to bring greater health to the Fresno community.

Genesis of a Movement: No Name Fellowship

Seared by the LA riots, and awakened to the potential for similar outbreaks in Fresno, two pastors named Bufe Karraker and G. L. Johnson convened a group of twelve civic leaders in Fresno. These two men had long pastored large congregations, and each brought thirty-five years of history and relationships to the table, along with a commitment to each other and to the city. They were able to gather together a diverse group, including the mayor, chief of police, sheriff, business and church leaders. H. Spees and Gordon Donoho were among the prime movers giving birth to this vision. Christian community development leader John Perkins delivered a hard-hitting challenge to the city's leaders to renew together. To avoid any proprietary claims, they called the group the "No Name Fellowship."

This movement pulled together people from diverse sectors to meet in the hot spots of the city, such as a rescue mission, an inner-city school, or a jail, to hear from a leader on the front lines. Pastors, government officials, and business leaders exchanged thoughts on the problem over lunch on site, and brainstormed potential solutions. Chief of Police Joseph Samuels challenged the group to do a "cops and clergy ride-along." On a Friday night, sixty businessmen and pastors rode the night shift in police cars, as they sped to shootouts and robberies. Some saw youngsters die and came back with their blood on their clothes. The effect was galvanizing.

The relationships built and ideas sparked through the pastors' prayer retreat and the No Name Fellowship led to several creative new initiatives that have borne tangible fruit. A participant in the initial mountaintop prayer retreat, Rev. Roger Minassian, left his pastorate in 1993 to attempt the unlikely task of finding employment for gang members. Since then, Hope Now for Youth has placed eight hundred gang members in jobs with 230 businesses. From cleaning streets for the City of Fresno to sterilizing surgical instruments at Children's Hospital Central California, gang youths and their families have left crime and violence for productivity in the American mainstream.

Apartment Intervention: Care Fresno

One of the other initiatives spawned from the retreat and the No Name Fellowship was Care Fresno. Pockets of trouble in several local apartment complexes drew a disproportionately high number of calls for police intervention. Care Fresno mobilized the police, local apartment owners, and pastors of local churches to intervene together in these distressed complexes to cut the crime. Owners agree to offer the use of one apartment in a complex free of charge, which local churches "adopt." Participating churches offer constructive activities for the would-be troublemakers, providing services like on-site youth and after-school programs, tutoring, music lessons, and adult education. The police have cracked down on drug traffickers and stepped up protection in the involved neighborhoods. Today twenty-five apartment complexes housing ten thousand people in Fresno are serviced by this partnership, which has reduced crime by a remarkable 65–70 percent in these complexes.

Downwardly Mobile Relocation

A number of families, including those of H. Spees and Randy White, decided in the early '90s to pick up their children and move from nicer high-income low-crime neighborhoods into Lowell, the multiracial region of Fresno with the highest crime and the lowest income. H. had spent eleven years working in Mississippi with John Perkins, living with the population he served. He had experienced the power of this kind of renewal. He and his wife and children agreed to move into Lowell, even though it had real consequences for all of them.

This was a tough task even for the stouthearted. Randy White, who heads InterVarsity for Fresno, says in the early years after the move he collected shell casings in his yard and "prostitutes who had been shot would come up to the door bleeding." There were ten murders on his street. Tom Sommers, an insurance executive who now chairs the No Name Fellowship, recalls, "When I heard about what H. and Randy were doing, I thought they were crazy." Randy bought an old house with enough room to do ministry in it, and founded a tutoring program for grade-school kids called Wise Old Owl—which has met ever since in his house—now reaching one hundred kids each week. He also oversees the Pink House, a residence offering a one-year opportunity for college students in Fresno to learn leadership skills and do urban ministry.

Another fifteen families have joined them, as have eight new ministries that have a visible presence in the neighborhood. Encouraged by their influx, some of the long-term Lowell residents have decided to tough it out and stay. Together, they form a critical mass for renewal from the grassroots up. The neighborhood has improved noticeably. Teams of volunteers have repainted more than twenty-five houses, graffiti has been removed, the blight has been abated, and crime has dropped by more than 50 percent.

Stewardship for the Soul of the City

After several years, the No Name Fellowship sent a delegation, including the mayor, chief of police, a school administrator, a seminary professor, and several pastors, to see the Pittsburgh Leadership Foundation in action. They came back convinced that the Leadership Foundation model was the best way for them to engage in civic renewal. A new action-oriented organization was created in 1994, initially as the Fresno Leadership Foundation, later rechristened One by One Leadership. H. Spees assumed the leadership role for the organization's "multi-sector stewardship for the soul of the city."

Assuming the function of a Nehemiah, H. Spees and his successor as the CEO of One by One Leadership, Kurt Madden, have taken on the task of identifying the places where the wall is down in the city. Their work has the blessing of the "king"—whether it's the mayor, the governor, or the president. They have obtained seed money for the tools, and they have systematically connected the workers at the wall. They have mobilized, trained, and equipped the frontline workers, deploying them in a strategy that encompasses the city. Just as the individual families and tradesmen worked on the wall in front of their homes and shops under Nehemiah, grassroots groups, neighborhood associations, pastors, and police are working on their piece of the city in Fresno.

The role One by One plays is that of catalyst, facilitator, trainer, and equipper for civic partners, whether they are drawn from the churches, the neighborhoods, the schools, or the streets. They do not own all the programs, but they provide a staff person or a team to serve as a moving hub, conveying a philosophy of civic renewal to a broader circle of other partners. Their job is to mobilize and equip the frontline street saints. One by One Leadership has been intentional in building relationships and has effectively fostered overlapping circles of influence. Within these circles, relationships and trust have grown, and with them, a willingness to engage the community together. People from the government, schools, businesses, law enforcement, and the faith community have been brought into relationship with each other, bridging races and denominations and sharing a commitment to seek solutions for the city together.

One by One Leadership currently has a budget of $2 million and a staff of twenty-one full-time and five part-time employees, as well as eighty-five volunteers. It is an accredited member of the Leadership Foundations of America. The current activities of One by One Leadership center around four areas of service:

1. Neighborhood-based community development
2. Mentoring of at-risk youth and families leaving welfare
3. Capacity building for congregational and faith-based nonprofits
4. Improving academic outcomes for inner-city public school children

Neighborhood-Based Community Development

The community of Jefferson lies just outside downtown Fresno, a pocket of poverty and transience for five thousand residents, largely Hmong, Laotian, and Hispanic families. Crime and prostitution are rampant on the streets. Resident Michael Lust, chairman of the recently developed neighborhood association, says, "When I first moved in it was a joke. Crime was high and street violence was a problem. One New Year's Eve I brought a tape recorder outside just to record the amount of gunfire. It sounded like a Hollywood movie. A tavern down the street was probably the murder capital of Fresno."[5]

Residents faced a potential initiative that was at once promising and threatening. Community Medical Centers wanted to build a massive Regional Medical Center costing $320 million, which would cover fifty-eight acres within the four-hundred-acre Jefferson neighborhood. The city had approved the plans in 1995, but the initial design necessitated a housing relocation strategy for residents. That had stymied both city planners and Community Medical Centers. No one wanted a hospital complex bordering a high-crime area to become a Taj Mahal surrounded by razor wire fence.

One by One sensed the potential in this neighborhood, despite its difficulties. At Jefferson Elementary School, 98.4 percent of the students' families are at the national poverty level. Many of them are undocumented, and 85 percent of the parents do not speak English. One by One Leadership began doing on-the-ground community organization training work in 1998, which eventually gave rise to the Jefferson Area Neighborhood Association (JANA). One by One Leadership staff taught residents the principles of community organization and how to engage the police and city officials to improve their neighborhood. The results were modest but visible improvements in the community: new sidewalks and stop signs, graffiti removal, parent patrols to and from school, and cleaner alleys and streets. But equally important was the change in the residents: they were finding their voice, and joining together to claim the neighborhood as their own. They experienced what Peter Drucker calls turning "geography into community."

When people participate in planning, they feel ownership in the project. So One by One embarked on a hands-on planning process to renew the area, bringing the residents into the discussion. An urban design architect facilitated the process, and a university professor of urban planning trained residents in the vocabulary of urban planning. Because many of the residents do not speak English, planning sessions were held with headphones and translators simultaneously giving the proceedings in Hmong, Laotian, and Spanish. Participants with headsets on excitedly came forward to the huge map of the area to sketch their proposals. These immigrants experienced the full value of civic participation, probably for the first time. The city government has approved their plan.

Fred Burkhardt, who became director of the city's Housing, Economic and Community Development office in 2001, was looking for partnerships in the Jefferson neighborhood, which the federal government has now designated as part of an Empowerment Zone for nine years. He says,

"We found that One by One had been on the ground in force for two or three years, and they had done an enormous amount of spade work, community grassroots-level work that would have taken us another two to three years to accomplish. . . . So being the organizational speed demon I am, I said why am I going out there to reinvent this wheel? I have a wheel right here. Let's use theirs."

Burkhardt has concluded that the city government can provide services like water, sewage disposal, garbage pickup, and parking, but "We are not built organizationally to do work at the level at the depth of the community that One by One and similar organizations are built to reach. We're simply not good at it." One by One brought to the table local schools, city planners, housing developers, residents, police, and the Community Medical Center. Together they produced a solution no one sector alone could have.

Rather than trying to keep the neighbors out, the Community Medical Center is now training them for work. Central California has a shortfall of nurses, coupled with an unemployment rate of 12–14 percent. The obvious solution: train people in nursing. To train residents for future jobs that will be created in the neighborhood, Community Medical Centers offers a six-month "boot camp" for job readiness, teaching residents how to apply for a job, write a resume, and go for an interview.

As parents have engaged in JANA and the classes at the medical center, there has been a ripple effect on their children. John Barber, principal of Tehipite Middle School, observes: "Children see their parents repositioning their goals, and see their mom is learning to speak English and use computers, and it has an effect on them. We now see fewer behavior problems, fewer absentees, and less tardiness." Academic performance is rising in tandem with parental civic engagement, as unlikely as that may seem. As Bryn Forhan, former vice president of government relations for Community Medical Centers, explains it, "Children are doing better because they see their parents making changes. There's a ripple effect, moving up the Maslow scale. Their basic needs are being met. And they are readying to participate in democracy."

Forhan sees that the neighborhood horizon has been brightened.

"One by One has given attention to the residents, given them hope, a direct link to information, a sense of empowerment, and creates an environment that changes outlook. They lived in hopelessness and despair and now they see options." If the community-renewal project plays out as planned, the net result for the community will be new jobs, improved educational opportunities, increased police protection, and affordable housing. One outcome now is hope.

Mentoring for Families and Youth

Welfare-to-Work Job Coaches and Mentors

Transitioning families from welfare to work is one of the earliest projects One by One Leadership undertook. The organization's research on best practices pointed it toward a model that recruited and trained job coaches from disenfranchised neighborhoods who had succeeded in making it up and out. They sent them back into the neighborhood to help others make the same transition. One by One forged a partnership with the local Fresno City Community College, which provided training; the Housing Authority to create neighborhood job centers, which provided space; and the Economic Opportunities Commission. The Workforce Investment Act provided funding for the Fresno Neighborhood Jobs Network program, and One by One Leadership provided job coaching. They added a volunteer mentoring component.

Four hundred men and women have been placed in unsubsidized jobs, with about 150 of them currently receiving job coaching from staff members and mentors. One by One recruits mentors from local churches, who receive twenty hours of training. Six neighborhood centers were established, fifty-seven mentors matched, and eleven job coaches were trained. Nearly all the job coaches came through the welfare system themselves, which gives them a degree of credibility that only comes from first-hand experience. Rose Orta serves as a job coach now, but remembers well what it was like to be on welfare. She tells her participants with conviction: "I was there and made it. You can, too." The job coaches stay with their clients a minimum of six months, during which time they call or visit them each week, troubleshoot problems that may be impeding the job search, and offer encouragement and advice. The coaches convene a roundtable once a month for all their participants to facilitate peer learning and connect the individuals to community resources.

Mentoring High-Risk Youth: ARMS

The At-Risk Ministries (ARMS) Network is a collaborative strategy that began in partnership with the sheriff, the chaplain of juvenile hall, the captain of the police department, and Youth for Christ. As is the case with several One by One projects, staff members interface as a hub for a number of civic partners, providing the infrastructure to keep the coalition in motion. These Nehemiah strategists keep checking in on the builders at the wall to get them what they need, and to keep the work moving.

Youth who have been in trouble with the law are taken to camps in the mountains, accompanied by probation officers. On this trip, which offers an intensive outdoor character-building experience, each youth is paired with a mentor. Mentors are recruited from local churches and trained for the relationship with a troubled teen, committing to at least six months. A modified version of the Search Institute tool for assessing developmental assets is utilized as an intake evaluation. So far, 240 youngsters have come through the camping program.

Records from juvenile hall in Fresno reveal that of those youth who are simply released from incarceration with no further intervention, 70 percent are rearrested in one year. If they go to the county "boot camp" program, the percentage of re-arrests drops to 17 percent. The participants in the ARMS mountain trip have been drawn from the pool of "boot camp" participants. Of those who have graduated from "boot camp," gone on the mountain trip, and worked with a mentor for half a year, only 1 percent have been rearrested. While the pool of participants is small—currently twenty-two youth, paired with twelve trained mentors—the preliminary evidence indicates that the combination of intensive intervention and sustained mentoring has a strong likelihood of reducing recidivism.

City Builders Roundtable

In another Nehemiah function, One by One facilitates a monthly round-table for leaders of faith-based groups throughout Fresno. The workers at the wall get a chance to get together in City Builders, where they are discovering they are stronger as allies than as competitors. Capacity-building workshops strengthen their competence in things like grant writing, as well as their connectedness. Randy White, director of InterVarsity, affirms that the City Builders process has provided a "steady stream of qualified people to provide training, as well as access to funding." But beyond that, he sees that One by One Leadership is serving as a catalyst in bringing together faith-based groups from throughout the city and fostering a growth process that intertwines their strengths. "They make things happen that none of the nonprofits alone could. This whole process generates relationships and momentum. It's like growing the interlocking roots of redwood trees, which grow in shallow soil but produce tremendous stability. Together we are producing things than no one organization could."

City as Parish

City as Parish (CAP) is a citywide collaborative to train parishioners to move outside the church and into the city in service. Launched in partnership with the Pittsburgh Leadership Foundation's City as Parish program, and headed in Fresno by Don Simmons, this training is equipping believers to put their gifts into action in a concerted strategy that embraces needs throughout the city.

Don has trained teams from eighty-seven churches, whose membership includes thirty thousand people. Participants receive weekly training totaling fifty hours, then, in collaboration with their own pastors, engage in ministries either within their own church or outside it. Since the project began, volunteers have fanned out into more than fifty agencies in Fresno, offering parent education, after-school programs, food distribution, English tutorials, a home for battered women, help overcoming substance abuse, and mentoring.

Don Simmons was the unexpected beneficiary of the training he had given. Bleeding in the brain caused him to fall unconscious, and he lay in his home more than a day until he was discovered. He was pronounced dead on arrival at the hospital. Resuscitation revived his heart, but he lay in a coma for three months. Fresno parishioners, whom he had trained, spontaneously rallied to orchestrate round-the-clock vigils by his bedside, pay his bills, and care for him. In the months as he slowly recuperated, these laypeople picked up the mantle from their pastoral leader and continued the city-wide work, coming in for coaching from Don at his bedside once he could speak. He was told he would never walk again, but he defied the prognosis. He has risen from his bed with a fervor for Kingdom work born from the intimate brush with death.

His work is engendering ripples of transformation within the faith community. "When people discover their style and gifts, then see a need for those talents, they just come alive," says Terrie Purgason, pastor of Equipping Ministries at Fresno First Baptist Church. Terrie says, "It changes the mindset of pastors to release their people into the city. We are moving people outside the doors of the church." The mindset of parishioners is changed as well, as Don Simmons explains. "The transformation is in the pew—the churches own it then. It's the natural next step from the prayer movement." Once the mindset is changed, CAP provides the means for mobilization. As Don says, "Some people are asking for opportunities for service—we provide the on-ramps."

The City as Parish process has helped clergy design creative solutions to neighborhood problems. As Rev. Willie Nolte, senior pastor of First Baptist, affirms, "Our community garden is a tangible outcome of our attempt to engage the community through CAP." A blighted drug house stood across the street from Nolte's church, close enough that kids watching from the windows of their Sunday school class could see crack being sold. Heroin syringes were thrown onto church property, and prostitutes walked the street. The church bought the lot and tore down the house. Taking the church members outside their walls, the church's youth groups then converted the vacant lot into a community garden. The church provides the water, while the neighbors plant and care for fruits and vegetables sprouting in individual plots. The parishioners have engaged their neighbors in a new way, and again, geography has been converted to community.

Scott Gillum, senior pastor of Sunnyside Church, appreciates the way CAP has stimulated his congregation's growing outreach ministries. "What CAP is enabling us to do is to expand and track opportunities and to evaluate the results of our service." In Fresno, CAP trainees go all over the city to serve. To assist people on the search, CAP has created a Web-based volunteer recruitment system called Volunteer Connect, which links nonprofits offering service-specific opportunities with people willing to serve. CAP Fresno has attracted diverse congregations: white, black, Hispanic, Evangelical, Protestant, Episcopalian, and southeast Asian including Lao, Kmu, Khmer, Cambodian, Chinese, and Korean.

Pastors Clusters

Pastors are sometimes the loneliest people in town. Always pouring out for other people, they seldom cultivate real relationships with their counterparts across the street, denominationally or geographically. One by One gathers groups of pastors of all races and denominations for fellowship, prayer, and unity. They have been bundled into eight geographic clusters throughout the city, involving about a hundred clergy who span the denominational spectrum. In a city with four hundred churches, that's a broad swath.

The relationships are slowly bearing fruit. Pastor Paul Binion, for example, says the relationships formed through the No Name Fellowship, One by One Leadership, and the Pastors Clusters "have moved me from my myopic perspective. I was a very Afro-centric kind of guy, born in a black community, living in a black church, all I wanted was black folk, black, black, black, black, black. . . . And so what the Lord has done is put people in my life who have made me open my perspective." His church is now attended by Latinos, Asians, and Caucasians. "We're not a black church anymore. We are a fellowship of different flavors." Pastor Binion is now in the process of starting a Hispanic congregation.

When Pastor Jim Franklin came to Fresno as a newcomer, he found the No Name Fellowship introduced him "into relationships with government, religious, and civic leaders it would have been difficult or impossible to meet." The population in downtown Fresno was an eye-opener for this small-town boy. The neighborhood he serves includes former gang members and prostitutes, and kids who have been shot, stabbed, and raped. Franklin's church accepted the challenge to welcome these people, and the numbers swelled. To accommodate the growth, the Cornerstone Church bought an old vaudeville theater downtown, which now is the home of a congregation of 3,000. In response to the community's needs, this church has launched ministries for prisoners, gang members, and the homeless. Their food ministry has fed 650,000 people and currently supplies 120 agencies throughout the city.

Coming from a small-town Oklahoma Assemblies of God background, Franklin admits he "had to overcome some spiritual prejudice engaging people with a different theological basis." He found that the No Name Fellowship and Pastors Clusters "gave me an opportunity to engage the city with a common cause, and cross theological and racial boundaries. It liberated me, and made me an ambassador to others, to bring other brothers to the table. It changed me philosophically, allowing me to cross the greatest barrier—the division in the body of Christ. Now we have the power of unity."

The spirit of cooperation fostered in the Pastors Clusters is manifested when Franklin sends out teams of two hundred volunteers and a huge load of food to a smaller church trying to start a neighborhood feeding program. Franklin says if they don't have a choir, he brings his, and doesn't care who gets the credit. "We can empower these churches with our resources if we act like a body." Some of the churches have doubled in size with such a boost.

Improving Achievement for Children

One by One has also used its collaborative strength to bring ministry and civic leaders to the table for community renewal affecting education, leveraging all their resources. One example is the CORAL project (Communities Organizing Resources for Advanced Learning). Fresno is one of five California cities chosen for this project, which is bringing $12 million into the region over six years. Working in conjunction with United Way and the Irvine Foundation, One by One Leadership has helped craft an approach to develop out-of-school programs that improve student achievement in up to twelve downtown and west Fresno elementary schools.

Rich Kriegbaum, president of the United Way of Fresno County, explained that this project is attempting to improve the level of learning through out-of-school programs that enhance the capacity of residents, producing learning results in their children that can be verified in improved standardized test scores. One by One Leadership is one of the architects for this strategy, which is building the capacity of neighborhood associations, enhancing parent training and adult literacy, and partnering with community development corporations. This initiative dovetails with efforts to train and mobilize laity across the city. Trained volunteers from the churches are improving both spiritual and civic health. CORAL is now in its third year, offering afternoon programs to nearly a hundred students at each of six sites.

A second example of leveraging resources by bringing other players to the table is the California Works for Better Health (CWBH) initiative, which is a collaboration of California Endowment and the Rockefeller Foundation. One by One Leadership and three other community-based organizations in Fresno—Catholic Charities, the Center for New Americans, and the Fresno West Coalition for Economic Development—will receive a total of $2.4 million over the next four years to improve health and employment development in the area.

City Builders Campus

One by One Leadership has forged partnerships to revitalize a city block in the historical section of Fresno to create a campus for faith-based and community organizations. Homes built at the turn of the century by Fresno's commercial entrepreneurs are being renovated by this group of social entrepreneurs to create a hub of activity for renewal. The CORAL initiative is housed in one of the homes, while another will be a center for early childhood learning. One by One Leadership is housed in the Bufe Karraker Center for Spiritual and Civic Renewal, and the Center for Faith-Based Nonprofits will have its headquarters nearby along with Care Fresno and the No Name Fellowship. The John Perkins Center for Community Transformation is another of the homes being renovated, which will serve as an equipping institute for urban ministry. Multipurpose housing, a charter school, and a retail support center round out the planned renewal of the neighborhood, which will include a community technology center and a social entrepreneurship center. Together, these efforts will transform a piece of Fresno's geography into community in a meaningful way.

Family Leadership Connection

The value that One by One Leadership adds accrues to individual organizations and people, as well as networks and neighborhoods. For example, Family Leadership Connection is an organization that was initiated under the wing of One by One, but has now spun off as a stand-alone nonprofit. Leaders Patty Bunker and Gladys Morris have coauthored a book on parenting based on the Search Institute's developmental assets for youth. This approach teaches parents how to systematically foster the development of their children to become whole, motivated, and stable. The curriculum has been translated from English into Hmong and Spanish, and has been used to teach 1,300 parents over the past six years. Because parenting is an important piece of the community-building strategy, the organization is a key element of the citywide holistic approach to renewal.

Individual Benefits

Building the capacity of individual people is an important part of the One by One strategy as well. Socorro Gaeta is one example of a neighborhood resident who has flourished with training. An immigrant from Mexico with minimal schooling, Socorro has lived in the Jefferson neighborhood for twenty-seven years, where she raised six children, and had seen no improvement in the area until One by One arrived. With One by One's encouragement, she joined the Jefferson Area Neighborhood Association and Fresno CORAL, and has become a leader, mobilizing three hundred of her neighbors to participate. She now serves on the boards of the Downtown Community Development Corporation and is an instructor in parenting for Family Leadership Connection. She is learning English and has a part-time job at Jefferson Elementary School.

As Socorro puts it, "When they start sending me to represent Jefferson I was so happy because I'm thinking who's me to represent Jefferson? There's more important people . . . I told them you can do better than me. But I never say no, I go on my way and I'm so happy because I learned for me." One by One sent her to training for ten days to learn how to interface with the mayor, police, and local officials. "I have a big change from that time to now, because I'm involved with the community and the school and the city and Parenting Partners. They call me a key leader for Jefferson." When asked what One by One Leadership has given her, she exclaims with a broad smile, "Ideas!" Socorro has caught fire, and is actively contributing to her community and motivating others to do likewise.

Lessons Learned

One by One Leadership has been nimble to reposition itself, based on its discoveries along the learning curve. Early on, the organization launched an effort to raise funds for a group of faith-based organizations (FBOs) in the city. Jim Westgate, who was then co-leading the organization, explains, "It was a kind of Christian United Way." They raised and re-granted close to $200,000 to other groups, but found that it created a dynamic that was not good. "It led to a kind of competitive spirit among the faith-based groups, which was not what we intended. We concluded that we did not want to do anything that would divide. So we tried to re-vamp our strategy to build up in unity instead." Collaborative projects and leadership training were born out of this frustration, and have yielded a more interwoven strategy that equips FBOs to obtain their own funding, while cooperating on shared strategies.

Prior to this shift, One by One was a pure intermediary, not offering any direct services itself. The group discovered that it is extremely diffi-cult to find funders who want to invest in intermediary work alone. So One by One decided to embark on a mixed model, working to provide some direct services with tangible (and fundable) results, while continu-ing to serve the intermediary function in the background.

Another lesson crystallized out of the early attempts at community re-newal. Teams of people had been mobilized to come into the Lowell neighborhood to paint houses, working with the local residents to scrape and prep them. Globe streetlights were put up. But because the impetus did not originate with the residents, they were not enthusiastic about maintaining the lights or the houses. One by One concluded that any ef-forts that were "outside in" were not going to yield lasting fruit. They backed off to reconsider what an "inside out" strategy would look like to empower residents to take responsibility for their own neighbor-hood. The Jefferson neighborhood project was born out of this learning pro-cess.

How One by One Works Citywide: Best Practices for Intermediaries
Spanning the Spectrum

The strategic way that One by One works as an intermediary demon-strates some best practices for other intermediaries throughout the coun-try. One by One Leadership builds capacity across several civic sectors of Fresno. It is unusual as a faith-based group to have both a strong presence in the church community, where faith is explicit, as well as a presence in the public square, where it is not. One by One Leadership has a consistent core anchored in faith that serves as its motivation, but which is manifested in a way appropriate to the forum. Its work spans the full spectrum of civic engagement, from full government collaboration to full church collaboration. It requires clarity of vision and conviction to work effectively across such a broad spectrum without diluting the faith content of faith-based programs or transgressing the boundaries of the public sector.

H. Spees makes a case for developing approaches appropriate for either private or public space, because, he asserts, "American public space is theistic and moral but not Christian or spiritual." He is convinced of the rightful place of evangelization and personal transformation that comes through in private space, as his organization demonstrated in collaborating to bring the Billy Graham Crusade to Fresno. Spees explains, "We need to embrace our role in this larger movement in America of restoring community, restoring the common good, taking our place as good citizens in that process. So what that means is that we can draw upon legitimately Judeo-Christian and, specifically, Christ-centered core values. And we can draw upon the values of civil society. Both are legitimate."

Relational Intentionality: Connecting Circles

One by One Leadership cultivates the city with relational intentionality. The leaders and staff have deliberately developed relationships in a number of different circles—including the mayor's office, the schools, the police, the churches, and the business community—and nurtured them, continually introducing people to one another and fostering relationships. They are keeping a number of plates spinning throughout the city, returning to give the pole a twist every week. By providing a staff member whose job it is to keep the relational coalitions in motion, they are able to serve as a catalyst for action that grows from relationship and trust. It is no accident that most of the major players throughout the One by One network simultaneously serve in several circles.

New initiatives come from relationship, which means they are much more likely to bear fruit over time. Randy White put it this way: "One by

One has created relationships, which are more important than programs. They are building something that can last. I can go out into my backyard and plant an orange tree, and it will put down roots and produce oranges year after year. Or I can go and buy a sack of oranges at the store. One by One is planting trees."

Deliberate Diversity and Unity

One by One Leadership has been intentional in assembling its staff as well as the boards of the various cooperating organizations. Because the population in Fresno spans Hispanic, Asian, black, and white populations, leadership has been drawn from these groups. Cultural competence is crucial to the mission, and the result has been active recruitment of diverse talent. One by One has been creative in drawing from the populations served, hiring former welfare recipients to work with families now transitioning from welfare, and a former gang member to reach out to those still involved in gangs and their families.

Equipping from the Inside Out

One by One serves as an equipper to give people the training they need to create widening circles of competence. Every leader trained by CAP goes back into his or her own church trained to create an equipping culture to mobilize scores of others. By providing community organization training and urban-planning instruction to the residents of the Jefferson neighborhood, One by One Leadership has built up their personal capacity and competence, while empowering them to engage in the process of renewing their own neighborhood. By providing networking opportunities and capacity-building training to leaders of faith-based groups citywide, an atmosphere of cooperation rather than of competition has been fostered. The "value-added" of One by One is the capacity that has been built in the individuals as well as in the institutions that serve them. This approach is transformation from the inside out.

Providing On-Ramps

One of the difficulties for the ordinary citizen, or the person in the pew of a local church, is to find a way to engage his or her own community at the flash point of need. One by One Leadership is providing on-ramps for people who want to engage by offering specific ways to use their time and talents. It provides a clearinghouse of opportunities as well as a framework of accountability for collaborating ministries. As Dr. Jim Aldredge, professor at Fresno State University, put it, "The usefulness of a movement like this is that it's difficult for church folks to get involved in poverty and community development efforts. This is an opening. One by One provides an escort service into the city, a way to go places you wouldn't be able to otherwise. Now there's a mechanism for what amounts to foreign ministry on the domestic scene."

Civic Catalyst

One by One Leadership has proven effective at bringing together a variety of organizations and serving as a facilitator and catalyst among them. As Rich Kriegbaum observed, "Their strength is awakening the community. One by One advances and enhances the civic efforts of the church, extending into the entire community. Faith-based organizations do what they do for their specific area—sheltering the homeless, feeding the hungry—but One by One does it across all those areas. No one else does this." By collaborating with the No Name Fellowship and the broad swath of civic partners who convene there, new initiatives are meeting the changing needs of the community. One by One Leadership then gives them "legs."

Changing the Culture

One of the more subtle changes in the city, but one which has had a clear effect, is a change in the culture. Ten years ago in Fresno, it was rare for a person in public office to talk about his or her faith, or to seek an alliance with faith-based groups. But with the steady influence of the No Name Fellowship and One by One Leadership, leaders have been nurtured who in later years have come forward to take on leadership roles and acknowledge their convictions. Fresno now has a mayor, chief of police, superintendent of schools, and fire chief who are all professing Christians. The cooperation between these officials and the faith community has contributed to the success of a number of civic initiatives over the past decade. The fruits of racial and denominational reconciliation have made it much easier to mobilize people of faith and people of good will throughout the city to work together.

One by One Leadership has concluded that solutions to the problems of the neighborhoods are to be found right there, in the neighborhood. The organization's strategy, like that of Nehemiah, is to equip local leaders, give them organizational tools, and connect them in relationship to people from all strata of the city. One by One moves from the mayor's office to police headquarters, from the university to the homeless shelter, without missing a beat. Staff and volunteers speak the languages of all these players, and build relationships among them. They have brought together pastors from all over the city to embrace the community as one body, while equipping the laity to mobilize the slumbering giant of the church. Because One by One serves as an intermediary between school principals, faith-based leaders, housing developers, the community college, pastors, foundations, and urban planners, initiatives have blossomed that no one of these sectors could have produced alone.

And while Fresno may have had the dubious distinction of being named "least livable" American city in 1983, that has all changed. Affirmed by the National Civic League's award as All-America City in 2000, with its faith-based initiatives highlighted in the city's winning application, Fresno is now one of America's most promising examples of comprehensive civic renewal anchored in faith.

One by One Leadership: Results at a Glance

- Trained equipping teams from sixty-two churches, with 4,100 individuals now actively engaged in outreach throughout Fresno
- Placed four hundred welfare-to-work participants in jobs

- Trained fifteen job coaches and 120 church-based job mentors
- Leveraging $14.4 million in new grants into the community over the next five years
- Capacity-building training for thirty leaders of faith-based organizations
- Building relational bridges among one hundred clergy of different denominations
- Mobilized neighborhood coalition to take advantage of a $320 million hospital expansion project
- Building character in 240 at-risk youth to reduce recidivism
- Cross-pollinating seventy-five civic, government, and faith leaders every month
- Revitalizing an entire city block through the City Builders Campus

A Conversation with H. Spees

One valuable asset that has emerged from the experience of One by One Leadership is the fusion of hands-on experience with an understanding of civic engagement grounded in theology. H. Spees has articulated this intersection in the city, drawing from his experience, his intellect, and his faith.[6] He led One by One Leadership as its CEO until November 2003, and is now a pastor at Fresno's Northwest Church.

Soon after Spees moved from the suburbs with his family into the low-income Lowell neighborhood, a neighbor's son was innocently walking near a gang conflict and was struck in the head by a stray bullet. This generated both anger and firmness in Spees, who concluded, "This is unacceptable for my neighbor's son Aurelio to die walking home from school." A city can be blessed with desperation, and some of the fortitude that was forged in this tragedy has urged him on in his service to the city. H. Spees reflects on city transformation from his experience.

Desperation causes great things to happen from a sense of identification with pain. Nehemiah was struck with grief over the report that he heard about Jerusalem and he wept. I have wept on numerous occasions. Cities that are disconnected from the desperation that's at their heart and soul don't have a chance for healing because power follows compassion. God didn't just come down and tell Moses to inflict ten plagues. At the burning bush, he said, "I have witnessed the suffering of my people. I have heard their cries. I'm concerned for them and I have come down and now I am sending you." There is a real identification there between God and his burning love for his people. That's really close to the heartbeat of why we do this work.

We can't disconnect our love for God and His brokenhearted concern. We need to be praying, "Lord, break my heart with the things that break your heart in my city." This work is about prayer. It requires prayer powerfully connected to people committing their lives, fortunes, and sacred honor around a burning, heartbroken love that God has put on their heart for their city and its people. That's the kind of love that is going to create revival, not a media event. This is something much higher and deeper. Authentic prayer is tied to action. The healing of a land is tied to prayer, which is vertical, but there's an engagement piece, which is horizontal. God never gives us the luxury of detaching them. Prayer is a uniquely vertical event that drives me to horizontal engagement, if it is real prayer.

It's important to understand that this kind of work is intensely relational. When God looks at a city, he sees people. It's about loving and valuing them. When Jesus had his last conversation with Peter it was not about strategy, tactics, organization, or structure. It was about love, and about intimacy with him. When he said "feed my sheep," in effect, he said, "Your intimacy, your capacity for loving people and serving them is going to be limited or expanded by your capacity to have intimacy with me."

Another thing that is important is the issue of connectedness. Every city has been gifted by God with the resources to heal itself. It's not about money. It's about connecting people relationally. The purpose of the body of Christ is to be the physical replacement of Jesus on earth, in the local community—ministering to people across all barriers in a powerful and positive way, while connecting them in his name.

The role of the church is to create a sacred space where people have the opportunity to make the life-changing decision to change their eternal address. The process of evangelism, spiritual formation, and discipleship nurtures that. But what is most desperately needed in our cities is face-to-face interaction through relationship, and the church has retreated from these spaces. Individuals of faith can work in a private role that knows no geographical boundaries.

The public role of the church is to be an example of Shalom—to fulfill the calling that Jeremiah gave on behalf of God to seek the prosperity and peace of the city for which you have been called to pray. Shalom means the wholeness that comes with community. That means we should model it in the way we live our lives, how we spend our money, how we raise and educate our children. We create models that are corporate in nature that can be visible and seen in the public space to give encouragement and hope to people.

That also means we begin to look prophetically through the eyes of God at the pain in our cities and ask questions that will lead us to strategically mobilize our resources on behalf of the poor, the hurting, and the marginalized. It means we accept the responsibility to influence our vocational institutions to work for the common good.

Peter Drucker says the church is the only institution that is capable of re-civilizing the broken urban city. It's important to see the three sectors—the public, the private, and the nonprofit or voluntary sector. Modern America has traded the relational interaction for the institutional kind. What we are doing is reversing that, re-localizing where care is given, taking it back to the neighborhood level Tocqueville saw when he came to America. The problem is that our communities are broken.

My experience is that a majority of people who are really passionate about civic renewal at the grassroots level are people who are motivated by their love of Christ. That's because it takes a supernatural love to get the job done. This is Jesus' work without Jesus' name on it. If you pan for gold, 50 percent of the leaders end up being his people.

The great gift of America is that American public space is a free and open marketplace of ideas. Many Christians founded America, but the public space itself is not Christian, and it's not spiritual. That means we have to compete in the public space for the hearts and minds of men and women. It's my experience that in the free and open marketplace of ideas, Jesus Christ wins because he can meet the competition. But we have to exercise extreme respect for people of other faiths or convictions whose rights are also guaranteed under the Constitution. We have to hold these two disciplines in tension, but if we do, we can have a huge impact.

part iv

THE BIG PICTURE

Faith at Work in America's History

The Beliefs That Motivate

Street Saints Today

chapter 12

The Roots of American Compassion

A debate is being waged in America to define the place of faith in the public square. Compassion motivated by faith has been a part of the American experience since the earliest days of its founding. And as the nation now considers the relationship of the sacred and the secular, it may be helpful to reconsider our roots. This debate does not take place in a vacuum. In fact, we have several hundred years of American experience since the earliest settlers came here. The role of religion in the founding of America is worth revisiting, as is the truth about the relationship between church and state.

Faith-based organizations in America today are doing their work in a long-standing tradition that began with the earliest settlers to our shores. The discussions on President George W. Bush's Faith-Based Initiative have prompted some soul searching on the part of people who see the benefits of such organizations but are trying to wisely determine how best to foster their fruits. As the previous chapters demonstrate, many of these organizations are producing civic value by coming to the aid of individuals who are in need, strengthening them, giving them job and life skills, helping them leave addiction, and transforming their lives. As faith-based organizations extend a hand to people in transition, decrease criminal behavior, and renew neighborhoods, these groups are clearly contributing to the common good. But the question is: What is the proper role of these groups in relationship to the government?

The question has deeper dimensions than merely the issue of funding, although that has been the lightning rod recently. A deeper consideration probes the relationship of faith and freedom, which in the minds of the founders were inextricably linked. The American founders believed that freedom must be linked to faith, or freedom would fail. They were convinced that a free nation can function well only if its citizens live by the fruits of faith, although they did not want the government to impose one church on the nation. They believed that individual men and women can live in liberty only if they are governed from within. They believed that faith fosters good character, and that without virtue and self-restraint, there would be conflict and chaos. The American founders were certain that religion is indispensable for freedom. The relationship of church and state is this: the state depends on the fruits of faith for its survival. Without virtue, freedom cannot be sustained. And faith is necessary to foster virtue.

George Washington said so plainly in his Farewell Address: "Of all the dispositions and habits which lead to political prosperity, Religion and morality are indispensable supports. . . . Let us with caution indulge the supposition, that morality can be maintained without religion. . . . Reason and experience both forbid us to expect that National morality can prevail in exclusion of religious principle."[1] That is exactly the same conclusion John Adams reached, and he drove the point home, saying, "Our Constitution was made only for a moral and religious people. It is wholly inadequate to the government of any other."[2]

The Truth about Church and State

The phrase "separation of church and state" appears nowhere in the U.S. Constitution or the First Amendment. It is cited today by people everywhere as a given, although many do not know its origin. The metaphor of a "wall of separation" stems from a private letter Thomas Jefferson wrote to the Baptists in Danbury, Connecticut, in 1802. The notion of "separation of church and state" was not, and is not, an amendment

Resurrecting Fresno's agricultural roots, One by One Leadership has provided land and water for neighborhood residents to tend a thriving vegetable garden. It is self-help paired with neighborhood improvement.

Luis Cortes (*second from left*) leads Nueva Esperanza in strengthening self-sufficiency among Latinos in North Philadelphia, fusing faith with civic values to help struggling families buy their first house, get an education, and receive job training.

A modern-day Nehemiah Robert Woodson identifies, encourages, and develops leaders of grass-roots organizations focused on community renewal, through his National Center for Neighborhood Enterprise.

The Star of Hope Transitional Living Center in Houston keeps parents together with their children, while moving them out of homelessness and into self-sufficiency.

Since 1988, Neighborhood Housing Opportunities has sold more than 200 affordable homes in Memphis to low-income families, providing first-time homeowners with coaching through the entire process.

The Brookwood Community gives handicapped adults in Texas, who require round-the-clock care, like Stacy, the opportunity to participate in on-site pottery production, horticulture, and other enterprises that teach skills while supporting the non-government funded institution.

To foster a sense of ownership in Fresno's residents, One by One Leadership mobilized local participants in community renewal planning sessions, using headphones and translators to break the language barriers for Hmong, Hispanic, and Vietnamese residents.

Reid Carpenter (*right*) heads the Leadership Foundations of America while John Stahl-Wert (*left*) has succeeded him as president of the Pittsburgh Leadership Foundation. Their work is focused on city transformation through people of faith.

Born of Reid Carpenter's passion for kids, the Pittsburgh Youth Network now tallies more than ninety youth workers and reaches about one-third of all the young people in Pittsburgh in a given year.

Resources in Brooklyn trains immigrants in the English language, then imparts job skills through apprenticeships in culinary arts, computer graphics, professional cleaning, or carpentry. The result is gainful employment and self-sufficiency.

The Pittsburgh Community Storehouse has mobilized a cooperative effort that provides donated material goods to non-profit organizations in return for monthly volunteer hours.

These children swim at Memphis Leadership Foundation's For the Kingdom Camp and Retreat Center. The camp serves as an oasis for kids who know only an urban environment.

Gwen Morris (*foreground*) of One by One Leadership joins local residents and Fresno's mayor, Alan Autry, in painting a homeowner's fence. Community renewal mobilizes stakeholders from local businesses and churches in a Nehemiah strategy.

Multinational Ministries serves refugee families with not only gifts, but youth ministry, medical care, education, job training, and placement, to make them self-sufficient.

LEFT: Men who leave the hospital after surgery with no home can find refuge at Open Door Mission's Healing Dorm in Houston, where the staff helps them recover and find permanent housing. Some arrive in hospital gowns with no possessions.

BELOW: John Sage (*left*), the founder of Bridges to Life, congratulates Enrique Salina, the 1000th graduate of the prison program that brings victims of crime face-to-face with inmates. The result has reduced recidivism to eight percent.

ABOVE LEFT: Kirbyjon Caldwell's Power Center in Houston has spawned 100 ministries to meet local needs, pumped $17.5 million into the economy, and created nearly 1,000 jobs. His success inspired George W. Bush as governor.

ABOVE RIGHT: Former mayor of Philadelphia, Wilson Goode, is the founder of Amachi, a program that mobilizes church members to mentor children of incarcerated parents.

Jobs Partnership provides an on-ramp to employment by pairing mentors from churches with willing job applicants. Now replicated in twenty-seven cities, the successful program has placed 1,800 graduates in jobs. Eighty-four percent were still employed one year later.

to our Constitution. It was a phrase in a letter with no legally binding power. The current application of the phrase to attempt to eradicate all traces of faith from the public square runs completely contrary to the founders' intentions.

The First Amendment reads: "Congress shall make no law respecting an establishment of religion, or prohibiting the free exercise thereof." The intent of the founders was specifically to prevent Congress from imposing one denomination on the entire nation from the federal level. The First Amendment was never intended to exorcise all traces of religion from public life. Quite the contrary. The founders believed that the practice of religion was essential to provide the moral content to fill the institutions of the newly formed government. They understood that in the absence of virtue, there could be no order in freedom. Gouvernor Morris put it this way: "Religion is the only solid Base of morals and Morals are the only possible Support of free governments."[3]

Even Jefferson, whose Deist convictions put him outside the mainstream of the founders, clearly articulated the necessity of reliance on God for the survival of our republic. His words are etched in the wall of the Jefferson Memorial in Washington, D.C.: "God who gave us life gave us liberty. Can the liberties of a nation be thought secure when we remove their only firm basis, a conviction in the minds of people that these liberties are a gift from God?" Jefferson's own convictions, even as a Deist, honored Christian teaching and specifically Jesus. Jefferson did not believe in the divinity of Christ, miracles in the Bible, or the Trinity, but he wrote, "The philosophy of Jesus is the most sublime and benevolent code of morals ever offered to man. A more beautiful or precious morsel of ethics I have never seen."[4]

While Jefferson was president, he regularly attended worship services on Sunday in the Capitol building. Rev. Ethan Allen, who lived nearby, wrote in his own hand an account of the following encounter. President Jefferson was on his way to church one Sunday morning with his large red prayer book under his arm when, after wishing him a good morning, Allen asked him which way he was walking.

Jefferson replied, "To church, sir."

He exclaimed, "You going to church, Mr. Jefferson? You do not be-lieve a word of it."

"Sir," said Mr. Jefferson, "No nation has ever yet existed or been gov-erned without religion. Nor can be. The Christian religion is the best reli-gion that has ever been given to man and I, as chief Magistrate of this na-tion, am bound to give it the sanction of my example. Good morning, Sir."[5]

Two dominant characteristics of early America were its deep Christian faith and its denominational diversity. So to encourage faith without dilut-ing it, while preserving the right of all individuals to practice their faith freely, the First Amendment prohibited Congress from imposing one de-nomination on the country. In fact, the right to establish churches at the state level was fully legal, and several states did so. Massachusetts, Con-necticut, Virginia, New Hampshire, and South Carolina had established state churches supported with taxes, the last of which ended only in the nineteenth century: Massachusetts in 1833.[6]

The First Amendment did not prohibit the use of government money or property for religious purposes. In fact, the founders wanted to encour-age religious belief and its practice. Public schools regularly taught from the Bible and offered character education based on it. Jefferson himself authorized the use of federal funds to purchase Bibles to "propagate Christianity among the Indians."[7] Worship services were held every Sun-day in the Capitol. The sessions of Congress opened with prayer, and presidents were sworn into office in a public inauguration with a hand on a Bible, just as they are now. The Northwest Ordinance of 1787 pro-claimed "Religion . . . [to be] necessary to good government and the hap-piness of mankind," and set aside land for churches.[8]

States had free reign to foster the practice of religion and its instruc-tion. John Adams in Massachusetts affirmed that "religious education was essential to survival of a free republic." His state's constitution "required the state to pay for religious education if there weren't any private groups able to do it."[9] The article of religion drafted by George Mason for the Virginia Declaration of Rights in 1776 and modified by James Madison reflects the climate of ideas at the time they worked through different drafts of the First Amendment: "Religion [is] the duty we owe to our Creator. . . . [A]ll men are equally entitled to the free exercise of religion, according to the dictates of conscience. . . . [I]t is the mutual duty of all to practice Christian forbearance, love and charity toward each other."[10]

Forbearance, love, and charity. These are the attributes that the founders wanted to foster in America.

Faith and the Founders

The faith of our forefathers played a very significant role in the birth of this young nation, shaping the hearts and minds of the founders. Faith and reason shaped the American soul, which has produced both civic order and compassion. Michael Novak writes that the American eagle mounts on two wings: humble faith and reason, mounting "upwards on both those wings in unison."[11] He goes on to say, "In one key respect, the way the story of the United States has been told for the past one hundred years is wrong. It has cut off one of the two wings by which the American eagle flies, her compact with the God . . . who brings down the mighty and lifts up the poor; . . . Believe that there is such a God or not, the founding generation did. . . . Their faith is an 'indispensible' part of their story."[12]

From the earliest colonial times, our citizens have lived out a tension between freedom and order, between selfishness and selflessness. Our founders believed that freedom can be lived out fruitfully only when it is paired with virtue. And the source of their virtue was faith in God. Their understanding was rooted in spiritual and intellectual history, the rich soil of civilization of the Western world. They did not invent a new order; they inherited one that had slowly ripened. Our nation is the fruition of centuries of wisdom that emerged long before our forefathers landed on North American shores.

Russell Kirk offers a magnificent overview of our intellectual and spiritual patrimony in *The Roots of American Order;* he takes us through five cities and civilizations that are sources for our rich heritage: Jerusalem, Athens, Rome, London, and Philadelphia.[13] In a philosophically panoramic view, we learn that from the ancient Hebrews we have inherited an understanding of the order of the soul and a purposeful existence. From Athens, we have an understanding of the order of the mind. From Rome, we have an understanding of personal virtue and the order of the polity. From Jerusalem, we received salvation and sanctification from the Savior. And from London, we have inherited our concepts of common law, private property, and constitutional order. Each of these layers of understanding built upon the previous one.

This wisdom of the ages was planted in American soil in Philadelphia. Here, free of the constraints of the Old World, it produced the unique flowering of our republic. We did not invent these truths, nor was our republic the product of wild-eyed ideologues. We inherited a rich patrimony, rooted in all of Western civilization, which was transplanted into a new continent. Kirk warns us that if we are to flourish, we must tend to these roots and replenish them. The covenant that shaped our civic order springs from transcendent order, and compassion manifests morality as it moves the human heart. But he thinks that the life force that has animated the best of America's soul is ebbing away.

A City on a Hill

The roots of America's convictions are in the Bible. John Winthrop delivered his famous "city on a hill" sermon on the deck of the ship *Arbella* halfway between England and Cape Cod in 1630, to remind the Pilgrims of the covenant they had made with God and with each other. He said, "We must delight in each other, make others' conditions our own, rejoice together, mourn together, labor and suffer together. . . . For we must consider that we shall be as a city upon a hill, the eyes of all people are upon us."[14] Like the Israelites, they had a covenant with their Creator.

The settlers who came here believed that their life and liberty were gifts from God and that they would be judged at the end of their days according to how they used these remarkable gifts. They believed that they would be held accountable for their actions, their sins of omission and commission, the care or negligence they showed their neighbors, and their honesty in dealing with each other. They knew God as not only a God of mercy, but also as the God of justice, and they feared his wrath. "I tremble," Thomas Jefferson wrote, "when I reflect that God is just."

The Pilgrims, separatists from the Puritan movement in England, settled in the northeast colonies. A small enclave of Roman Catholics settled in the northeast as well. The settlers in the middle colonies tended to be members of the Anglican Church, while the South had a greater concentration of Baptists and Calvinists. There were Presbyterians, Lutherans, and Quakers who also populated the colonies, along with a sprinkling of Jews. Because so many settlers had come here with ferociously independent denominational convictions, albeit overwhelmingly Christian ones, they found it useful to adapt Old Testament language and imagery. Novak tells us that in "national debate, lest their speech be taken as partisan," Christian leaders usually adopted the "idiom of Abraham, Isaac, and Jacob" as the "religious *lingua franca* for the founding generation."[15] This shared language of Judaism "came to be the central language of the American metaphysic—the unspoken background to a special American vision of nature, history and the destiny of the human race."[16]

The colonists knew the Bible well, both Old Testament and New. The influence of biblical teaching on early America was profound. At the time of the American Revolution, 84 percent of the pamphlets circulating were reprints of sermons, generously peppered with scriptural references. Even in the secular pamphlets, 34 percent of the quotations were from the Bible.[17] It was the book often used to teach youngsters how to read, starting with the Gospel of John. Biblical imagery permeated the language and the culture. Sermons were the main form of spiritual, intellectual, and civic formation.[18] The settlers had a clear understanding of theology in which the family was the primary unit ordained by God for mutual care. They believed they had been given property and ability as gifts of God, which were to be released through work. Producing prosperity was an expression of the fullness of a godly life. And they believed that they should be openhanded with neighbors in need.

Conditions were rugged, and the settlers were ravaged by disease and hunger, which meant their dependence on each other was great. Shortly after landing at Plymouth Rock in 1620, nearly all the Pilgrims became deathly ill. Only six or seven of them could still move about, and the rest languished in their beds in misery. But the few who were still on their feet, despite the hazard to their own health, fetched the wood, cooked the meals, washed the linens, bathed and clothed the ill, caring for them day and night. As the Pilgrim leader William Bradford wrote, they did this "willingly and cheerfully, without any grudging in ye least, shewing herein true love unto their friends & brethren."[19]

The colonists were pledged to care for one another, and neighbors joined forces to drain the swamp on one man's property, and clear trees on that of another. If the parents of a child fell ill or died, it was understood that another family would care for the child as their own.[20] These Good Samaritans were often reimbursed from the town coffers for their out-of-pocket expenses in caring for the needy. The town fathers agreed that the individuals' costs of caring for a neighbor could be shared with the community. This is a precedent worth noting, in light of contemporary debates.

The early Americans felt obligated to give wisely, for the sake of both giver and receiver. They linked the formation of character to acts of charity. Assistance was almost always given in the form of time, food, cloth, or coal, but not money. They looked at a person's motivation, whether they could get assistance from friends or relatives,[21] and whether they were willing to work to support themselves. This was all in keeping with the biblical teaching to give to those who ask, but that those who do not work should not eat.[22]

The Fruits of Faith

Sermons of the founding era, whether Anglican, Congregationalist, Methodist, or Presbyterian, regularly noted that faith without works of compassion was dead. Benjamin Colman warned in a sermon, "God values our Hearts and Spirits above all our Silver or Gold, our Herds and Flocks. If a Man would give all the Substance of his House instead of Love, . . . it would be contemned."[23] When Methodism spread in the eighteenth century, American followers urged their countrymen to follow John Wesley's advice to "put yourself in the place of every poor man and deal with him as you would have God deal with you."[24] It is clear that faith was expected to produce fruits.

In fact, the fruits of liberty prompted by faith are exactly what the founders had in mind. As Gleaves Whitney has pointed out, the intention of the founders was not only to protect the practice of religion, but to foster the fruits of its practice as well: the virtues of forbearance, love, and charity. The preamble of the Constitution is to "provide the common defense, promote the general welfare, and secure the blessings of liberty to ourselves and our posterity." Here we see that the founders sought not mere liberty, but the blessings of liberty.

Whitney points us deeper.

If the Founders seem as interested in securing "the *blessings* of liberty" as in liberty itself, then it is because they viewed liberty as instrumental. It is a means, not the end—rather like money. Most people want money, not for its own sake, but for what it allows one to have: status, security, power, material comforts, and so on. It is not the money per se but the blessings of money that we want. By analogy, the Preamble suggests that the Founders viewed liberty not as an end in itself, but as the means to the end, which is the good life.[25]

The good life consists in the virtues of forbearance, love, and charity—fruits of the spirit.

Compact and Covenant

Before the first settlers even set foot on Plymouth Rock, they bound themselves to each other and to God in a form of governance derived from covenant theology of the Old Testament. In the words of the Mayflower Compact of 1620: "Having undertaken for the glory of God, . . . and advancement of the Christian faith, a voyage to plant colony . . . in the presence of God and of one another, we do Covenant and Combine ourselves together into a Civil Body Politic, for our better ordering and preservation."[26] As Donald Lutz asserts in the *Origins of American Constitutionalism,* this was a defining moment for America because of the character of a covenant and its civic counterpart, a compact.[27] The Mayflower Compact and other compacts implemented by the original colonies were derived directly from the covenant of the Old Testament, which bound Abraham, Isaac, and Jacob to the great I AM and obligated themselves to live in accordance with his law. Our Constitution has the same roots.

The names for God referenced in the Declaration of Independence were Old Testament names: Lawgiver, Creator, Judge, and Providence. Michael Novak points out, "If these Hebraic texts of the Declaration were strung together as a single prayer, the prayer would run as follows: 'Creator, who has endowed in us our inalienable rights, Maker of nature and nature's laws, undeceivable Judge of the rectitude of our intentions, we place our firm reliance upon the protection of divine Providence, which you have extended over our nation from its beginnings.'"[28] This is no secular document: our Declaration of Independence has embedded in it this subtext, a prayer.

Conclusive Christian Convictions

The signers of the Declaration of Independence were almost all devout Christians, despite the contemporary spin on history that tells us otherwise. Professor M. E. Bradford researched their lives thoroughly, including their correspondence, wills, and writings, and found conclusive evidence that the signers, with very few exceptions, were firmly committed to the traditional practice of Christianity.[29] Bradford found that the references by the founders to "Jesus Christ as Redeemer and Son of God" are "commonplace in their private papers, correspondence, and public remarks."[30] Their faith was evident not only in their words, but in their lives. For example:

• Patrick Henry wrote in his will, "This is the inheritance I can give to my dear family. The religion of Christ will give them one which will make them rich indeed."[31]

• John Jay of New York in his will thanked "the author and giver of all good . . . for His merciful and unmerited blessings, and especially for our redemption and salvation by his beloved Son."[32]

• Elias Boudinot of New Jersey was "heavily involved in Christian missions and was the founder of the American Bible Society."[33]

• Roger Sherman "was a ruling elder of his church."[34]

• Richard Bassett "rode joyfully with his former slaves . . . singing on the way to Methodist camp meetings."[35]

• Charles Cotesworth Pinckney "set aside money to evangelize slaves" and "distributed Bibles to blacks" as president of the Charleston Bible Society.[36]

• During the Revolution, Abraham Baldwin of Georgia "served as chaplain in the American army."

• Luther Martin declared "his devotion to 'the sacred truths of the Christian religion.'"[37]

• James Madison and Alexander Hamilton "regularly led their households in the observance of family prayers."[38]

• David Brearly of New Jersey and William Samuel Johnson of Connecticut "devoted themselves to reorganizing the Episcopal Church in their states."[39]

• John Witherspoon educated Presbyterian clergy with treatises such as "The Absolute Necessity of Salvation Through Christ."[40]

Their lives are the proof of their Christian faith, which permeated the founding and their intentions for the country.

What Alexis de Tocqueville Saw

When the Frenchman Alexis de Tocqueville visited America in the 1830s, he marveled at the faith that motivated civic life. He wrote, "For the Americans the ideas of Christianity and liberty are so completely mingled that it is almost impossible to get them to conceive of the one without the other."[41] He was dazzled by the array of voluntary associations—civic, philanthropic, political, neighborly, moral, educational—and the vibrant goodwill they harnessed. This kind of engagement was unique to America in this era, quite unlike the European culture. In old Europe, it was much more likely that the nobility or the church hierarchy would take on a project, but seldom would individuals simply band together. But in the years since the first colonials stepped ashore, these European immigrants had been helping one another survive, settle, and thrive. It had become a way of life.

In the famous passage that illustrates the voluntary vibrancy of America, de Tocqueville wrote:

> Americans of all ages, all stations in life, and all types of disposition are forever forming associations. There are not only commercial and industrial associations in which all take part, but others of a thousand different types—religious, moral, serious, futile . . . immensely large and very minute. Americans combine to give fêtes, found seminaries, build churches, distribute books, and send missionaries to the antipodes. Hospitals, prisons, and schools take shape in that way. Finally, if they want to proclaim a truth or propagate some feeling by the encouragement of a great example, they form an association.[42]

The variety of such associations was truly staggering. In *The Tragedy of American Compassion,* Marvin Olasky gives us a snapshot of the kinds of groups Tocqueville would have seen on his visit here.

- In New York, the Society for the Relief of Poor Widows with Small Children was founded in 1797.[43]
- In Boston, the Fragment Society, founded in 1812, provided material for clothes and assisted more than 10,200 families in need.[44]
- The St. Vincent de Paul societies set up hospitals and orphanages, and built the New York House of the Good Shepherd for what they delicately called "fallen women and girls."[45]
- The Female Domestic Missionary Society for the Poor, founded in 1816, distributed Bibles and provided schooling in poor parts of New York.
- In Baltimore, a group of Catholic women founded the Maria Marthian Society in 1827 to assist "all denominations, ages, sexes and colours."[46]
- In 1822, the Presbyterian women of Petersburg, Virginia, established an Education Society, a Ladies' Missionary Society, and a Dorcas Society, all to help the poor.
- The Baltimore Female Association for the Relief of Distressed Objects, founded in 1808, assisted women in need.
- In Charleston, beginning in 1813, the Ladies' Benevolent Society aided the senile, both black and white.[47]
- Jewish settlers established a Hebrew Benevolent Society in Charleston in 1784, a Hebrew Benevolent and Orphan Asylum Society in 1822, and a Hebrew Relief Society in New York in 1831, as well as other societies to assist "destitute pregnant women."[48]

These associations sprang up across the countryside to meet every imaginable need, and their roots bound people together at the community level. They worked irrespective of denominational lines, racial or class barriers. But Americans were modest about what they did in serving each other, seeking no public fanfare. They realized it had a value not only for others, but also for themselves.[49]

Fostering America's Soul

De Tocqueville observed that this kind of action has a steadying effect in encouraging people toward virtue, building their character as they practice it. He wrote, "The doctrine of self-interest properly understood does not inspire great sacrifices, but every day it prompts some small ones; by itself it cannot make a man virtuous, but its discipline shapes a lot of orderly, temperate, moderate, careful, and self-controlled citizens. If it does not lead the will directly to virtue, it establishes habits which unconsciously turn it that way."[50] This is the acquisition of civic virtue. In caring for one another voluntarily, Americans foster their own character development.

De Tocqueville dubbed these little units of interaction "voluntary associations." He wrote in the tradition of Edmund Burke, who called them "little platoons" and "subdivisions" of society. Others today call this sector "civil society." It is expressed in all the many ways people come together freely, in families, neighborhoods, schools, clubs, and communities. Burke and de Tocqueville agreed that human beings interact best with each other when they engage in small civic units. To love mankind is abstract, but one can love particular people. Trying to help "the poor" is overwhelming, but helping one family in need is a manageable task. It is the most effective way of reaching individuals: face to face.

Civil society operates at the intersection of faith and free human action. This way of looking at civil society rests upon Christian thinking, both Catholic and Protestant. One of the core principles of Catholic social teaching is the concept of "subsidiarity," which means in essence that if people closest to the problem can solve it through face-to-face relationships, particularly at the neighborhood level, that is where it should be solved. Catholic teaching says it is "both a serious evil and a disturbance of right order to assign to a larger and higher society what can be performed successfully by smaller and lower communities."[51] This is altogether consistent with Protestant teaching by Calvin, who advocated people "dwelling together in community under the dominion of God."[52] Scottish Enlightenment writer Adam Ferguson valued civil society "as a moral sphere."[53] Christian teaching across the denominational spectrum promotes interaction that creates a civic good while strengthening virtue.

From the beginning, it has been crucial for the health of America's soul to have vibrant manifestations of faith that both reflect virtue and inculcate it. Founder Benjamin Rush put it this way: "The only foundation for a useful education in a republic is to be laid in religion. Without it there can be no virtue, and without virtue there can be no liberty, and liberty is the object and life of all republican governments."[54]

The founders' syllogism is this:

Liberty is the object of the Republic.
Liberty needs virtue.
Virtue among the people is impossible without religion.[55]

The Contemporary Conflict Zone

If we "fast forward" to contemporary America, we discover a very different picture. The scope of the civic realm has shriveled in the past century. People who were once connected through voluntary relationships no longer are. We see the "little platoons" overwhelmed by big cities as urbanization has replaced the agrarian culture. Unbridled materialism and politicization have overwhelmed the public philosophy of life. This trend accelerated over the course of the twentieth century, peaking in the 1960s. It has unraveled the private sector and its morality, and shifted civic engagement from voluntary associations toward the centralized city, county, state, and federal bureaucracy.

At the same time, there was a push in the name of efficiency to turn over the care of the poor to the government, shifting the responsibility from the civic space, where actions are personal, to the public space, where they are not. What individuals once did became the responsibility of a vast institution. As we have decreased our civic engagement, our expectations of government have risen. The weaker our horizontal local ties are in the community, the stronger the dependency on the vertical ties of the state.[56] A ripple effect has resulted, Charles Murray tells us: "When the government takes away a core function, it depletes not only the source of vitality pertaining to that particular function, but also the vitality of a much larger family of responses."[57] The middle sector of civic engagement and the mediating institutions have shriveled. Underlying all of these shifts is the broad secularization of our culture, the post-Enlightenment mentality writ large. We see an overt ejection of faith from the public square. We see that the First Amendment, which was intended to preserve freedom of religion, has now become interpreted as a mandate to protect Americans *from* religion. And we see the private voluntary sector severed from its religious roots.

The centrifugal forces of modernity have accelerated at a dizzying pace from the 1960s to the present. What has happened in just forty years has been the demise of the traditional family, which has been replaced by a culture of "alternative lifestyles." We see skyrocketing rates of illegitimate births and abortion, an explosion of divorce and domestic violence, and the evaporation of multigenerational families in one place together. Quite often, those living in poverty are single mothers with their children. In the tonier parts of town, neighborhood has been replaced by "lifestyle enclaves" and gated communities for those who can afford them, where it is never necessary to encounter poverty. Private civic engagement has radically atrophied, with fewer true volunteers. Women, who had been the backbone of volunteerism, are increasingly in the workforce instead, with no spare time.

Americans Are "Bowling Alone"

Civic engagement in America remained relatively strong well into the twentieth century. Robert Putnam tells us in *Bowling Alone*[58] that from the Moose and Elk Lodges to the Salvation Army, from the Knights of Columbus to Hadassah, Americans historically have been deeply engaged in civic organizations. They flourished well into the twentieth century, diminished slightly during the Depression, and then rose smartly after World War II and through the 1950s. But Putnam has discovered that since the late '60s, civic engagement has taken a free-fall. A nation that volunteered together or bowled in leagues has abandoned these activities and is now "bowling alone"—hence Putnam's title.

The Harvard professor has examined patterns of political and religious participation, volunteering, community activity, and philanthropy as indicators of "social capital." In graph after graph, he presents visible evidence of the decline of civic engagement over the past forty years in everything from churches to political organizations and service clubs. He finds that more Americans are living in cities but are relationally alone, severed from their extended families, surrounded by people, but living a life in isolation.

There are several contributing factors to this malaise, Putnam concludes. Most markedly, there has been a stark change of mindset between the generations born before the end of World War II and the Baby Boomers born between 1946 and 1964. The plummet began as the boomers began to reach adulthood and showed little of the civic engagement of their parents, who were still volunteering actively. Putnam looks at the entry of women into the workplace and the pressures of two-career families; he concludes that this is a significant factor, but not the only one. Urban sprawl is another, because it necessitates longer commutes and thins out the sense of community. Putnam finds a striking correlation between the amount of time spent watching television and slack civic engagement.

The religious community has been hit harder than it would appear. Over the past four decades, church membership has slipped by a mere 10 percent. But more telling is the fact that "actual attendance and involvement in religious activities has fallen by roughly 25 to 50 percent."[59] What used to be a commitment beyond Sunday worship no longer is. This one-time pillar of American life has been "hollowed out," Putnam tells us. "Seen from without, the institutional edifice appears virtually intact—little decline in profession of faith, formal membership down just a bit, and so on. When examined more closely, however, it seems clear that decay has consumed the load-bearing beams of our civic infrastructure."[60]

Mall as Modern Temple

But the drive toward material consumption is alive and well. Over the same period, Putnam finds that 70 percent of young people have decided that making a lot of money is their top priority. Participating in the community is a priority for only one in five.[61] In an eerily prophetic insight, de Tocqueville could already see these conflicting tendencies in the bosom of America. At the same time he admired the thriving voluntary associations and the selfless impulse of Americans, he also saw that a strong streak of individualism and materialism ran through the character of the country. Tocqueville detected the early signs of civic stagnation when he observed, "Individualism is a calm and considered feeling which disposes each citizen to isolate himself from the mass of his fellows and withdraw into the circle of family and friends; with this little society formed to his taste, he gladly leaves the greater society to look after itself."[62] Add a television, and you have a perfect recipe for inaction.

We see the modern man around us everywhere today. Robert Bellah calls this creature the "radically unencumbered and improvisational self," cut off from any ties to community, history, tradition, or civic engagement. The culture of the "self" has grown, as have the publications, spas, therapists, and support groups to massage our bodies and egos. What Tom Wolfe described as the "Me Decade" has turned into several decades of self-absorption by the Baby Boomers, and now Generations X and Y. The "pursuit of happiness" in America is increasingly expressed by material consumption. De Tocqueville foresaw this also, warning that a decrease in religion was likely to "lay the soul open to an inordinate love of material pleasure."[63] His words were prophetic. The shopping mall has become the new American temple.

The market economy has created a higher standard of living, materially speaking, and has created many lucrative jobs. But as the nation has become more intensely market driven, it has also exacted a price on civil society. Markets tend to undermine what makes them work. Economist Joseph Schumpeter characterized market processes as "creative destruction." Trust is necessary for a marketplace to function, but the market depends on a driving self-interest, which can rupture trust. Cooperation is necessary for the market, but a climate of competition can fracture cooperation. The quieter personal attributes can be jeopardized by a stampede toward wealth. This cuts to the heart of the contemporary dilemma in

America. At some point, the human conditions that allow markets to flourish are undone by the market's success.

Dislocation and ruptured families severed from geographic community roots have also weakened the fabric of our nation. People who move every seven years on average, regardless of how much they earn, are relationally impoverished. The mobility that has been efficient for the marketplace has been slowly unraveling the rootedness of American people. Community is dissolved by constant geographic relocation. As small shopkeepers are driven out of business by large chains, the character of our towns is homogenized and depersonalized. It is a delicate order that makes markets sustainable in a free country, and we in America teeter in a precarious balancing act.

Economist Wilhelm Roepke addressed these concerns in *A Humane Economy*,[64] concluding that there is a point of diminishing returns with unfettered economic growth. Roepke observed that as economic improvement grows, discontentment rises in proportion to expectations. He contends that a growing economy does not necessarily improve the welfare of individuals, because other costs accompany economic growth. The creation of more goods creates new wants, envy, and the social compulsion to acquire. This discontent, however, comes from a mindset that equates our satisfaction with our material goods, and assumes that our possessions define our worth.

But the real question is the human heart and our attitudes toward wealth, not prosperity itself. From the biblical perspective, wealth is bestowed as a blessing, but with it comes responsibility to use it both wisely and compassionately. If we do not, the result is an atrophied soul, and materialism writ large. The bitter fruit is alienation.

Historically, mediating institutions have provided a bridge between individuals and the overarching structures above them. But in the push of the modern age toward big business and big bureaucracy, the bridges of mediating institutions have fallen into disrepair or disappeared. Mediating institutions are the antidote to isolation and alienation of the individual and the dissolution of society by the centrifugal forces of modernity.

They are crucial in preserving the good character of the country. We live in a fragile institution.

One of the most powerful mediating institutions was always the church. But over the course of time, this beam in our nation has become hollow. Marginalized in the drive toward secular materialism, which appears to be the new national religion, the transformational power of the church has less influence on the culture. Fewer and fewer people venture outside the pews in any other manifestation of their faith. The voice of self-interest and self-indulgence has become louder to fill the space left in the retreat of virtue.

We have increasingly placed our faith in the power of government to provide solutions for human misery. What was once a strong level of responsibility and autonomy at the city, county, and state level has shifted toward a concentration at the federal level, with only modest attempts since to change the tide. The responsibility for caring for the poor is no longer that of the community, but that of the federal government, diminishing the need for community. So we see another kind of polarization taking place—the mediating institutions have shriveled, leaving at one end alienated individuals, and, at the other end, a vast bureaucracy, in which we have placed our hopes, but which by its nature cannot meet individual, personal needs.

Seeking Secular Salvation

Deep beneath this shift toward the political realm was a philosophical drift that began in an undercurrent several centuries ago. Eric Voegelin, one of the most astute critics of modernity, argues that the modern age has been characterized by the emergence of politics as a secular means of salvation. He traces the unraveling of order back to Joachim of Flora, a medieval mystic who depicted man's history in three ascending ages, which would bring about the final age of perfection. According to Voegelin, "He and his successors replaced faith in God with faith in man's ability to build heaven on earth. The new earthly faith depended upon the fallacious notion that history itself has a purpose: the achievement of human perfection. Salvation was to be sought in this world, through the pursuit of temporal achievements aimed at making material the transcendent world of God."[65] Hobbes and Rousseau took the next steps, claiming that the political order could provide the means to rescue man from his fallen state and remake his image.

This train of thought took a cunning twist at the turn of the century in America through the Social Universalists. Professor Richard Ely urged economists and theologians to converge in support of "coercive philanthropy," which he saw as the "duty of government" to "establish among us true cities of God."[66] William G. Fremantle expounded this approach, lifting up the "Nation as the Church, its rulers as ministers of Christ, its whole body as a Christian brotherhood, . . . material interests as Sacraments, its progressive development, especially in raising the weak, as the fullest service rendered on earth to God, the nearest thing as yet within our reach to the kingdom of heaven."[67]

This approach is a perversion of the natural order. The government can never bring about the kingdom of heaven. The political realm is incapable of inculcating virtue. Law can draw the dividing line between human beings and their actions, and can punish infractions that violate a person or his or her property. But it is incapable of directly influencing the human heart to desire good or to avoid evil. Government can provide boundaries for human action and can guarantee rights, but it cannot write its laws in the hearts of its citizens. Government can protect the freedom for people to seek their own good, but it cannot mandate the appetite to seek the highest good. These tasks must remain squarely in the private sector.

It is an odd paradox, but the success of America depends on these private virtues, and the theological truths that shape them, for its very existence. But it is outside the realm of the government to provide the character formation that is necessary for the survival of the republic. This is what people of faith in the private sector must do. That which is essential for the survival of our civic order must be provided in the private realm, in individuals and families, and through the armies of compassion, the street saints. There are thousands of houses of worship, faith-based organizations, schools, and community associations that educate, nurture, and care for people, shaping their hearts and souls. It is crucial that they succeed in planting the seeds of virtue.

Renewers in America are now seeking appropriate ways to foster the "fruits of liberty"—forbearance, love, and charity—in a way that is consistent with the overarching principles of the country. People of faith are necessary to instill the values and convictions that make people responsible individuals. Without faith, virtue cannot be sustained. We walk this precarious balancing act, suspended in the tension between church and state, with a push to eradicate all public traces of faith, while the nation depends on the vibrancy of faith for its survival.

The Ambiguous Embrace of Government

What then is the relationship between faith and the public square in America? Although the founders clearly proclaimed faith to be essential in fostering virtue, and virtue to be necessary for the functioning of the republic, the linkage has been severed today. For 350 years from the arrival of the earliest settlers, Americans acknowledged their dependence on God's grace for the human governing institutions to function. Only in the past fifty years has the dependency of the state on the fruits of faith been called into question.

Jefferson's old metaphor of a "wall of separation between church and state" lay dormant in his letter of 1802, with no legal significance or binding power whatsoever. It suddenly appeared in an opinion of the Supreme Court in 1947. Justice Hugo Black wrote, "The First Amendment has erected 'a wall between church and state.' . . . That wall must be kept high and impregnable. We could not approve the slightest breach."[68] With this opinion, Jefferson's words in private correspondence assumed a power that the founding generation and Jefferson himself never intended.[69] The following year, the Supreme Court again quoted this metaphor, blithely imbuing it with constitutional power. Ever since, this metaphor has defined church-state jurisprudence. A spate of court decisions have expanded the concept to roll back manifestations of faith in public life in myriad ways, to the point that Chief Justice Rehnquist has noted that the Court "bristles with hostility to all things religious in public life."[70] As Daniel Dreisbach has pointed out, the metaphor of a wall is troublesome because it is inaccurate. A wall blocks in both directions. The First Amendment as formulated by the founders meant to restrain Congress from intruding on the religious domain, not to evict religion from the public ethic. Dreisbach underscores "the widespread assumption of the age that republican government and civic virtue were dependent on a moral people and that morals could be nurtured only by the Christian religion." He claims, "The 'high and impregnable' wall constructed by the modern Court" has been used to "silence the religious voice in the public marketplace of ideas and to segregate faith communities behind a restrictive barrier."[71]

We see now a court order that has mandated the removal of a monument of the Ten Commandments, and a secular feeding frenzy that aims to sanitize the public square from all traces of religion, particularly if it is Christian. There have been a few decisions bucking that trend, affirming voluntary religious clubs in schools or universities if they are led and initiated by students; permitting public school teachers to do remedial classes in private faith-centered schools; and procuring computers and library books for such schools.[72] But these are the rare exceptions.

We have experienced a White House that has actively sought to reverse the tide that has swept faith away from its rightful place as the cornerstone of America's civic order. The George W. Bush administration has trumpeted the successes of the "armies of compassion." It set out to create a "level playing field" for faith-based and community organizations in the country to provide social services, and to remove the obstacles for them to apply for federal contracts to do so. Faith-based groups may compete like any other agency or organization for grants to provide social services the government contracts out, and the funding may be used for the secular part of faith-based organizations' work. Bush told participants in a Washington conference on Faith-Based Initiatives in 2004, "I do believe that groups should be allowed to access social service grants as long as they don't proselytize or exclude somebody simply because they don't share a certain faith," he said. "In other words, there's a way to accomplish the separation of church and state and at the same time accomplish the social objective of having America become a hopeful place and loving place."[73]

Through Executive Orders, President Bush has established offices in ten departments of the federal government to assist faith-based and community initiatives to gain access to appropriate funding for the kinds of services they provide. By competing through the bidding process to provide social services, faith-based organizations have received contracts for $1.1 billion since Bush took office. Approximately $75 million has been allocated through the Compassion Capital Fund to build up the capacity and competence of faith-based organizations through intermediary organizations.

But one of the most useful things President George W. Bush has done is to simply focus the national spotlight on faith initiatives, raising their visibility in the country and increasing their legitimacy through his public blessing. President Bush says "One of my most important initiatives is the Faith-Based and Community Initiative, because I recognize that government can hand out money, but what it cannot do is put hope in people's hearts or a sense of purpose in people's lives. What I want to do is unleash the great compassion of America, by changing America one heart, one soul, one conscience at a time."[74]

Faith-based organizations are providing results with clear civic value. The results are being expressed in decreased recidivism of criminal offenders, reduced drug addiction, successful transition from welfare to work, decreased disciplinary infractions of at-risk youth, fewer teen pregnancies, and reunited families. These are the tangible fruits of faith, and they are improving the quality of life for citizens throughout the country. The Bush administration has been attempting to foster these fruits in a way appropriate to its mission to serve the common good. But the Faith-Based Initiative has received a hailstorm of criticism from opponents. Jim Towey, director of the White House Office of Faith-Based and Community Initiatives, says the losers in the controversy are the people who need the services faith-based organizations provide. "The administration wants to make sure citizens have access to effective programs. There's always going to be the need for careful monitoring so this remains constitutional. But . . . the defenders of the status quo that have tried to raise constitutional concerns to protect the status quo need to provide an accounting to the poor who are being denied access to effective programs."[75]

There are clear restrictions on the kinds of activities the federal government may fund. The rules of engagement since the "Charitable Choice" provisions of welfare reform in 1996 dictate that federal funds may not be used for religious instruction, purchase of Bibles or other religious materials, or for proselytizing. Recipients of federal funds agree to comply with these restrictions. Faith-based agencies have been advised to establish separate 501(c)3 nonprofit organizations as a firewall to handle the work under government contract. But not all providers are in a position to administer a separate organization well. While some ministries can segregate out the secular aspects of their work for budgetary purposes, for others it is an onerous task and, in some cases, philosophically impossible. If faith is not only the motivation but also the method, how do you divide the mission? Many of the smaller grassroots organizations doing good work at the neighborhood level would be overwhelmed with the burden of compliance in administering a sizeable federal grant. Some critics are concerned that faith-based providers would become dependent on government funding or would trim their mission to accommodate future funding streams.

But there is a deeper issue.

If faith-based groups receive significant federal funding, it may be a Faustian bargain. Overt faith—preaching, teaching, evangelizing—must be sanitized from the portions of programs that receive federal dollars.[76] What remains is the delivery of social services, which undoubtedly have value, but can become decoupled from their spiritual origin. Faith-based organizations that receive a significant portion of their budget from federal funding run the risk of a new application of Lord Acton's famous maxim on the corrupting tendencies of power (let's call it Elliott's law): "federal funding tends to secularize, and absolute federal funding secularizes absolutely." By definition, faith-based organizations exist because of faith. But if they are funded fully by the federal government, they may not teach the source of their faith.[77] If they do keep the faith factor, they have to fund it separately with private funding. It requires a certain degree of sophistication to walk the tightrope of maintaining spiritual integrity and passion while complying with the necessity of separating the sacred from the secular. Some groups appear to be keeping their balance. Many others have decided simply not to apply for public funding.

There are alternatives to direct program funding. Acknowledging that the faith-saturated programs[78] have a particularly successful track record in treating drug addiction, for example, the Bush administration has set out to create vouchers for addicts, who can redeem them at a faith-based program if they so choose. This solution preserves the integrity of the faith-saturated program because it is not directly funded by the government, while giving the addict the option of receiving treatment at whatever kind of facility he or she chooses.

It's crucial to maintain the distinctive characteristic of this kind of work. If you take the faith out of faith-based organizations, they do not differ from their secular counterparts and they lose the dynamism that makes them effective. Part of the power of people of faith walking into prisons and schools as volunteers comes from the fact that they are not agents of the government, but private citizens moved by their hearts. The work of people of faith is too important to the soul of the nation for it to be neutered or diluted. It is a delicate task to preserve this unique power of faith-based work as it intersects with public funding.

What's Needed Is a Change of Heart

But the more important question is not what the government can do. The question is how the private sector can respond. The real solution for funding faith-based work is for street saints to turn to the foundations, corporations, and individuals who are free to give in their own communities. Corporations and some foundations have behaved as if they were prohibited from making grants to faith-based work, although there are no constitutional constraints. If these groups are providing work with a clear civic value, they are worthy of support. Individuals, more than any other sector, can maneuver freely with their giving. People of faith can do a great deal to revitalize a rapidly decaying culture from the inside out. The heavy lifting has to be done by individual people who act because of their faith and are at liberty to give an account of the source of their hope.

The glue that held this society together for as long as it flourished was found in personal, face-to-face relationships. This is where civil society grows. To the extent that we have lost these face-to-face relationships to care for people in need, we have lost an important part of what made America personal, warm, even luminescent. We need to nurture this part of the American soul. Only if we can reignite a passion for vibrant personal faith, which produces virtue manifested in action, can we maintain the fragile order that has been bequeathed to us by our forefathers. We need to quicken the spiritual life of lukewarm believers and light a fire to mobilize the laity to care for individuals in their own communities. The reasons for doing this are compelling. But what is needed is a change of heart.

We hold in our own hands the threads of our tattered civil society. Reweaving the threads of relationship through face-to-face encounters in our own communities can be a joyous and fulfilling engagement. The antidote to so much of the modern malady is right there, contained in the fragile string of relationship. Abandoned children in the inner city, blasé Baby Boomers, isolated elderly, and disenchanted Gen-Xers are all yearning for a better way of living. And yet we do not connect the threads. In the corners of communities where street saints are quietly knitting up relationships, there is a renewal of the fabric of our country.

Until our culture demonstrates the virtue of *agape*, it will not move to help its forgotten. Until we do so as individuals, we will never know the joy that comes in serving others. The American culture has an opportunity now for renewal through its people of faith. We are being called to care for one another because of our faith. We are being called to live out our virtue in service. The American soul has withered, and awaits an infusion of the lifeblood of love. Whether or not we respond may determine the very survival of our civilization. "Just look at history," Peter Kreeft warns. "Each civilization has survived and thrived in proportion to its virtue. It has decayed when its virtue decayed. Israel, Greece, Rome and the modern West are examples."[79]

America inherited such a rich patrimony, spanning more than twenty centuries, intellectually and spiritually. We have had the benefit of understanding the mind and spirit in the context of human institutions, and we have had the gift of freedom to develop our capabilities with an unparalleled dynamism. We have witnessed a remarkable outpouring of generosity in charity and the warmth of human engagement through a proliferation of private associations, armies of compassion on our streets. Trust and cooperation flourished in a way that we almost took for granted, but that surprised visitors and newcomers from other shores. We had a nation that was not only strong, but gentle and good. But the soul of America is in peril now.

The question is whether we will heed the call to renew America's soul.

Conclusion

A Kingdom Vision

Our journey through the world of street saints has taken us from the people who do the work, through the programs they are engaged in and the cities where they work, to a perspective on their effects on the soul of America since its earliest days. And as important as the framework of the government is in setting the boundaries for human activity, in the end, the care of our neighbor rests with each individual. Why should men and women care for people in their own communities? There are several reasons. The most compelling motivation for compassion is faith in God. People of faith reach out to others because they have received divine love and they share it with others in gratitude. Those who do so enter into a reciprocal relationship that changes not only the person who receives, but also the one who gives. Henri Nouwen and Mother Teresa have both described in different ways a surprising ellipse of love received and given, and received again. This last chapter looks at the spiritual roots and the lives of street saints as they illustrate compassion in action.

The "Wounded Healer": Henri Nouwen

In a mysterious way, deeds of compassion transform both the giver and the receiver. What one person initiates as a healing gesture may accom-

plish the healing of both giver and recipient. This opens a rich dimension
in the life of compassion: it is less about meeting needs than it is about
changing hearts, and the process is reciprocal. Henri Nouwen articulated
this process of mutual healing better than anyone in the modern era, because he wrote from personal experience. Nouwen chronicles his journey
from the classrooms of the Ivy League to a surprising destination in his
book, *In the Name of Jesus*.[1]

There he writes: "After twenty-five years of priesthood, I found myself
praying poorly, living somewhat isolated from other people, and very
much preoccupied with burning issues. Everyone was saying that I was
doing really well, but something inside was telling me that my success was
putting my own soul in danger. I began to ask myself whether my lack of
contemplative prayer, my loneliness, and my constantly changing involvement in what seemed most urgent were signs that the Spirit was gradually
being suppressed" (10). He joked about hell but realized that he "was living in a very dark place and that the term 'burnout' was a convenient psychological translation for a spiritual death" (10–11).

Nouwen continues:

> In the midst of this I kept praying, 'Lord, show me where you want me to go
> and I will follow you, but please be clear and unambiguous about it!' Well,
> God was. In the person of Jean Vanier, the founder of the L'Arche communi-
> ties for mentally handicapped people, God said, "Go and live among the poor
> in spirit, and they will heal you." The call was so clear and distinct that I had
> no choice but to follow. So I moved from Harvard to L'Arche, from the best
> and the brightest, wanting to rule the world, to men and women who had few
> or no words and were considered, at best, marginal to the needs of our socie-
> ty. (11)

Nouwen was in for a culture shock. This man, who had written many
learned books, was surrounded by mentally handicapped people who
could not read or did not care to. He found that his ecumenical experience was not appreciated, as he overheard one of the residents remark to
another in the dinner line, "Don't give him meat—he's Presbyterian." All
of his intellectual prowess was useless there. Nouwen floundered, learning

to swim in this new milieu, and said, "[I]t forced me to rediscover my true identity. These broken, wounded and completely unpretentious people forced me to let go of my relevant self—the self that can do things, show things, prove things, build things—and forced me to reclaim that unadorned self in which I am completely vulnerable, open to receive and give love regardless of any accomplishments" (16).

Nouwen began to find a way of relating agape, and whose success was not quantifiable. As one of the preeminent theologians, Nouwen had been driven by head faith, but was starving for heart faith. Even his ministry had been oriented toward a success model, and the result was the bitter fruit of competition. As Nouwen saw it, this malady characterized the entire culture. He wrote, "Beneath all the great accomplishments of our time there is a deep current of despair. While efficiency and control are the great aspirations of our society, the loneliness, isolation, lack of friendship and intimacy, broken relationships, boredom, feelings of emptiness and depression, and a deep sense of uselessness fill the hearts of millions of people in our success-oriented world" (21).

The key to healing, says Nouwen, is understanding that "we are not the healers, we are not the reconcilers, we are not the givers of life. We are sinful, broken, vulnerable people who need as much care as anyone we care for. The mystery of ministry is that we have been chosen to make our own limited and very conditional love the gateway for the unlimited and unconditional love of God. Therefore, true ministry must be mutual" (43–44).

We are all wounded healers, Nouwen writes. He points us toward one of the deepest wellsprings of compassion ministry. If we are real, we will acknowledge that we have broken, hurting places inside us. Every person has been bruised by life, maybe even mortally wounded by failed relationships, abusive partners, unjust circumstances, or cruelty. We may have done great damage to ourselves—through bad decisions, weakness, or malice. We may have suffered through disease or abandonment. We may have struggled with depression or addiction. We may have wounded others gravely. As soon as we can be honest about our failures and our wounds and can accept the fact that we need Christ like every other sinner, we open ourselves to the possibility of a real conversion, and a real conversation with another hurting person.

Nouwen writes:

> Through compassion it is possible to recognize that the craving for love that men feel resides also in our own hearts, that the cruelty that the world knows all too well is also rooted in our own impulses. Through compassion we also sense our hope for forgiveness in our friends' eyes and our hatred in their bitter mouths. When they kill, we know that we could have done it; when they give life, we know that we can do the same. For a compassionate man nothing human is alien: no joy and no sorrow, no way of living and no way of dying.[2]

Compassion changes our hearts.

The Kingdom at Hand: Dallas Willard

Part of the problem is our understanding of what it is we are supposed to be doing in this life. Is our life in fact purpose driven? Dallas Willard reminds us that the purpose for followers of Christ is to be useful in accomplishing Kingdom purposes here and now, not just waiting for the future heavenly realm. In his book *The Divine Conspiracy*, Willard explains that God's Kingdom "is the range of his effective will, where what he wants done is done."[3] Where God's will is being realized is where his Kingdom is. "The Kingdom is at hand," he tells us. But we don't live as if that were so. Insofar as most people think about it at all, we think of the Kingdom as some ethereal afterlife, the heavenly reward for the faithful. But Jesus told parable upon parable to explain what the Kingdom was like—a treasure buried in a field, a pearl of great value—a discovery here and now (Matthew 13:44–45). But the human mind is so trapped by the linear concept of time that we don't grasp the fact that eternity encompasses time in its sphere. The Kingdom exists both in the future and in the present, intersecting with time. It is present now, among us.

Willard says the Kingdom is accessible, like going into a house. "Think of visiting in a home where you have not been before," he says.

It is a fairly large house, and you sit for a while with your host in a living room or on the veranda. Dinner is announced, and he ushers you down a hall, saying at a certain point, "Turn, for the dining room is at hand," or more likely, "Here's the dining room." Similarly, Jesus directs us to his kingdom. . . . There is no suggestion that . . . the dining room hasn't happened yet but is about to happen or about to be there. . . . And similarly, the Kingdom of God is also right beside us. It is indeed The Kingdom Among Us.[4]

From the UN to the Inner City

Wherever people are following God's will and cooperating by doing what he intends them to do, the Kingdom is at hand. This realization struck me one wintry day in New York in the '80s. A delegation of members of various European parliaments had come over for the National Prayer Breakfast in Washington, D.C., and, as a part of their tour, we visited New York together. For this group of political figures, visiting the headquarters for international policy had a particular luster. The impressive edifice of the United Nations, with its marble floors, vast murals, opulent conference rooms, and rich gifts from the nations conveyed the impression that this was truly the locus of power for all the kingdoms of the world. An hour later, after a bus ride across town, we found ourselves in a run-down inner-city neighborhood with clapboard houses and broken glass on the streets. In a real study of contrasts, we stepped into a shabby two-story learning center with a well-worn carpet and furniture that didn't match. Kids from the neighborhood were tapping away at donated computers, laughing gleefully when the right answer in their math program fired a clown from a cannon on their screens. Another group of children clustered in a circle to practice reading aloud, sitting with the arms of volunteers around them. The warmth of the people who worked with the youngsters made up for what was lacking in material wealth.

The former head of the Congressional Black Caucus, Barbara Williams, had married a former gang member turned evangelist, Tom Skinner, and the two of them had embarked on this ministry together. The love that Barbara and Tom gave these children surrounded them, and it had a tangible effect. One life at a time, this love was freeing the children from the limits of their bullet-pocked neighborhood, its failed schools, and their dysfunctional families. These street saints were transforming lives in a way that no international policymakers could. As the delegation of European politicians drank in the experience, stepping outside their usual parameters, the contrast with our earlier foray into the UN was clear. We had seen where the center of power appeared to be, in those plush conference rooms and towering marble halls. What seemed to be important had an echo that was cold and hollow. But here, in this modest building in a tattered neighborhood across town, God's will was being done. We had turned a corner and the Kingdom was at hand.

Why the Seepage after Sunday?

If the Kingdom is where God's will is being realized, why are the glimpses of it so rare? With so many street saints across America, why are most laboring in relative isolation? In a country where churches are abundant, why is there a gap between worshippers and the transformational power that is supposed to go out the doors with them? Houses of worship draw millions of people Sunday after Sunday for joyous music, teaching that may even be inspiring, and discussions of questions of faith in Sunday school classes. Why then, with all these trained legions, is the church militant so puny in its battle for the souls of our cities? Somehow, there is seepage between the messages that are preached and the actions that should flow from them. After Sunday, the great giant of the church universal slumbers.

One reason is that many people have not taken biblical admonitions into their hearts deeply enough to be transformed by them. Christianity in America has become for many people a kind of candy coating, a veneer. Even the term "Christian" doesn't always tell you anything about the content of belief beyond a vague cultural nod, which is why some believers prefer to describe themselves as "followers of Christ" and their work as "Christ-centered." Nonbelievers see little difference in the behavior of people who call themselves Christians, many of whom seem to have been inoculated with just enough Christianity to achieve immunization against the real thing.

Lacking Discipleship

What has gone awry? Dallas Willard tells us the answer lies in the Great Commission: "Therefore go and make disciples of all nations, baptizing them in the name of the Father and of the Son and of the Holy Spirit, and teaching them to obey everything I have commanded." Willard says the key phrase we have overlooked is *go and make disciples.* A disciple is someone who has been trained by the master to become like him, to be capable of working alongside him. It means becoming capable of making other disciples who are mature and fully equipped to do the same.[5]

We have churches full of people who have heard a lot of teaching, but few have seriously attempted to become disciples. It is not required for membership, nor does it automatically happen with baptism, confirmation, or answering an altar call. It requires an act of will, coupled with spiritual diligence, to engage fully with mind and soul, to retrain the habits of the heart in the imitation of Christ. Discipleship is a process, not an event. The goal is nothing less than being conformed to Christ's image. Through faith, disciples participate in the kind of eternal life that flows through Christ.

The original disciples spent enough time with the Master that he transformed them. Their character was conformed to his over time, as they learned from him. Their desires and thoughts and old ways as fishermen and tax collectors were reshaped to reflect his intentions for them. They walked with him, listened to him, and learned to minister from him as they grew in faith. They practiced, learning to do the things he taught them. With the gift of the Holy Spirit on Pentecost, they were fully empowered to be sent out as his emissaries to the world.

The journey of faith should take followers deeper into Christ's character, his habits, and his ways of handling situations. The journey leads to communion with the Trinity, which is in itself complete relationship. The point of this process is to make true disciples, seasoned in the walk of faith. A disciple has had the milk of the easy teachings but has gone on to grapple with the meaty spiritual disciplines and train his or her spirit for service. A disciple is no longer blown about by every wind of doctrine or knocked off course by temptation or by a season of hardship.

Discipleship is necessary to train a serious cadre of believers who are mature in faith, serious in their intention to serve, and willing to step out in faith to do whatever God wants them to do. It takes a very special kind of person who is willing to pray with complete abandon, "Thy will be done." It takes the faith of a young teenage girl in a dusty Middle Eastern village who was willing to say, "let it be done unto me according to his will" (Luke 1:38). It takes a willingness to recognize the Savior at work and do whatever he tells you (John 2:5). We are of little use to the Kingdom if we do any less.

The Crucial Intersection

The entire history of humanity turns on two axes, the vertical and the horizontal: the relationship with God and the relationship with our neighbor. Jesus summed this up when he said to "love the Lord your God with all your heart and with all your soul and with all your mind and with all your strength" and to "love your neighbor as yourself"(Mark 12:30–31). Together these two commandments constitute the crucial intersection of the horizontal and vertical in human relationships: the relationship between God and humankind, and the relationships among people. Because we have been created as relational beings, our deepest essence seeks loving relationships. Our relationship to God is the vertical, the primary relationship. Only if we are rightly related to God can our relationship to humankind, the horizontal, be at a right angle. If the relationship to him is right, the relationship to other humans can be right as well.

God initiates the relationship. "We love because he first loved us" (1

John 4:19). But accepting the love brings with it the responsibility to act on it. Keeping his commandments is a response to love, and also the evidence of it (John 14:21). We are asked to give a loving response to the love we receive, extending it to our neighbor. As the story of the Good Samaritan shows, our neighbor may not be of our faith, of our ethnicity, or come from our neighborhood. He may turn up in our path at an inconvenient time when we are on our way elsewhere. But when we encounter people in distress, we are supposed to bind their wounds, bring them to safety, and, if necessary, entrust them to someone else's care until they can stand again. We are to take personal action with our own hands, with our own hearts, and with our own money.

Faith Is the Root, Love Is the Fruit

One of the hallmarks of Kingdom people is the presence of love—deep, transforming love. Jesus said, "I give you a new commandment: love one another; you must love one another just as I have loved you. It is by your love for one another that everyone will recognize you as my disciples" (John 13:34). This should be the distinguishing characteristic, the unmistakable evidence of citizenship in the Kingdom of God. Love should shine as a natural manifestation of Christ's presence.

Deeds of love should be the natural outgrowth of receiving love. As Peter Kreeft explains it, "The three theological virtues are a single plant. Faith is its root. Hope is its stalk, its life-thrust. Love is its fruit. The plant is God's own life in us. . . . Faith, hope and charity are the hands that receive God."[6] Love is not just a feeling. It embraces, it lifts up, it works. James writes, "What good is it, my brothers, if a man claims to have faith but has no deeds? Can such faith save him? Suppose a brother or sister is without clothes and daily food. If one of you says to him, 'Go, I wish you well: keep warm and well fed,' but does nothing about his physical needs, what good is it? In the same way, faith by itself, if it is not accompanied by action, is dead" (James 2:14–17).

What people do is a manifestation of their spiritual substance. Whatever is in the human heart ultimately will be expressed in action of some kind. People give evidence of the presence of God in their lives by doing the things that please him. John echoes James when he writes, "If anyone is well off in worldly possessions and sees his brother in need but closes his heart to him, how can the love of God be remaining in him? Children, our love must be not just words or mere talk, but something active and genuine. This will be the proof that we belong to the truth" (1 John 3:17).

People who have a heart rooted in love for Christ will love the things he loves, and do the things he would have them do. Richard Foster tells us that "white-hot love of God compels us into compassionate love of neighbor."[7] Followers of Christ are called to be human torches of divine love, bearers of heat and light in a world grown tepid. Deeds of love are supposed to flow out from the animating source. Vibrant faith should produce a visible outpouring. This is not a theology of salvation by works. It is a way of taking the temperature of people who claim to be believers. The Lord does not like lukewarmness. He warns the Laodiceans in the book of Revelation: "I know your deeds, that you are neither cold nor hot. I wish you were either one or the other! So, because you are lukewarm—neither hot nor cold—I am about to spit you out of my mouth" (Revelation 3:15–16). (Some translations are even stronger: "vomit you out of my mouth.")

The answer to the faith-works issue is very clear. Paul writes "it is by grace you have been saved, through faith; not by anything of your own, but by a gift from God; not by anything that you have done, so that nobody can claim the credit. We are God's work of art, created in Christ Jesus for the good works which God has already designated to make up our way of life" (Ephesians 2:8–10). The same living water that is God's spirit gives life to the soul. Those who receive this spirit by faith are to pour it out in the Kingdom work that he entrusts to his people. Those who do not use the spiritual capital they have been given are like the slothful servant who buried his master's money rather than investing it.[8]

The Lord has a special love for the poor, and he asks us to honor that in our care for others by participating in his nature. More than four hundred verses in the Bible speak of his real and tender concern for the poor. He says to "be openhanded to your brothers in need" (Deuteronomy 15:11) because "he who oppresses the poor shows contempt for his maker. He who is kind to the needy honors God" (Proverbs 14:31). Out of sheer gratitude for the love that he showers on us, we are asked to take a portion of it and give it away.

Apparently, this is not an optional program. In a story that grates modern sensibilities of tolerance, Matthew 25 tells the story of the Last Judgment, when Christ is separating the sheep from the goats. He says to those on his right, "Come, you who are blessed by my Father; take your inheritance, prepared for you since the creation of the world. For I was hungry and you gave me something to eat, I was thirsty and you gave me something to drink. I was a stranger and you invited me in. I needed clothes and you clothed me. I was sick and you looked after me. I was in prison and you came to visit me." They ask him, "Lord when did we see you hungry . . . thirsty . . . a stranger . . . needing clothes . . . sick or in prison?" He replies, "Whatever you did for one of the least of these brothers of mine, you did for me." He says to the rest, "Depart from me, you who are cursed, into the eternal fire prepared for the devil and his angels." Those who do not respond are not welcome in the Kingdom. "Whatever you did not do for one of the least of these, you did not do for me." He hands down the judgment. "They will go away to eternal punishment, but the righteous to eternal life" (Matthew 25:31–46).

The Tao: C. S. Lewis

The admonition to care for the weak is a moral truth that has emerged in the teachings of not only Christian and Hebrew scriptures, but throughout history. In *The Abolition of Man*,[9] C. S. Lewis compiled quotations supporting this value from other religious traditions—not as a syncretistic approach, but as an illustration of Natural Law. They illustrate that transcendent truth has been discovered by civilizations in different times and places. Lewis calls this the Tao, or the way. The examples quoted below from his book illustrate Lewis's point.

"Men were brought into existence for the sake of men that they might do one another good." (Roman. Cicero, *De Off.* I.vii)

"He who is asked for alms should always give." (Hindu. Janet, i.7)

"What good man regards any misfortune as no concern of his?" (Roman. Juvenal, xv.140)

"Never do to others what you would not like them to do to you." (Ancient Chinese. *Analects of Confucius,* trans. A. Waley, xv.23; cf.xii.2)

"Speak kindness . . . show good will." (Babylonian. *Hymn to Samas.* ERE v. 445)

"Love thy neighbor as thyself." (Ancient Jewish. Leviticus xix.18)

"Love the stranger as thyself." (Ancient Jewish, ibid., 33,34)

"You will see them take care of their kindred [and] the children of their friends . . . never reproaching them in the least." (Redskin. Le Jeune, quoted ERE v. 437)

"I ought not to be unfeeling like a statue but should fulfill both my natural and artificial relations, as a worshipper, a son, a brother, a father, and a citizen." (Greek. Epictetus, III. li)

"The union and fellowship of men will be best preserved if each receive from us the more kindness in proportion as he is more closely connected with us." (Roman. Cicero, *De Off.* I.xvi)

"The poor and the sick should be regarded as lords of the atmosphere." (Hindu. Janet, i.8)

"Whoso makes intercession for the weak, well pleasing is this to Samas." (Babylonian. ERE v. 445)

"I have given bread to the hungry, water to the thirsty, clothes to the naked, a ferry boat to the boatless." (Ancient Egyptian. ERE v. 478)

"They never desert the sick." (Australian Aborigines. ERE v. 443)

"You will see them take care of . . . widows, orphans, and old men, never reproaching them." (Redskin, ERE v. 439)

"When thou cuttest down thine harvest . . . and has forgot a sheaf . . . thou shalt not go again to fetch it: it shall be for the stranger, for the fatherless, and for the widow." (Ancient Jewish. Deut. xxiv.19)

"There are two kinds of injustice: the first is found in those who do an injury, the second in those who fail to protect another from injury when they can." (Roman. Cicero. *Dr. Off.* I.vii)

"The foundation of justice is good faith." (Roman. Cicero, *Dr. Off.* I.vii)

"Verily, verily I say to you unless a grain of wheat falls into the earth and dies, it remains alone, but if it dies it bears much fruit. He who loves his life loses it." (Christian. John xii.24,25)

Within the history of the Christian Church, there are a number of streams that have emphasized care for the poor. Rooted in the Hebrew scriptures of the Old Testament, and continuing through the life of Christ and his followers since, the manifestations in the Christian Church have flowed in great streams, according to Richard Foster.[10] The social justice tradition, the evangelical tradition, and the contemplative tradition are three to consider which foster compassion ministry.

The Social Justice Tradition

As Jesus inaugurated his public ministry, he spoke using the words of Isaiah: "He has sent me to proclaim freedom for the prisoners and recovery of sight for the blind, to release the oppressed, to proclaim the year of the Lord's favor."[11] The concepts of righteousness, justice, and peace have always been interwoven, because where there is injustice there cannot be peace. The psalmist describes the place where the Lord's people honor him: "Love and faithfulness meet together; righteousness and peace will kiss each other" (Psalm 85:10). Throughout the Bible, there are scores of references to the righteous treatment of people in need. The prophet Zechariah tells us, "Administer true justice, show mercy and compassion to one another. Do not oppress the widow or the fatherless, the alien or the poor" (Zechariah 7:9).

One tradition that has developed in response to these Old Testament roots is that of social justice.[12] In the New Testament, the first social justice controversy that erupts in the young church is the distribution of food among the widows. The Greek widows contended that they were not fairly fed in relation to the other widows. The solution was to create deacons to look after them, all of whom had Greek names, meaning that the new caregivers were raised up from the community of the aggrieved. Deacons were tasked with their care, in a new role added to the church. This was an institutional response as well as a personal one.[13] God has charged us to care for our fellow humans, including for their physical needs, and sometimes institutions have to be changed to accomplish this. The Roman Catholic Church has historically held social justice issues at the forefront of its teaching. "Justice will never be fully attained unless people see in the poor person, who is asking for help to survive, not an annoyance or burden," says Pope John Paul II, "but an opportunity for showing kindness and a chance for greater enrichment."[14] The emphasis on social justice was also a potent strain in the Methodism of the latter nineteenth and early twentieth centuries.

Faith has often moved people to take action on behalf of the oppressed. Slavery is an example that summoned forth courageous people to lead the forces to unshackle its victims. William Wilberforce worked incessantly for much of his life to lift the yoke of slavery. John Newton joined him, once his soul as a slave trader had been convicted by the Holy Spirit. John Woolman had deeply influenced his fellow Quakers in the American colonies, which led them to abolish slavery in 1758.[15]

In the United States, the work of African American churches has effectively moved into issues of social justice. New community development corporations have been spun out of the churches to address subsistence issues like affordable housing, job skills training, transitioning from welfare to work, and small business ownership. Inspired by leaders like John Perkins, leaders are stepping forward with solutions to local problems that are built on the agents of health in their own neighborhoods.

There has been a strong push in some churches to equate economic and political action with issues of faith. Social justice issues address the material needs of the oppressed and poor, and these concerns often intersect with the political world. There is a great temptation to focus on the policy issues and lose sight of the spiritual dimension. John Perkins warns, "We can get caught in the shallows of welfare or paternalism if we help meet people's physical needs without sharing with them the understanding that they can have a new quality of life with God that lasts forever. God wants people to develop into whole human beings."[16]

Richard Foster writes that the greatest pitfall in the social justice tradition is "caring for social needs without reference to the condition of the heart." He warns that those who do not "minister to both physical and spiritual needs . . . end up severing the spiritual underpinnings of their efforts." If they neglect the spiritual, Foster laments, "The only thing these organizations have left is a kind of social salvation that leaves people rooted in spiritual despair and alienated from God."[17] But if the approach maintains its focus on God, it can be a powerful agent of change in a broken and often unjust world.

The Evangelical Tradition

"Repent, for the kingdom of heaven has come near" (Matthew 4:17). This is the message Jesus brought, the good news for proclamation to a world awash with sin. In the years since Jesus uttered these words, the evangelical tradition has mobilized scores of people who take this message to the unchurched, the unwashed, and the unloved. For anyone who has sin in his or her life, this is the clarion call to confess and seek a new life in Christ. The evangelical tradition is rooted in the Bible as the unerring word of God. It is centered in the person of Christ, his life and ministry, his crucifixion and resurrection. This teaching proclaims the substitutional atonement accomplished on the cross. It offers us the chance to be born again in the Spirit if we acknowledge our guilt, ask the Lord's forgiveness, and enter into a new life with him. Willfulness causes people to seek their own way and not that of God, and the resulting sin creates an abyss that separates us from him. Jesus Christ is the bridge over the abyss. Those who accept him are charged to take this good news and share it with the world.

This tradition has birthed faith-based organizations throughout America and the world whose mission has been to take the message of the need for repentance to sinners. It is the impetus of the message in homeless shelters that offer "soup, soap, and salvation" to street people. It is the message that priests, pastors, and volunteers take into prisons. This is what is preached at the Salvation Army and in their shelters. It is the message of Gospel Rescue Missions throughout the country. Ministries like

Prison Fellowship International offer convicts the chance to confess their wrongs and receive God's forgiveness. This is the message in faith-based drug treatment programs that confront addicts with the need to change their hearts and their lives. The message is straightforward: "Drugs aren't the problem. Drugs are the symptom. Sin is the problem. Jesus Christ is the answer."

The evangelical approach addresses the people it serves with the firm conviction that the state of the human soul is the main concern, and that unless a person is "born again" in a personal relationship with Christ, they cannot be whole. If, however, a person makes that commitment, they can begin a new life. Conversion is the goal, and faith in God is the medium of change.

The Contemplative Tradition: Mother Teresa

Mother Teresa is the quintessential street saint. Her example and the world-wide movement she inspired by her example are evidence that the contemplative approach can be an important motivation for compassion. At first glance, the contemplative tradition and the life of active compassion would appear to have little to do with each other. But Mother Teresa described herself as a "contemplative in the world." For her, there was a clear linkage between a spiritual life rooted in contemplative prayer, and compassion in action. It was in prayer that she first heard the call to go and live among the poorest of the poor, and it was in prayer that she drew the strength each day to live it out. It was not her love of the poor that compelled her, but her love of God.

Born as Agnes Bojaxhiu, she entered the Irish order of the Sisters of Loreto at the age of eighteen, and bid her family a tearful farewell as she left for Ireland to learn English. She feared that she would never see them again, and that proved to be the case. She was sent to Calcutta in 1929, where she taught geography and catechism at St. Mary's High School, and later became the principal. She observed the bone-crushing poverty and squalor of the city, where dead bodies were collected from the streets as the weakest fell to disease or starvation. It seared the heart of the nun who lived cloistered away in the safety and relative comfort of the convent.

Mother Teresa was on a train on September 10, 1946, when she received what she called "the call within the call." It became clear that she was to follow Jesus into the poorest slums of the city, live among the poor, and do his work there. But there is a story behind this well-known story. Mother Teresa had made a secret vow in 1942 that she wanted to give a gift, "something very beautiful . . . something without reserve." She promised to give God "anything that He would ask—not to refuse Him anything."[18] She carried this private vow within her for four years. When she received the "call within a call" to go and live among the poorest of the poor in Calcutta, this was what God was asking her to give. As she was in prayer, he spoke to her in an interior voice that she sensed rather than heard. *You have become my spouse for My love. Will you refuse to do this for me? Refuse me not.*[19] She kept a journal of these inner locutions. Later, she wrote, "One day at Holy Communion I heard the same voice very distinctly: *I want Indian nuns, victims of my love, who would be Mary and Martha, who would be so very united to me as to radiate my love on soul. . . . Wilt thou refuse to do this for me?*[20]

What has come to light only recently in the investigation for her canonization is that she had a much more difficult time answering this call than was previously known. She struggled first with her own uncertainty, and then with the church, from which she had to receive permission for this unconventional ministry. Father Brian Kolodiejchuk of the Missionaries of Charity has documented her story, based on interviews and correspondence with her spiritual advisor, Father Van Exem, and with Archbishop Perier.

She wrote to Perier in 1947, citing these things God had put in her heart. "These words, or rather, this voice frightened me. The thought of eating, sleeping, living like the Indians filled me with fear. I prayed long—I prayed so much. . . . The more I prayed, the clearer grew the voice in my heart." Another day the words of this voice were: *Do not fear. I shall be with you always. You will suffer and you suffer now, but . . . you will have to bear these torments on your heart. Let me act. Refuse me not. Trust me lovingly, trust me blindly.*[21]

When Mother Teresa asked to be released from the convent to go onto the streets, she was denied permission. She was told to say nothing and go back and pray, which she did obediently. As she waited, the outlines of what she was to do became clearer. She knew that she would need nuns equipped to move about in the city, and began to make plans for them to learn to drive vehicles, which was highly unusual for nuns in Calcutta in the 1940s. She asked again, but her superiors in the church still doubted the authenticity of her call. Once again, she went back in obedience to pray. Again, permission was not granted.

In a vision, she saw a crowd with their hands lifted to her in their midst, as they cried out, "Come, come, save us. Bring us to Jesus." She wrote in her prayer journal, "I could see great sorrow and suffering in their faces." She could see the crowd in darkness with Christ on the cross before them, as she stood as a little child next to Jesus' mother, Mary, facing the cross. The Lord said, *I have asked you. They have asked you and she, my mother, has asked you. Will you refuse to do this for me, to take care of them, to bring them to me?* She answered, "You know Jesus, I am ready to go at a moment's notice."[22]

Mother Teresa's perseverance and prayer finally sufficed to persuade Father Van Exem of the authenticity of her call. And when Archbishop Perier received Mother Teresa's letter with the excerpts from her prayer journal cited above, and many others, he no longer doubted that it was the will of God, either. But when the permission to move out of the convent to live among the poor finally came from Rome, her struggles for acceptance were not over. She encountered serious resistance from her fellow believers in Calcutta. "One convent where she stopped by to eat her lunch ordered her to eat under the back stairs like a common beggar. A Yugoslav Jesuit, of the very nationality and order that had first inspired her love for India, commented brusquely, 'We thought she was cracked.'"[23]

A Pencil in God's Hand

Mother Teresa embarked on the ministry that the world now knows, the outreach to the unloved, the lost, the unwanted, the lepers, the untouchables. She called herself a pencil in God's hand. She did what he asked of her, and he wrote a compelling message through her obedient life. She picked up the dying and brought them to the home she founded to give them love and dignity in death. She picked up babies and infants that had been abandoned in the garbage heaps, like human refuse, and nursed them back to life. She once encountered a man who lay dying in a gutter, half eaten by worms, rotting. Mother Teresa herself carried him to her home for the sick and dying, and gave him what he had not known until then, a clean place to lie, unconditional love, and dignity. "I have lived like an animal all my life," the man told her, "but I will die like an angel." One of the sisters found eight fetuses from an abortion clinic in Calcutta that were still alive. They took them in, nurtured them, and three lived for a time. One eventually grew into a healthy girl and they found a family to adopt her.

Mother Teresa always insisted that the work she and the sisters did was not social work, but the fruit of their contemplative life of prayer. There were many people eager to push a label of social activism on her, or engage her in political issues centered on the poor. But she would have none of it. She said, "We are contemplatives in the world." The work she did was rooted in prayer, and was an outpouring of the love she received in mystical union with Christ. She saw him in the destitute people she touched. As she explained it, she served "Christ in the distressing disguise of the poorest of the poor." In touching their filthy and diseased bodies, she was touching his body.

Dark Night of the Soul

One of the greatest mysteries in Mother Teresa's life is a phenomenon that was almost entirely unknown to others during her lifetime. Only her spiritual directors knew. She suffered from a spiritual darkness that lasted more than forty years. This woman whose radiant smile lit up the world around her was in fact walking by faith, and not by sight. Her communication with her spiritual directors in the 1960s, '70s, and '80s describe a "darkness and nothingness" that eclipsed her spirit. In her "dark night of the soul" that lasted for nearly four decades, she had an overwhelming thirst for God that caused her great anguish. She likened her suffering to that of souls in hell, parched for God. She questioned whether he had rejected her. And yet, she remained surrendered to him, and persevered despite the darkness.[24]

Father Kolodiejchuk says, "She understood that the darkness she experienced was a mystical participation in Jesus' sufferings." She described in her prayer journal the sense of aloneness that Jesus experienced, the pain and darkness that he endured. In a moment of unfiltered candor, she voiced her cry to God: "When you asked to imprint your passion on my heart, is this the answer? If this brings you glory, if you get a drop of joy from this, if souls are brought to you, if my suffering satiates your thirst—here I am, Lord. With joy I accept all to the end of life and I will smile at your hidden face—always."[25] She offered up the profound pain of separation from Christ to him as a gift.

There are two words written on a sign that hangs on the walls of the Missionaries of Charity homes all over the world: "I thirst." The Missionaries of Charities have taken these words uttered on the cross as their own, enshrining them in their constitution. "Our aim is to quench the infinite thirst of Jesus Christ on the Cross for love of souls. We serve Jesus in the poor, we nurse Him, feed Him, clothe Him, visit Him." It was this profound love, deepened in contemplative prayer, and nourished daily by the Eucharist, which sustained Mother Teresa through what would have been a crushing burden for lesser souls.

She warned that it is not possible to do this kind of work "without being a soul of prayer." Time for silence and contemplative prayer was crucial for her work. "We need to find God, and he cannot be found in noise and restlessness. God is the friend of the silence," she said. "We need silence to be able to touch souls."[26]

She pointed us toward what she calls "A Simple Path."

The fruit of silence is prayer.
The fruit of prayer is faith.
The fruit of faith is love.
The fruit of love is service.
The fruit of service is peace.[27]

Although Mother Teresa labored in relative obscurity for much of her life, she won the Nobel Peace Prize and the Templeton Prize for Religion, and the respect for her saintliness rapidly spread throughout the world. She was beatified by the Roman Catholic Church in October, 2003.

The Missionaries of Charity now work in 130 countries, including some in the West that did not think of themselves as home to the "poorest of the poor." But the spread of AIDS, drugs, and the squalor of urban slums in first world countries has spawned pockets of third world conditions. Beyond the pockets of material poverty in otherwise affluent cities, there is a quiet, crippling poverty of the soul that is less visible but every bit as devastating. Spiritual and relational impoverishment is often found in materially wealthy countries. Mother Teresa was once asked what the worst disease was. Instead of replying leprosy or AIDS, she answered, "loneliness." She saw people who were lonely and hungry not only for food but for the word of God and for the touch of another human being. They were thirsty not only for water but for knowledge, truth, and love. They lacked not only clothes but also human dignity. In materially affluent countries, Mother Teresa reached out to the spiritually poor—the unwanted child, the victim of racial discrimination, the alcoholic, the drug addict, and all those who have lost hope.[28]

It's about Our Hearts

Likewise, the street saints in America are called to both the "up-and-outers" and "down-and-outers." One of the most remarkable phenomena of compassion ministry is the way that boundaries fall away for those who enter into the world of outreach. In a priceless moment, an investment banker turned up with his church members for a Christmas party in the homeless shelter. That day the banker was unshaven and wearing an old, ratty sweater as he sat smoking and chatting with the other men at the table. A homeless man at the table turned to his neighbor and asked, "Is he one of us?" We chuckled, but realized that at a deeper level this is not a world of "them" and "us." A newly separated woman who turns up at an airport with two suitcases and two children, not knowing where to begin a new life, is not much different than a refugee. People who go into the inner city to mentor at-risk teenagers may figure out that their own kids are just as much at risk. The person who is in a home, severely disabled because of an automobile accident, could have been any of us. It is a world of hurting, wounded people all around us, and we are right in the middle of it, participants ourselves.

Compassion shatters the boundaries between rich and poor, black, white, Hispanic, and Asian. It spans the great divide of income, denomination, or political party. A mother whose son was killed in a drive-by shooting in the inner city knows anguish, as does a mother in the suburbs whose son commits suicide. Kids doing drugs break the hearts of the parents in lovely homes and in unlovely homes. Children abandoned by their dads hurt just as much, regardless of which zip code they live in. Broken families leave a trail of human wreckage. We are in this jostling, pushing and pulling, weeping, howling valley of tears together. And until we are willing to learn in compassion, we will be victimized by pain rather than perfected by it.

For whatever reasons, God has chosen to manifest his light through the cracks in the vessels he has created. It takes an admission of our brokenness for us to be useful to him in this process, and a willingness to seek his love to fill us. Only then can it shine out on others, not as merely our own, but as his love that radiates from within us. Admitting our own brokenness allows God to fill the empty places, completing us, and allows us to hear the brokenness in another human soul. A person who listens from the experience of deep personal pain can say to someone else not merely "That's too bad" or "I'm sorry for you," but, from the depth of his or her heart, "I understand." The deepest kind of empathy can emanate from another soul who has been wounded deeply.

In admitting our own brokenness, we are prepared to go to the Lord and ask for his healing love. When we receive it, a part of the healing process is being able to share it with other wounded souls. A remarkable dynamism is unleashed when we are willing to admit our own weakness, accept the love, and reach out to others in humility to share it with them. Instead of leadership by power, it is leadership from humility. It is servant leadership.[29]

Street saints are sent out to be vessels of love to people who hurt. Service is a manifestation of love. Christ fills us with love to give away, not to squander on ourselves. If we do not move to give to others, it may be because we have not loved deeply enough or realized how deeply we are loved. Nouwen puts his finger on this, and he takes us back to the preeminent question. It is the question Jesus put to Peter over breakfast on the shore of the Sea of Galilee, just after the resurrection. "Do you love me?" he asked him. Not once, but three times. Once for each time Peter had denied him. "Do you love me?" There is no more important question if we are truly serving Jesus. Only if we can answer it with a joyous, resounding "Yes," can we be of any use to him at all.

Serving others in compassion has a purpose in changing the heart because it is both a manifestation of love and a means of deepening it. The deepest kind of unity with God is surrender to him, joyful surrender of our own will to do his. Those who obey and rely on his guidance will find joy walking in the center of his will, right in the middle of the Kingdom Among Us. We can aspire to become street saints or to work alongside one—giving our time, talent, or treasure.

How Do You Hear a Call?

But how is one to know what God may want them to do? In the absence of a burning bush, how can we know when he is calling us? God often speaks through scripture. On a given day a particular passage of the Bible may leap off the pages and galvanize conviction through words that penetrate the heart with crystalline clarity. He may choose to speak through life circumstances, doors that swing open while others slam shut. He often speaks through other people, in whose mouths he places words that are clearly directed toward us.

Prayer is a way to discern what God may be asking us to do. We often utilize prayer to pour out petitions, praise God with thanks, beg his forgiveness, and intercede for others. But it is also an important way to align one's will with that of the Lord in an ongoing conversation. While some people do well with their side of the conversation, not all take the time to listen. It is a little like hanging up the receiver before the person you called has had time to respond. In a world of noise and too many words, there seems to be little time to listen for God in silence.

This can be found only when a person can push down deep enough to leave the layers of daily noise behind, after all the words are finished. Prayer can be a wordless adoration that emanates from the deepest places of the soul to simply rest in God's presence. Teresa of Avila describes this place as the "interior castle of the soul." This is where God's barely perceptible whispers may come to direct the one who prays. The listening kind of prayer is where God may nudge "halftimers" to take their time, talent, and treasure and put it to use for Kingdom purposes. This is where the whisper may come to build a clinic, start an inner-city school, or be a mentor. Thomas Merton writes that one who prays here "has risked his mind in the desert beyond language and beyond ideas where God is encountered in the nakedness of pure trust."[30] If one intends to serve, this is a good place to discern what to do, and how.

What to Expect If You Go

The attitude with which you go is important. You have to go with a willingness to be changed. Anyone who goes with an open heart will find it stretched to embrace and understand. The experience may challenge your assumptions and knock you out of your comfort zone. You need to go with the certainty that you do not have all the answers and that your own strength will not suffice. You may discover that you need God in a way you never have before because your own resources are clearly inadequate. You will probably be driven to your knees in prayer.

It is good to go with other people, because the task is so huge that no one alone can do all that needs to be done. It becomes apparent that the true brothers and sisters in Christ are those who have heard his word and who are doing it. And if people work side by side in unity, God mobilizes remarkable talent from very diverse sources.

Above all things, we are called to be a presence of love. The aroma of Christ is with those who dwell in him, and those who are truly rooted in him will exude this fragrance in their words, their touch, their demeanor. This alone speaks volumes to the lives touched, and it communicates the presence of the Spirit that dwells within. Remember St. Francis's advice to preach always, and only when necessary to use words.

Necessary Attitudes of the Heart to Serve with Street Saints

- Love is the medium and the message
- You don't have all the answers
- Money will not solve the most important problems
- Rely completely on God for direction
- Don't get ahead of God; timing is everything
- Prayer is a lifeline
- Have the teachable heart of a student and servant
- You need other people to do this
- Don't expect to be thanked
- You will be drawn into suffering

Money will not solve the most important problems, which are often problems of the heart. What appears to be material need often has a deeper, spiritual dimension. But physical needs are real, and unless we are giving sacrificially to meet these needs, our own hearts have not been captured. A person can not hear the preaching if he or she is hungry.

It is important to resist the temptation to get ahead of what God is doing and not force your need for action on his plan. Timing is everything. So many seemingly good ideas have produced nothing but dust because someone has raced ahead without being guided.

Only the heart of a servant and a student is helpful. We need hearts willing to serve others unselfishly, untiringly. A teachable spirit acknowledges that we have limited knowledge. Humility reminds us we don't have all the answers, and that we have a great deal to learn. We should honor others above ourselves. We do other human beings a great disservice if we approach them with an attitude of coming from above them.

Don't expect to be thanked. Anybody who thinks there are people out there just waiting for random acts of kindness who will be incredibly grateful for what we do are in for a disappointment. Nobody wants to be needy, and it is almost always harder to receive than to give. God sees what we do, and he knows our hearts. It should be enough to know that we have given him joy, even if it is in secret.

Make no mistake: anyone who ventures to reach out to other human souls who suffer will be drawn into their suffering. This is the meaning of the word "compassion." It comes from Latin: *com,* meaning "with," and *patior,* meaning "to suffer." To suffer with someone is the essence of compassion. If we pray to God to be useful in the lives of those we serve, we need to be willing to pray the prayer: "Lord, help me to see what you would have me see, and break my heart for the things that break your heart." If the sight of a battered child grieves us, how much more must it grieve the Creator? If injustice makes us want to cry out, how much more must God want to cry out when he sees the injustices we have permitted?

Nouwen writes, "Who can save a child from a burning house without taking the risk of being hurt by the flames? Who can listen to a story of loneliness and despair without taking the risk of experiencing similar pains in his own heart? . . . The great illusion of leadership is to think that man can be led out of the desert by someone who has never been there. . . . [W]e have forgotten that no God can save us except a suffering God, and that no man can lead his people except the man who is crushed by its sins."[31]

There is a purpose in suffering. This is one of the hardest things to accept, particularly when we see it up close and respond viscerally. But to short-circuit suffering by charging in as an amateur providence can thwart God's intentions in a given situation. The refiner's fire does in fact burn, and it is burning all of us, but it will never burn away that which is essential. It only removes the dross, and the silver emerges gleaming.

The process of engaging with others in service opens us up to participate in the life that flows from God. There is a torrent of love that he pours out on us all, like a waterfall cascading over us. He pours this out in abundance, showering us with abandon, urging our souls to drink. If only we would. This abundance is available, and in serving, we come to fill our hearts with this living water. An apt metaphor for our spiritual lives is found in the Holy Land, where water flows into two lakes. The Sea of Galilee and the Dead Sea are fed by the same source, the River Jordan. But there is one crucial difference. The Sea of Galilee has an outlet, and it is continually refreshed as new water flows in to replace that which has poured out. The Dead Sea is static: water pours in but nothing flows out, and nothing can live within it. So it is with our souls. Only if we are pouring out the living water that is poured into us are we capable of receiving more, and sustaining fresh life.[32] God wants to open our hearts to receive the rivers and let them flow through us, give us joy, and complete ourselves in him. But he cannot if we do not cooperate. He will not force himself on us. But he is seeking us constantly, nudging, whispering, quietly calling.

If you feel a nudge to come and serve, don't quench the spirit. Respond. Don't ignore him. Open your heart and go where there is a need, go to be a presence of love. Make yourself available to be a participant in the Kingdom Among Us in your city now, where it is hidden away but vibrant. Street saints can show you where. Offer one of them your time, talent, or treasure. Hear the call to serve the unloved and say, "Here I am, Lord, send me." Step out to become a part of what he is already doing in our cities. Anyone who goes to serve with street saints discovers the joy that comes from being in their presence—refreshment from their contagious laughter and their spiritual warmth that beckons. We all have time, talent, or treasure to give. The question is whether we are willing.

The call is urgent. The need is great, but the joy in fulfilling it is even greater. Go, as Mother Teresa urged us, and do "something beautiful for

God." What you do is less important than how you do it. She said, "There are no great deeds. Only small deeds done with great love."

God is with us if we go. In the words of Isaiah:

> If you spend yourselves in behalf of the hungry
> and satisfy the needs of the oppressed,
> then your light will rise in the darkness,
> and your night will become like the noonday.
> The Lord will guide you always:
> He will satisfy your needs in a sun-scorched land
> And will strengthen your frame.
> You will be like a well-watered garden,
> Like a spring whose waters never fail.
> Your people will rebuild the ancient ruins
> And will raise up the age-old foundations:
> You will be called Repairer of Broken Walls,
> Restorer of Streets with Dwellings. (Isaiah 58:10–12)

Appendix

Contact Information for Street Saints

An online directory provides more information on these, and other faith-based organizations, at www.streetsaints.com.

Aldine Y.O.U.T.H.

Sylvia Bolling (Executive Director and Founder)
Mailing Address: PO Box 11044
Houston, TX 77293-1044
Physical Address: 4700 Aldine Mail Rd.
Houston, TX 77039
(P) 281-449-4828 / (F) 281-449-4886
sbolling@aldineyouth.org
www.aldineyouth.org

Amachi

Rev. Dr. W. Wilson Goode Sr. (Director)
2000 Market St., Suite 600, Philadelphia, PA 19103
(P) 215-557-4400 / (F) 215-557-2270
wgoode@ppv.org / *www.ppv.org*

Association of Gospel Rescue Missions

Rev. Stephen Burger (Executive Director)
1045 Swift St., Kansas City, MO 64116-4127
(P) 816-471-8020 / (F) 816-471-3718
agrm@agrm.org / *www.agrm.org*

Bridges to Life

John Sage (Executive Director and Founder)
9426 Old Katy Rd., Building 7, Houston, TX 77055
(P) 713-463-7200 / (F) 713-465-5658
Jsage1@aol.com
www.bridgestolife.org

Brookwood Community

Yvonne Tuttle Streit (Executive Director and Founder)
1752 FM 1489, Brookshire, TX 77423
(P) 281-375-2100
(P) 800-726-3234 (toll-free)
(F) 281-375-2162
info@brookwoodcommunity.org
www.brookwoodcommunity.org

Care Fresno

Gordon Donoho (Executive Director)
1727 L St., Fresno, CA 93721

(P) 559-233-2000 / (F) 559-233-2810
Gordon@onebyoneleadership.com
www.Onebyoneleadership.com

Casa de Esperanza de los Ninos, Inc.
Kathleen Foster (Director)
Mailing Address: PO Box 66581,
    Houston, TX 77266-6581
Physical Address: 1407 Wichita St.,
    Houston, TX 77004
(P) 713-529-0639 / (F) 713-529-9179
casa@casahope.org
www.casahope.org

Christ Community Health Services
Burt Waller (Executive Director)
2953 Broad Ave., Memphis, TN 38112
(P) 901-260-8500 / (F) 901-260-8599
burt.waller@christchs.org

Christian Community Development Association
Gordon Murphy (Executive Director)
3827 W. Ogden Ave., Chicago, IL
    60623
(P) 773-762-0994 / (F) 773-346-0071
info@ccda.org / *www.ccda.org*

City as Parish
One by One Leadership
Dr. Don Simmons
1727 L St., Fresno, CA 93721
(P) 559-233-2000 / (F) 559-233-2810
don@onebyoneleadership.com
*www.onebyoneleadership.com/city_as_*
    parish.htm

City as Parish
Pittsburgh Leadership Foundation
Marilyn Mulvihill (Executive Director)
100 Ross St., 4th Floor, Pittsburgh, PA
    15219
(P) 412-281-3752 / (F) 412-281-2312
marilynmulvihill@comcast.net

City of Refuge Evangelical Presbyterian Church
Rufus Smith (Senior Pastor)
3150 Yellowstone Blvd., Houston, TX
    77054
(P) 713-664-5033 (Church)
(P) 713-664-5054 (Community
    Development Center)
(F) 713-664-5253
mmcnierhall@cityofrefuge.org (office
    manager)
www.cityofrefuge.org

Cornerstone Schools Association
Ernestine L. Sanders (President) and
    Clark Durant (CEO)
6861 East Nevada, Detroit, MI 48234
(P) 313-892-1860
(F) 313-892-1861
Ernestine.Sanders@
    cornerstoneschools.org
www.cornerstoneschools.org

Craine House, Inc.
Suzanne K. Milner (Executive
    Director) and Priscilla Ferguson-
    Wagstaff (Board President)

3535 North Pennsylvania,
   Indianapolis, IN 46205
(P) 317-925-2833 / (F) 317-925-2834
CraineHouse1@aol.com

Family House, Inc.
Cordelia Taylor (CEO)
3269 N. 11th Street, Milwaukee, WI
   53206
(P) 414-374-5212 / (F) 414-374-1294
familyhouseinc@cs.com
www.always.org.uk/familyhouse

Goodcity
Michael Ivers (President)
5049 West Harrison Street, Chicago,
   IL, 60644
(P) 312-322-3000 / (F) 312-573-8881
mjtivers@goodcitychicago.org
www.goodcitychicago.org

Good Samaritan Ministries
Janet DeYoung (Executive Director)
513 East 8th St., Suite 25, Holland, MI
   49423
(P) 616-392-7159 / (F) 616-392-5889
info@goodsamministries.com
www.goodsamministries.com

Harambee Christian Family Center
Rudy Carrasco (Executive Director)
1581 Navarro Ave., Pasadena, CA
   91103
(P) 626-791-7439 / (F) 626-628-3138
rudy@harambee.org
www.harambee.org

Homeboyz
Stephen Foltz (Executive Director)
731 W. Washington, Milwaukee, WI
   53204
(P) 414-672-3346 / (F) 414-672-5234
steve@homeboyz.com
www.homeboyz.com

Hope Christian Community Foundation
James Daughdrill (CEO)
5100 Poplar Ave., Suite 2412,
   Memphis, TN 38137
(P) 901-682-6201 / (F) 901-682-8098
www.hopeccf.org

Hope Now for Youth, Inc.
Rev. Roger Minassian (Executive
   Director)
PO Box 5294, Fresno, CA 93755-5294
(P) 559-434-8125 / (F) 559-434-8125
info@hopenow.org
www.hopenow.org

InnerChange Freedom Initiative (IFI) – Iowa
Sam Dye (Director)
Newton Correctional Facility, 307 S.
   60th Ave. W., Box 218, Newton,
   Iowa 50208
(P) 641-792-7552, ext. 761
(F) 641-787-1114
sam_dye@pfm.org / *www.pfm.org*

InnerChange Freedom Initiative (IFI) – Kansas

Don Raymond (Director)

Ellsworth Correctional Facility, 1607 State St., PO Box 107, Ellsworth, KS 67439-0107

(P) 785-472-3991 / (F) 785-472-3992

ifi.Kansas@ifiprison.org

www.ifiprison.org

InnerChange Freedom Initiative (IFI) – Minnesota

Mark Early (Director)

Minnesota Correctional Facility, Lino Lakes, MN 55014

(P) 651-717-6722 / (F) 651-717-6725

dkingery@pfm.org / www.pfm.org

InnerChange Freedom Initiative (IFI) – Texas

Tommie Dorsett (Director)

Carol S. Vance Unit, Jester 2 Rd., Richmond, TX 77469

(P) 281-277-8707 / (F) 281-277-8701

phillip.dautrich@ifiprison.org

www.ifiprison.org

Inner City Youth

Prince Couisnard (President)

Mailing Address: PO Pox 14575, Houston, TX 77221

Physical Address: 6311 Allegheny, Houston, TX 77021

(P) 713-747-0705 / (F) 713-747-1010

info@innercityyouth.net

www.innercityyouth.net

Interfaith Housing Coalition

Ben Beltzer (Founder) and Linda Hall (Executive Director)

PO Box 720206, Dallas, TX 75372-0206

(P) 214-827-7220 / (F) 214-827-1347

IHCD@sbcglobal.net

www.interfaithhousingcoalition.org

Jobs Partnership

Rev. Skip Long (CEO and President)

4208 Six Forks Rd., Raleigh, NC 27609

(P) 919-571-8614 / (F) 919-786-4912

national@tjp.org / www.tjp.org

John M. Perkins Foundation for Reconciliation

Dr. John M. Perkins (President and Founder)

1831 Robinson St., Jackson, MS 39209

(P) 601-354-1563 / (F) 601-352-6882

jmpoffice@jam.rr.com

www.jmpf.org

Kids Hope USA

Dr. Virgil Gulker (Executive Director) and Jinny DeJong (President)

PO Box 2517, Holland, MI 49422-2517

(P) 616-546-3580 / (F) 616-546-3586

vgulker@kidshopeusa.org

www.kidshopeusa.org

L'Arche Canada

381, Rachel Est, Montreal, QC, H2W IE8, CANADA

(P) 514-844-1661 / (F) 514-844-1960

office@larchecanada.org
www.larchecanada.org

Leadership Foundations of America

Reid Carpenter (President)
100 Ross St., 4th Floor, Pittsburgh, PA
  15219
(P) 412-562-9070 / (F) 412-281-2312
info@lfofa.org / www.lfofa.org
www.larchecanada.org

Mediation and Restitution/ Reconciliation Services (MARRS)

Adriann W. Wilson (Executive
  Director)
MARRS, 4488 Poplar Ave., Memphis,
  TN 38117
(P) 901-261-7128 (MARRS)
(P) 901-261-2165 (Executive Director)
(F) 901-261-4393
awilsonmarrs@yahoo.com
www.mlfonline.org

Memphis Leadership Foundation

Howard Eddings (President)
1548 Poplar Ave., Memphis, TN 38104
(P) 901-729-2931 / (F) 901-729-2933
howard@mlfonline.org
www.mlfonline.org

Missionaries of Charity

Sister M. Dominga, M.C.
335 E. 145th St., Bronx, NY 10451
(P) 718-292-0019
*http://www.cmswr.org/member_
  communities/MC.htm*

My Friend's House

Jim Ortiz (Pastor)
6525 S. Norwalk Blvd., Whittier, CA
  90606
(P) 562-692-0953 / (F) 562-692-1983
jomfh@juno.com
www.myfriendshouse.org

National Center for Neighborhood Enterprise

Robert L. Woodson Sr. (President and
  Founder)
1424 Sixteenth St. NW, Suite 300,
  Washington, D.C. 20036
(P) 202-518-6500 / (F) 202-588-0314
info@ncne.com / www.ncne.com

National Ten Point Leadership Foundation

Jacqueline Rivers (Executive Director)
Rev. Eugene F. Rivers III (President
  and Cofounder)
360 Huntington Ave., Suite 140SC-
  401, Boston, MA 02115
(P) 617-373-7273 / (F) 617-373-7575
info@ntlf.org / www.ntlf.org

Neighborhood Housing Opportunities, Inc.

Howard Eddings Jr. (Executive
  Director)
1548 Poplar Ave., Memphis, TN 38104
(P) 901-729-2934 / (F) 901-729-2933
ybholt@mlfonline.org or
howard@mlfonline.org
www.mlfonline.org

New Focus National
Jenny Forner
6837 Lake Michigan Dr., PO Box 351,
    Allendale, MI 49401-0351
(P) 616-895-5356 / (F) 616-895-5355
data@newfocus.org
www.newfocus.org

No More Victims
Marilyn Gambrell (Founder)
9680 Mason, Houston, TX 77078
(P) 713-807-8287 / (F) 713-807-7762
nomorevictimsinc@mail.ev1.net
www.nomorevictimsinc.org

Nueva Esperanza
Rev. Luis Cortes (President)
4261 N. 5th St., Philadelphia, PA 19140
(P) 215-324-0746
(P) 877-574-5322 (toll-free)
(F) 215-324-2542
lcortes@nueva.org
www.esperanza.us

The Oaks Academy
Andrew N. Hart (Head of School)
2301 N. Park Ave., Indianapolis, IN
    46205
(P) 317-931-3043 / (F) 317-931-3050
hlee@theoaksacademy.org
www.theoaksacademy.org

One by One Leadership
Kurt Madden (CEO)
1727 L Street, Fresno, CA 93721
(P) 559-233-2000 / (F) 559-233-2810

contact@onebyoneleadership.com
www.onebyoneleadership.com

Open Door Mission Foundation
Richard H. Hill (Executive Director)
5803 Harrisburg, Houston, TX 77011
(P) 713-921-7520 / (F) 713-921-4206
info@opendoorhouston.org
www.opendoorhouston.org

Pittsburgh Community Storehouse
Justin Brown (Executive Director)
16 Doverlake Dr., Pittsburgh, PA
    15206
(P) 412-362-0290 / (F) 412-362-0293
justinbrown@plf.org
www.storehousepittsburgh.org

Pittsburgh Leadership Foundation
Dr. John Stahl-Wert (President and
    CEO)
100 Ross St., 4th Floor, Pittsburgh, PA
    15219
(P) 412-281-3752 / (F) 412-281-2312
mail@plf.org / www.plf.org

Pura Vida Partners
John K. Sage (President and
    Cofounder)
2724 First Ave. S., Seattle, WA 98134
(P) 877-469-1431 (toll-free)
(P) 206-328-9606 / (F) 206-328-2284
contact@puravidacoffee.com
www.puravidacoffee.com or
www.puravidacoffee.org

Resources

Rev. Msgr. Ronald T. Marino
(Founder)
1258 65th St., Brooklyn, NY 11219
(P) 718-236-3000 / (F) 718-256-9707
migration@aol.com
www.catholicmigration.org

Star of Hope Mission, Inc.

Randall L. Tabor (President and
CEO)
6897 Ardmore, Houston, TX 77054
(P) 713-748-0700 / (F) 713-747-4381
sohmission@sohmision.org
www.sohmission.org

Step 13

Bob Coté (Director and Founder)
2029 Larimer St., Denver, CO 80205
(P) 303-295-7837 / (F) 303-296-6415
info@step13.org / www.step13.org

Streets Ministries

Ken Bennett (Founder)
769 Vance Ave., Memphis, TN 38126
(P) 901-525-7380 / (F) 901-525-9628
kenstreets@yahoo.com
www.streetsministries.org

Teen Challenge International

John Castellani (President)
Mailing Address: PO Box 1015,
Springfield, MO 65801
Physical Address: 3728 W. Chestnut
Expressway, Springfield, MO
65802

(P) 417-862-6969 / (F) 417-862-8209
tcusa@teenchallengeusa.com
www.teenchallenge.com

Urban Ventures Leadership Foundation

Art Erickson (President and CEO)
3041 Fourth Avenue S., Minneapolis,
MN 55408
(P) 612-822-1628 / (F) 612-822-2507
info@urbanventures.org
www.urbanventures.org

Urban Youth Initiative, Inc.

Sheryl Beard (Executive Director)
1548 Poplar Ave., Memphis, TN 38104
(P) 901-729-3988
(F) 901-869-0726 or 901-729-2933
Sharon@mlfonline.org
www.mlfonline.org

Victory Fellowship

Freddie Garcia and Ninfa Garcia
(Founders)
659 N. San Dario, San Antonio, TX
78228
(P) 210-433-0028 / (F) 210-433-6268
info@victoryfellowship.com
www.victoryfellowship.com

Victory Home

Joe Hernandez, Director
Physical Address: 15402 Sellers Rd.
Nr. 20
Houston, TX 77060
Mailing address: 4103 Northfield

Houston, TX 77092
(P) 713-691-2209
jhernandez188@houston.rr.com

Wheeler Mission Ministries
Richard A. Alvis (President and
Executive Director)
245 N. Delaware St., Indianapolis, IN
46204
(P) 317-635-3575 / (F) 317-686-6238
cathyrohrer@wmm.org
www.wmm.org

Windsor Village United Methodist Church
Kirbyjon H. Caldwell (Pastor)
6000 Heatherbrook Dr., Houston, TX
77085
(P) 713-723-8187 / (F) 713-728-9923

*an affiliation of Windsor Villiage United
Methodist Church:*
Power Center
12401 South Post Oak Rd., Houston,
TX 77045

(P) 713-723-6837 / (F) 713-551-8600
e-mail@kingdombuilders.com
www.kingdombuilders.com

World Vision U.S.A.
Richard Stearns (President)
PO Box 78481, Tacoma, WA 98481-
8481
(P) 253-815-1000 / (F) 253-815-3447
info@worldvision.org
www.worldvision.org

Youth-Reach Houston
Curt Williams (Founder)
PO Box 9631, Houston, TX 77231
(P) 281-459-4555 / (F) 281-459-4440
admin@youth-reach.org
www.youth-reach.org

Notes

Foreword

1. Samuel Adams to John Trumball, October 16, 1778, quoted in *The Founders' Almanac* (Washington DC: Heritage Foundation, 2002), 190.

2. Alexis de Tocqueville, *Democracy in America,* trans. George Lawrence (New York: Harper & Row, 1966), 527.

Introduction

1. There are many people of other faiths in America who are doing compassionate work in caring for the needy. Their work is valid and valuable, but the focus of this book is Christ-centered work.

2. Robert Woodson, founder of the National Center for Neighborhood Enterprise, first pointed out the "zipcode test" in looking for authentic neighborhood renewers.

3. Ram Cnaan, "The Role of Religious Congregations in Providing Social Services" (address at a meeting of the Roundtable on Religion and Social Welfare Policy at the Rockefeller Institute of Government in Albany, NY, 30 April 2003), 1–2.

4. Ram A. Cnaan, *The Invisible Caring Hand: American Congregations and the Provision of Welfare* (New York: New York University Press, 2002), 9. These congregations include all religions in America: Christian, Jewish, Muslim, Buddhist, and other.

5. Ibid., 62.

6. See http://fact.hartsem.edu.

7. Bridges to Life in Texas has documented this rate in statistics compiled by the Texas Department of Justice in 2003.

8. Scott Vander Stoep and Laurie Van Ark, "Evaluation of the Mentoring Program Kids Hope USA," Carl Frost Center for Social Science Research (Holland, MI: Hope College, 2003).

9. Aaron Todd Bicknese, "The Teen Challenge Drug Treatment Program in Comparative Perspective" (Ph.D. thesis, Northwestern University, Evanston, IL, June 1999).

10. Management expert Peter Drucker's phrase.

11. See Barbara von der Heydt (Elliott), *Candles Behind the Wall: Heroes of the Peaceful Revolution That Shattered Communism* (Grand Rapids: Eerdmans, 1993).

Chapter 1

1. Kirbyjon Caldwell, interview with author, February 19, 2003, Houston, TX.

2. Kirbyjon Caldwell, *Gospel of Good Success* (New York: Simon & Schuster, 1999), 59.

3. The *Wall Street Journal* did a front-page article on Caldwell underscoring his entrepreneurial talents. See Rick Wartzman, "A Houston Clergyman Pushes Civic Projects along with Prayers: The Rev. Kirbyjon Caldwell Uses His Financial Skills to Aid Black Community," February 20, 1996.

4. *Imani* is the Swahili word for faith.

5. Caldwell, *Gospel of Good Success,* 13.

6. Ibid.

7. Freddie and Ninfa Garcia, interviews with author, 1996–2003, San Antonio, TX.

8. For Freddie and Ninfa's story, see *Outcry in the Barrio* (San Antonio, TX: Freddie Garcia Ministries, 1988).

9. Ibid., 59.

10. Victory Fellowship affiliates are in these locations: 23 in Texas, 1 in New Mexico, 1 in California, 28 in Peru, 5 in Puerto Rico, 7 in Mexico, and one each in Colombia, Argentina, Venezuela, Nicaragua, and Guatemala.

11. *Outcry in the Barrio,* 217.

12. Cordelia Taylor, interview with author, April 15, 2003, Milwaukee, WI.

13. Eugene Rivers (address to the Council of Leadership Foundations, Washington, DC, June 15, 2001); interview with author, June 15, 2001.

14. "The Dorchester Miracle: Eugene Rivers & One Neighborhood," BreakPoint interview with Charles Colson, Commentary #000802, August 2, 2000.

15. Adapted from "Ten Point Plan to Mobilize the Churches," www.ntlf.org/ten_point_plan.htm.

Chapter 2

1. John Perkins, *A Quiet Revolution* (Wentzville, MO: Network Unlimited International, 1976), 15. In this autobiography, John Perkins tells his story as a living history of the Christian community development movement.

2. This portrait is based on the author's interview with John Perkins, October 9–10, 2003. All information and quotes not otherwise attributed are from this interview.

3. An echo of Romans 10:1–2; see Perkins, *A Quiet Revolution,* 20–21.

4. Judge John R. Brown, *Perkins v. State of Mississippi,* 455 Federal Reporter, 2d Series, 49–50.

5. "Journey Toward Forgiveness: From Rage to Reconciliation," ABC-TV video produced by Mennonite Media Productions, 2001.

6. Ibid.

7. Ibid.

8. John Perkins (speech to Intersections conference of One by One Leadership, Fresno, CA, April 2002).

9. Ephesians 2:18–19.

10. Perkins, Intersections speech.

11. A Gathering of Friends was organized by Susan (Mrs. James) Baker, drawing together believers from throughout the world who met in Israel and Jordan for prayer and reconciliation to usher in the new millennium.

Chapter 3

1. This portrait is based on the author's interview with Brian King, April 9, 2002, Fresno, CA.

Chapter 4

1. See "Children at Risk: State Trends 1990–2000," published by the Annie E. Casey Foundation. The report designates at-risk kids as having three of the following four risk factors: 1) child lives in a family with income below the poverty line; 2) child lives in a single-parent family; 3) child lives in a family where no parent has full-time, year-round employment; or 4) child lives with a household head who is a high school dropout.

2. Compiled by the Children's Defense Fund and the National Fatherhood Institute.

3. Joe Loconte and Lia Fantuzzo produced an excellent study. See "Churches, Charity and Children: How Religious Organizations Are Reaching America's At-Risk Kids" (Center for Research on Religion and Urban Civil Society, 2003).

4. "As simply and directly as water to a thirsty child, food to a hungry child, and medicine for a sick child give that child life, so does attachment," *Casa de Esperanza de los Ninos*, Summer/Fall 2003, 1.

5. "More Memorable Moments," *Twenty Years, Twenty Stories* (Casa de Esperanza de los Ninos, 2002), no. 20.

6. George Will, "Disconnected Youth," *Washington Post*, September 21, 2003, B7.

7. Ibid.

8. Ibid.

9. ". . . Water to a Thirsty Child . . ." *Casa de Esperanza de los Ninos*, Summer/Fall 2003.

10. "Our Nurse," *Twenty Years, Twenty Stories,* no. 16.

11. This profile is based on author's interviews with Virgil Gulker, 1998–99, 2001, and 2003, and on thirty-eight additional interviews with participants in the Kids Hope program, including teachers, principals, pastors, and mentors throughout the country.

12. Kids Hope USA was initiated by International Aid, USA, and is now a stand-alone organization.

13. Scott Vander Stoep and Laurie Van Ark, "Evaluation of the Mentoring Program Kids Hope USA," Carl Frost Center for Social Science Research (Holland, MI: Hope College, 2003).

14. See Daniel Goleman, *Emotional Intelligence: Why It Can Matter More Than IQ* (New York: Bantam Books, 1997).

15. Wayne Brouwer, "A Kids Hope USA Case Study" (Holland, MI: Kids Hope USA, 2003).

16. Todd Svanoe, "When Business Aims for Miracles," *Christianity Today,* May 21, 2001.

17. Art Erickson, president's letter, *Urban Venture News* (Summer 2003), 2.

18. Sources: Public/Private Ventures, *Washington Post,* and Prison Fellowship.

19. "A block is transformed one choice at a time," www.urbanventures.org.

20. See "Community" (December 2002), 3, www.cornerstoneschools.com.

21. See Samuel Casey Carter, "No Excuses: Seven Principals of Low-Income Schools Who Set the Standard for High Achievement," www.noexcuses.org.

22. See www.noexcuses.org for the full report.

23. See Samuel Casey Carter, "No Excuses," 65.

24. Ibid.

25. David C. Butty, "Schools: Cornerstone President Wins Citizenship Prize," *Detroit News,* May 19, 1999.

26. "Prisoners of Time" (September 1994), www.ed.gov/pubs/PrisonersOfTime/PoTschool/chap1-6.

27. "Motown Classic," *Wall Street Journal,* October 12, 2001.

28. Tenisha Mercer, "Impact on Learning: Corporate Leaders Help Inspire Young Detroiters," *Detroit News,* December 19, 2001.

29. Ibid.

30. Ernestine Sanders, interview with author, September 26, 2003.

31. Author site visit, September 23, 2003, Indianapolis, IN.

32. See www.theoaksacademy.org.

33. Isaiah 61:3.

34. See Byron Johnson, "The Role of African-American Churches in Reducing Crime among Black Youth," "The Great Escape: How Religion Alters the Delinquent Behavior of High-Risk Adolescents," and "A Better Kind of High: How Religious Commitment Reduces Drug Use Among Poor Urban Teens," all published by the Center for Research on Religion and Urban Civil Society (CRRUCS).

35. Mark D. Regnerus, "Making the Grade: The Influence of Religion upon the Academic Performance of Youth in Disadvantaged Communities," CRRUCS (2002), 3.

36. Dr. David B. Larson and Dr. Byron R. Johnson. "Religion: The Forgotten Factor in Cutting Youth Crime and Saving At-Risk Urban Youth," *Jeremiah Project Report 98-2* (New York: Center for Civic Innovation, Manhattan Institute, 1998), 8-10.

37. Ibid., 20.

38. Byron Johnson and Marc Siegel, "The Great Escape: How Religion Alters the Delinquent Behavior of High-Risk Adolescents," CRRUCS (2003), 9.

39. Ibid., 11.

40. Byron Johnson, "A Better Kind of High," 14.

41. Ibid., 9.

42. Ibid.

43. Ibid.

44. John DiIulio, in the introduction to Johnson's "A Better Kind of High," 4.

45. See also Mark D. Regnerus, "Living up to Expectations: How Religion Alters the Delinquent Behavior of Low-Risk Adolescents," CRRUCS (2003).

46. Johnson, "A Better Kind of High," 10. See also Johnson, "The Role of African-American Churches in Reducing Crime Among Black Youth," CRRUCS (2002), 9–10.

Chapter 5

1. Washington DC: Bureau of Justice statistics (2002), http://www.ojp.usdoj.gov/bjs/glance/tables.

2. Bureau of Justice statistics (2002), http://www.ojp.usdoj.gov/bjs/reentry/recidivism.

3. Ibid. See also Fox Butterfield, "Prison Boom Has Not Deterred Crime, Report Suggests," *New York Times*, June 2, 2002.

4. Bureau of Justice statistics (2002), http://www.ojp.usdoj.gov/bjs/reentry/recidivism. See also Charles Colson, "An Exodus in Search of Moses: 630,000 Released Prisoners," BreakPoint January 20, 2002, #020129.

5. Ibid.

6. Bureau of Justice statistics, http://www.ojp.usdoj.gov/bjs/reentry/recidivism. The 2002 report by Patrick Langan and David Levin for the Department of Justice examined 272,111 former inmates in fifteen states during the first three years after their release.

7. Bureau of Justice statistics (2002), http://www.ojp.usdoj.gov/bjs, indicates that there are 1.5 million children with a parent in federal prison. In its 2003 fact sheet, Amachi, an initiative of Public/Private Ventures in Philadelphia, adds to that the children who have incarcerated parents in state prisons or local jails, and arrives at a current total of 2.5 million.

8. Wade F. Horn, Assistant Secretary for Children and Families, U.S. Department of Health and Human Services, "Responsible Fatherhood and the Role of the Family" (remarks, Serious and Violent Offender Reentry Initiative Grantee Conference, Washington, DC, September 30, 2002); available at http://www.ojp.usdoj.gov/reentry/responsible.

9. Ibid.

10. Ibid.

11. Byron R. Johnson with David B. Larson, *InnerChange Freedom Initiative: A Preliminary Evaluation of a Faith-Based Prison Program* (Philadelphia: University of Pennsylvania Center for Research on Religion and Urban Civil Society, 2003).

12. Tony Fabelo, "Overview of the InnerChange Freedom Initiative: The Faith-Based Prison Program within the Texas Department of Criminal Justice," Criminal Justice Policy Council, February 2002, 1. This paper gives a thorough overview of the structure of the program; available at www.cjpc.state.tx.us/reports/alphalist/IFI.pdf.

13. Interviews by author with inmates at Carol Vance Unit, Richmond, TX, 1999–2001; and with Jack Cowley, 2003.

14. See www.ifiprison.org.

15. Dr. Henry Brandt and Kerry L. Skinner, "InnerChange Freedom Initiative White Paper," available at www.ifiprison.org.

16. Ibid.

17. Charles Colson, *Loving God* (Grand Rapids: Zondervan, 1987), 166.

18. Brandt and Skinner, "White Paper."

19. See ibid. for a more extensive listing.

20. Quoted in Johnson and Larson, *InnerChange Freedom Initiative,* 26.

21. See Brandt and Skinner, "White Paper," for a more detailed explanation.

22. Johnson and Larson, *InnerChange Freedom Initiative,* 4.

23. Ibid., 22.

24. Ibid., 50.

25. Bill McGurn, "Jesus Saves," *Wall Street Journal,* June 20, 2003.

26. Johnson and Larson, *InnerChange Freedom Initiative.*

27. John Sage, interview with author, 2001.

28. John Sage, "A Deeper Surrender," *Guideposts,* August 2000.

29. John Sage, "Bridges to Life: A Unique Restorative Justice Process," www.bridgestolife.org.

30. Jennifer Lim, "Finding Forgiveness: In Murder's Aftermath, Faith-Based Program Helps Families, Offenders Heal," *Texas Catholic Herald,* April 13, 2001.

31. Ibid.

32. For more on Connie Hilton's story, see her article, "Aftermath," *Guideposts,* September 2002; and Ed Timms, "Victims Hope to Turn Inmates Around," *Dallas Morning News,* March 10, 2002.

33. Bridges to Life participants, interviews with author, 2003.

34. Fox Butterfield, "Prison Boom Has Not Deterred Crime, Report Suggests," *New York Times,* June 2, 2002. The article references a study released by the Department of Justice on June 2, 2002, quoted earlier. Bureau of Justice statistics (2002), http://www.ojp.usdoj.gov/bjs/reentry/recidivism.

35. According to John Sage, executive director and founder of Bridges to Life.

36. Marilyn Gambrell, interview with author, April 2003.

37. No More Victims is not a faith-based program, but does effectively care for the children of prisoners.

38. W. Wilson Goode Sr. served as the mayor of Philadelphia from 1984 to 1992.

39. From the 2003 Amachi fact sheet. See also Wade F. Horn, "Responsible Fatherhood and the Role of the Family."

40. Rev. Dr. Wilson Goode Sr., interview with author, August 18, 2003.

41. See Joseph P. Tierney and Jean B. Grossman, *Making a Difference: An Impact Study of Big Brothers Big Sisters of America* (Philadelphia, PA: Public/Private Ventures, 1995).

42. Joseph Loconte and Lia Fantuzzo, "Churches, Charity and Children: How Religious Organizations are Reaching America's At-Risk Kids," Center for Research on Religion and Urban Civil Society (2003), 19.

43. Ibid., 11.

44. Muriel Dobbin, "Mentors Help Kids with Parents in Prison," *Sacramento Bee,* March 10, 2000.

45. Public/Private Ventures News, Spring 2001.

46. Ibid.

47. Dobbin, "Mentors Help Kids."

48. Kathleen Brady Shaw, "Former Mayor Pitches Outreach," *Philadelphia Inquirer,* May 14, 2003.

49. See S. H. Fishman, "The Impact of Incarceration on Children of Offenders," *Journal of Children in Contemporary Society* 15 (1982): 89–99.

50. For a discussion of the literature, see William H. Barton, "The John P. Craine House: A Community Residential Program for Female Offenders and Their Children" (annual meetings of the American Society of Criminology, San Francisco, November 16, 2000), 2–4.

51. See C. Jose-Kampfner, "Post-traumatic Stress Reactions in Children of Imprisoned Mothers," in K. Gabel and D. Johnston, eds., *Children of Incarcerated Parents* (New York: Lexington Books, 1995), 89–100.

52. Site visit by author, September 2003.

53. T. J. Banes, "A Second Chance," *Indianapolis Star,* June 29, 2003, J1.

54. Barton, "The John P. Craine House," Fig. 3.

Chapter 6

1. Ronald J. Sider and Heidi Rolland Unruh, "No Aid for Religion? Charitable Choice and the First Amendment," *Brookings Review* (Spring 1999), 48.

2. See Amy Sherman's excellent work in this area, including *Restorers of Hope: Reaching the Poor in Your Community with Church-Based Ministries That Work* (Wheaton, IL: Crossway Books, 1997); *Establishing a Church-based Welfare-to-Work Mentoring Ministry: A Practical "How-to" Manual* Indianapolis, IN: Hudson Institute, 2000); as well as *Workbook and Supplemental Guide: Applying the Principles Found in the Welfare of My Neighbor* (Washington, DC: Family Research Council, 1999). See also Deanna Carlson, *The Welfare of My Neighbor: Living Out Christ's Love for the Poor* (Washington DC: Family Research Council, 1999).

3. Carlson, *Welfare of My Neighbor,* 74.

4. John M. Cummins, Ph.D., research project manager, Southwest Health Technology Foundation, interview with author, January 28, 2004, Houston, TX.

5. See "So Help Me God: Substance Abuse, Religion and Spirituality," a report of the National Center on Alcohol and Substance Abuse at Columbia University, which compiles results of a two-year study and concludes that religion and spirituality have power in preventing and treating drug addiction. Available at www.casacolumbia.org.

6. For a study on this approach, see V. Shannon Burkett, John M. Cummins, Robert M. Dickson, and Malcolm H. Skolnick, "EEG Biofeedback as an Adjunctive Therapy in

the Treatment of Crack-Cocaine Dependence," Southwest Health Technology Foundation, preprint. In this study, eighty-seven treatment completers indicated that one year later 10.4 percent had relapsed to regular crack use, but the others were clean.

7. Ibid.

8. Ibid., abstract, 2.

9. John Cummins, interview with author.

10. According to Dr. John Cummins, who runs the program at Open Door Mission, it is one of two places in the United States using this technique to treat drug addiction. The technique was pioneered by Dr. Eugene Penison in 1989, who treated twenty alcoholics with biofeedback, resulting in an 80 percent success rate, verified in three follow-up tests over ten years. Other applications include treatment of depression and children with attention deficit disorder.

11. Catherine B. Hess, "Teen Challenge Training Center: Research Summation," *Services Research Report* (Washington, DC: National Institute on Drug Abuse, United States Department of Health, Education and Welfare, 1976).

12. Roger D. Thompson, "Teen Challenge of Chattanooga, TN: Survey of Alumni" (1994). Dr. Thompson, associate professor and head of the Criminal Justice Department, conducted the independent survey in conjunction with the University of Tennessee at Chattanooga.

13. Dave Batty, "Research on the Effectiveness of Teen Challenge" (1994), Springfield, MO.

14. Aaron Todd Bicknese, *The Teen Challenge Drug Treatment Program in Comparative Perspective* (Ph.D. thesis, Northwestern University, Evanston, IL, June 1999).

15. Quoted in Jane Lampmann, "A Frontier of Medical Research: Prayer," *Christian Science Monitor,* March 25, 1998.

16. See Byron Johnson, "Objective Hope: Assessing the Effectiveness of Faith-based Organizations." This excellent study gives a detailed overview of all the relevant studies published. (Philadelphia, PA: CRRUCS, 2002) The facts cited here are from pp. 10–15.

17. Ibid., 9.

18. H. G. Koenig, J. C. Hays, D. B. Larson, L. K. George, H. J. Cohen, M. E. McCullough, K. G. Meador, and D. G Blazer, "Does Religious Attendance Prolong Survival? A Six-Year Follow-up Study of 3,968 Older Adults," *Journal of Gerontology: Medical Sciences* 54A, no. 7 (1999), M370–M376.

19. "Analysis of Studies Shows That Religious Involvement May be a Factor in Living a Long Life," American Psychological Association, June 4, 2000. See Michael E. McCullough, David B. Larson, William T. Hoyt, Harold G. Koenig, and Carl E. Thoresen, "Religious Involvement and Mortality: A Meta-Analytic Review," *Health Psychology* 19, no. 3 (2000).

20. Harold G. Koenig, "Religion, Congestive Heart Failure and Chronic Pulmonary Disease," *Journal of Religion and Health* 41, no. 3 (2002): 263–78.

21. H. G. Koenig, H. J. Cohen, L. K. George, J. C. Hays, D. B. Larson, D. G. Blazer, "Attendance at Religious Services, Interleukin-6, and Other Biological Indicators of Immune Function in Older Adults," *International Journal of Psychiatry in Medicine* 27 (1997): 233–50.

22. H. G. Koenig, L. K. George, K. G. Meador, D. G. Blazer, and S. M. Ford, "The Relationship between Religion and Alcoholism in a Sample of Community-Dwelling Adults," *Hospital and Community Psychiatry* 45 (1994): 225–31.

23. Quoted in Charles Colson, "Can Prayer Heal? Science Looks at Prayer," *BreakPoint*, October 12, 2001, #011012.

24. M. W. Krucoff, S. W. Crater, C. L. Green, A. C. Maas, J. E. Seskevich, J. D. Lane, K. A. Loeffler, K. Morris, T. M. Bashore, H. G. Koenig, "The Monitoring & Actualization of Noetic Trainings (MANTRA) Feasibility Pilot," *American Heart Journal* 142 (2001): 760–97.

25. H. G. Koenig, L. K. George, B. L. Peterson, "Religiosity and Remission of Depression in Medically Ill Older Patients," *American Journal of Psychiatry* 155, no. 4 (1998): 536–42.

26. "Depressed Patients Benefit from Religion and Prayers," *Visions: BC's Mental Health Journal* 12 (2001).

27. John H. Christy, "Prayer as Medicine," *Forbes Magazine*, March 23, 1998.

28. George Washington Institute for Spirituality and Health, available at www.gwish.org.

Chapter 7

1. See Daniel Pryfogle, "Prophets of Profit," at www.faithworks.com/articles.

2. Venture Fund Initiative, www.redf.org.

3. John K. Sage, interviews with author, April 17, 2000, in Houston, TX, and phone interview, Sept. 12, 2003. An earlier version of this story was published in Barbara Elliott, "From Success to Significance: FaithWorks," *Compassion & Culture*, Capital Research Center (August 2000).

4. An earlier version of this section on Resources was published in Barbara von der Heydt (Elliott), "A Job Tree Grows in Brooklyn," *Policy Review*, Heritage Foundation (January/February 1997): 16–17. This profile is based on site visits to Brooklyn in 1996, 1999, and phone interviews 2002–4.

5. Bob Coté, interview with author, June 10, 1997, in Denver, CO, and phone interview, October 28, 2003.

6. Skip Long, interviews with author, June 14, 2003, in Colorado Springs, CO, and phone interview, October 17, 2003.

7. At this writing, Jobs Partnership has been replicated from Raleigh, NC, to Brenham, TX; Buffalo, NY; Charlotte, NC; Chattanooga, TN; Clarksville, TN; Cleveland, OH; Colorado Springs, CO; Henderson, NC; Indianapolis, IN; Knoxville, TN; Little Rock, AR; Miami, FL; Minneapolis MN; Orange County, CA; Orlando, FL; Oxford, NC; Palm Beach County, FL; Peoria, IL; Petersburg, VA; Philadelphia, PA; Richmond, VA; St. Louis, MO; Topeka, KS; Tulsa, OK; Tucson, AZ; and Washington, DC.

8. Amy L. Sherman, "Collaborating for Employment among the Poor: The Jobs Partnership Model," Hudson Institute (2001). For copies, contact The National Jobs Partnership, national@tjp.org.

9. An earlier version of this section on Brookwood Community was published in Barbara Elliott, "The Brookwood Community: Healing through the Dignity of Work," *Philanthropy, Culture & Society*, Capital Research Center (November 1999). The information is based on annual site visits to Brookshire, TX, 1998–2004.

Chapter 8

1. The Council of Leadership Foundations changed its name to Leadership Foundations of America in 2003.

2. Robert L. Woodson Sr., "Faith in Action: How Neighborhood Leaders Are Reviving Our Streets and Neighborhoods," *Principles & Perspectives* (Fall/Winter 2000): 5–6.

3. Robert L. Woodson Sr., "Why Welfare Reform Can't Succeed Without the Help of Religious People," http://robtshepherd.tripod.com/taejf98j.htm.

4. Robert L. Woodson Sr., *The Triumphs of Joseph: How Today's Community Healers Are Reviving Our Streets and Neighborhoods* (New York: Free Press, 1998).

5. Woodson, "Faith in Action," 5.

6. Ibid.

7. Ibid.

8. Robert L. Woodson Sr., "The Second Underground Railroad" (speech, Independent Black Majority Conference, Washington, DC, January 15, 2001).

9. Robert L. Woodson Sr., "Wealth and Power Offer No Protection from Societal Disintegration," *Washington Times;* available at http://ncne.com.

10. Luis Cortes, interview with author, October 2003.

11. Rodolpho Carrasco, "Catching Up with Hispanics," *Christianity Today,* November 12, 2001. The figures cited are from a Gallup poll.

Chapter 9

1. Brian Miller, "The Investor: Pittsburgh Leadership Foundation," *Empowering Compassion: The Strategic Role of Intermediary Organizations in Building Capacity Among and Enhancing the Impact of Community Transformers*, ed. Amy L. Sherman (Indianapolis: Hudson Institute, 2002).

2. Pittsburgh Leadership Foundation, "Mustard Seed II Kingdom Venture Fund: Investing in the Future" (Pittsburgh, PA: Stahl-Wert, 2003).

3. See Carl I. Fertman, "Project 40: Challenges and Opportunities for Youth Ministry: An Evaluation of the Pittsburgh Leadership Foundation's Project 40" (Pittsburgh, PA: University of Pittsburgh, 2001).

4. Pittsburgh Leadership Foundation, "Mustard Seed II."

5. John Stahl-Wert, "Restoring the Soul of the City," *Care America* 1 (2002).

6. Pittsburgh Leadership Foundation, "Mustard Seed II."

7. 1 Corinthians 12–14, Romans 12, Ephesians 5.

8. John Stahl-Wert, "City as Parish: An Urban, Inter-Congregational Curriculum for

Collaborative Lay Ministry Equipping" (Ph.D. thesis, Eastern Baptist Theological Seminary, 2000), 80.

9. The Leadership Training Network has formulated these steps, which are quoted in ibid., 82.

10. Ibid., 91.

11. Stahl-Wert, "Restoring the Soul of the City."

12. Ibid.

13. Pittsburgh Leadership Foundation, "Mustard Seed II."

14. Reid Carpenter (Presidents' Retreat, Council of Leadership Foundations, Laity Lodge, TX, March 2001).

15. Leadership Foundations are in Pittsburgh, Philadelphia, Memphis, Fresno, Chicago, Knoxville, Denver, Minneapolis, Milwaukee, Seattle, Dallas, Phoenix, Baltimore, Springfield (OH), New York, and Tacoma are fully accredited partners. Associate members are in Akron, Atlanta, Austin, Boston, Denver, Erie (PA), Kerrville (TX), Houston, Lexington, New Orleans, Oklahoma City, Orlando, Raleigh, Ontario (CA), Salem, Yuma, Wilmington (NC).

16. Ray Bakke, *A Theology as Big as the City* (Downers Grove, IL: InterVarsity Press, 1997).

17. Reid Carpenter (speech to annual conference of Leadership Foundations of America, Memphis, TN, May 29, 2003).

18. Richard Seltzer, *Mortal Lessons* (New York: Simon & Schuster, 1974), 45-46.

Chapter 10

1. Based on interviews with author, Memphis, TN, March 17-18, and May 28-29, 2003.

2. Melissa A. Barker and Greg Owen, "Urban Youth Initiative, Inc.: A Support Organization of the Memphis Leadership Foundation," Wilder Research Center, Amherst H. Wilder Foundation (St. Paul, MN: March 2002).

3. "Halftimer" is derived from Bob Buford's book *Halftime,* which describes successful business executives reaching a midway point in their life when they want to move "from success to significance" and put their faith to work. (Grand Rapids, MI: Zondervan, 1994)

Chapter 11

1. An earlier version of this study by Barbara J. Elliott appears in *Empowering Compassion: The Strategic Role of Intermediary Organizations in Building Capacity among and Enhancing the Impact of Community Transformers,* ed., Amy L. Sherman (Indianapolis: Hudson Institute, 2002), and in *Compassion and Culture,* published by the Capital Research Center. This chapter is based on thirty-eight interviews conducted in Fresno in 2002, with follow-up interviews in 2004.

2. "What Does God See When He Looks at the San Joaquin Valley?" (briefing paper prepared for Billy Graham on Fresno), 4.

3. Ibid, 5.

4. *Soul of the City*, vol. 1 (Fresno, CA: One by One Leadership, 2001).

5. Ibid., 5.

6. H. Spees, interview with author, Fresno, CA, April 2002.

Chapter 12

1. George Washington, "Farewell Address," in W. B. Allen, ed., *George Washington: Collection* (Indianapolis: Liberty Classics, 1988), 521.

2. John Adams, "Address to the Military," October 11, 1798, quoted in *The Founders' Almanac,*(Washington, DC: Heritage Foundation) 191.

3. Gouvernor Morris to George Gordon, June 28, 1792, quoted in *The Founders' Almanac,* 190.

4. Quoted in Michael Novak, *On Two Wings: Humble Faith and Common Sense at the American Founding* (San Francisco: Encounter Books, 2002), 29.

5. From Rev. Ethan Allen's handwritten history, "Washington Parish, Washington City," Library of Congress MMC Collection, 1167 MSS, in James H. Hutson, *Religion and the Founding of the American Republic* (Washington, DC: Library of Congress, 1998), 96. Quoted in Novak, *On Two Wings,* 31.

6. M. E. Bradford, "Religion and the Framers: The Biographical Evidence," in *Original Intentions: On the Making and Ratification of the United States Constitution* (Athens: University of Georgia Press, 1993), 93–94.

7. Robert L. Cord, *Separation of Church and State: Historical Fact and Current Fiction* (New York: Lambeth Press, 1982), 41–45.

8. *American Legacy: The United States Constitution and Other Essential Documents of American Democracy* (Calabasas, CA: Center for Civic Education, 1997), 38–39.

9. Charles Colson, "Walls of Our Own Making: The Founders and Religion," *BreakPoint* January 4, 2002, #020104.

10. Quoted by Russell Kirk, *The Roots of American Order* (LaSalle, IL: Open Court, 1974), 436.

11. Ibid., 6. The image comes from John Paul II's *Fides et Ratio.*

12. Ibid., 5.

13. Kirk, *Roots of American Order.*

14. John Winthrop, "A Model of Christian Charity" (1630), in Perry Miller, ed., *The American Puritans: Their Prose and Poetry* (New York: Doubleday, 1956), 78.

15. Novak, *On Two Wings,* 7.

16. Ibid., 7.

17. Donald Lutz (lecture, Center for the American Idea Seminar, Del Lago, TX, June 2000). See his book, *The Origins of American Constitutionalism* (Baton Rouge: Louisiana State University Press, 1988).

18. See Ellis Sandoz, *Political Sermons of the American Founding Era: 1730–1805* (Indianapolis: Liberty Press, 1991).

19. William Bradford, *Of Plimoth Plantation* (Boston: Wright & Potter, 1898). Quoted in Marvin Olasky, *The Tragedy of American Compassion* (Washington, DC: Regnery Publishing, 1992), 6.

20. Eleanor Parkhurst, "Poor Relief in a Massachusetts Village in the Eighteenth Century," *The Social Service Review* XI (September 1937): 452; quoted in Olasky, *Tragedy of American Compassion*, 7.

21. The laws of the Northwest Territory required relatives to care for members of their family in need.

22. 2 Thessalonians 3:10.

23. An echo of 1 Corinthians 13. Benjamin Colman, *The Merchandise of the People: Holiness to the Lord* (Boston: J. Draper, 1736), from sermons preached in 1725 and 1726; quoted in Olasky, *Tragedy of American Compassion*, 8.

24. Olasky, *Tragedy of American Compassion*, 7–8.

25. Gleaves Whitney (lecture, Center for the American Idea Seminar, Del Lago, TX, June 2000).

26. *American Legacy*, 5.

27. Lutz, *Origins of American Constitutionalism*.

28. Novak, *On Two Wings*, 17–18.

29. M. E. Bradford, *Original Intentions*, 87–102.

30. Ibid., 89

31. Norine Dickson Campbell, *Patrick Henry: Patriot and Statesman* (New York: Devin-Adair Co., 1969), 418; quoted in M. E. Bradford, *Original Intentions*, 89.

32. William Jay, *The Life of John Jay with Selections from His Correspondence*, 3 vols. (New York: Harper, 1833), 1:519–20; Quoted in M. E. Bradford, *Original Intentions*, 89–90.

33. George Adams Boyd, *Elias Boudinot: Patriot and Statesman, 1740–1821* (Princeton, NJ: Princeton University Press, 1952). Referenced in M. E. Bradford, *Original Intentions*, 91.

34. Christopher Collier, *Roger Sherman's Connecticut: Yankee Politics and the American Revolution* (Middletown, CT: Wesleyan University Press, 1971), 325–29; referenced in M. E. Bradford, *Original Intentions*, 91.

35. M. E. Bradford, *Original Intentions*, 91.

36. Marvin R. Zahniser, *Charles Cotesworth Pinckney: Founding Father* (Chapel Hill: University of North Carolina Press, 1967), 272–74; quoted in M. E. Bradford, *Original Intentions*, 91.

37. M. E. Bradford, *Original Intentions*, 91.

38. Ibid.

39. Ibid.

40. Ibid.

41. Alexis de Tocqueville, *The Old Regime and the French Revolution* (New York: Doubleday, 1955), 153; quoted in Novak, *On Two Wings*, 31.

42. Alexis de Tocqueville, *Democracy in America,* trans. George Lawrence (New York: HarperPerrenial-Harper, 1969), 513.

43. Olasky, *Tragedy of American Compassion,* 13.

44. Ibid., 14.

45. *The Charities of New York, Brooklyn, and Staten Island* (New York: Hurd & Houghton, 1873), 46; quoted in Olasky, *Tragedy of American Compassion,* 17.

46. Olasky, *Tragedy of American Compassion,* 16–17.

47. Ibid., 15.

48. *Charities of New York, Brooklyn, and Staten Island,* 48.

49. de Tocqueville, *Democracy in America,* 525.

50. Ibid., 527.

51. *Quadragesimo Anno, 79;* quoted in *Encyclopedia of Catholic Doctrine,* ed. Russell Shaw (Huntingdon, IN: Our Sunday Visitor Publishing, 1997), 650.

52. Don E. Eberly, ed., *The Essential Civil Society Reader* (Lanham, MD: Rowman & Littlefield, 2000), 24.

53. Ibid., 24.

54. Benjamin Rush, "Of the Mode of Education Proper to a Republic" (1798), cited in William J. Bennett, *Our Sacred Honor* (New York: Simon & Schuster, 1997), 412.

55. Quoted in Novak, *On Two Wings,* 34.

56. See Robert Nisbet, *Quest for Community* (San Francisco: ICS Press, 1999).

57. Charles Murray, *In Pursuit of Happiness and Good Government* (New York: Simon & Schuster, 1988), 274.

58. Robert Putnam, *Bowling Alone* (New York: Simon & Schuster, 2000).

59. Ibid., 72.

60. Ibid.

61. Putnam, *Bowling Alone,* 260.

62. de Tocqueville, *Democracy in America,* 506.

63. Ibid., 444.

64. Wilhelm Roepke, *A Humane Economy: The Social Framework of the Free Market,* 3rd ed. (Wilmington, DE: ISI Books, 1998).

65. Eric Voegelin, *The New Science of Politics* (Chicago: University of Chicago Press, 1952), 110.

66. Richard Ely, *Social Aspects of Christianity* (New York: T.Y. Crowell, 1889), 92, 77; quoted in Olasky, *Tragedy of American Compassion,* 121.

67. William G. Fremantle, *The World as the Subject of Redemption,* 2nd ed. (New York: Longmans, Green, 1895), 281; quoted in Olasky, *Tragedy of American Compassion,* 122.

68. *Everson v. Board of Education,* 330 U.S. 1. (1947).

69. See Daniel L. Dreisbach, *Thomas Jefferson and the Wall of Separation Between Church and State* (New York: New York University Press, 2002).

70. *Doe v. Santa Fe Independent School District* (2000).

71. Daniel L. Dreisbach, "How Thomas Jefferson's 'Wall of Separation' Redefined Church-State Law and Policy" (paper presentation, Philadelphia Society, October 4, 2003).

72. See *Widmar v. Vincent,* 454 U.S. 263 (1981); *Westside Community Schools v. Mer-*

gens, 496 U.S. 226 (1990); *Capitol Square Review Board v. Pinette,* 515 U.S. 753 (1995); *Rosenberger v. Rector,* 515 U.S. 819 (1995); *Agostini v. Felton,* 521 U.S. 203 (1997); and *Mitchell v. Helms,* 120 Supreme Court Reporter 2530 (2000).

73. George W. Bush (speech, White House Conference on Faith-Based and Community Initiatives, Washington, DC, June 1, 2004).

74. George W. Bush, "Guidance to Faith-Based and Community Organizations on Partnering with the Federal Government," (Washington, DC: White House, 2004), 2.

75. Jim Towey, speaking in Pittsburgh at a conference of the White House Office of Faith-Based and Community Initiatives, April 21, 2004. See Allison Schlesinger, "Religious, Community Leaders Attend Conference on Faith-based Initiatives," Associated Press, April 22, 2004.

76. The rights of faith-based providers to wear religious garb or have religious symbols on the wall have been preserved, as has the right to hire in accordance with their faith convictions, as guaranteed by the Civil Rights Act. However, these rights are under fire from critics of the Faith-Based Initiative. Manifestations of faith outside the federally funded portion of the work are permitted, as is worship, but federal funds may not be comingled for these activities. The provision of services may not be predicated upon participation in such activities. And alternative sources of service must be available for participants who do not want to work with a faith-based provider.

77. The purists insist any government funding would potentially corrupt the faith mission. In practice, there are FBOs that have received such funds and remain true to their purpose. The key seems to be the clarity of the leadership in maintaining the faith character through a commitment to avoid "mission creep" that shifts the goals to follow funding streams. Limiting the proportion of the budget from government sources helps to maintain both integrity and independence.

78. Faith-saturated programs are defined as those that provide a total immersion in faith, in which spiritual transformation is the goal of the process and the means of accomplishing change.

79. Peter Kreeft, *Back to Virtue* (San Francisco: Ignatius Press, 1992), 193.

Conclusion

1. Henri J. M. Nouwen, *In the Name of Jesus: Reflections on Christian Leadership* (New York: Crossroad, 1989).

2. Henri J. M. Nouwen, *The Wounded Healer* (New York: Doubleday, 1979), 41.

3. Dallas Willard, *The Divine Conspiracy: Rediscovering Our Hidden Life in God* (New York: Harper Collins, 1998), 25.

4. Ibid., 31.

5. For an excellent discussion of discipleship, see Willard, *Divine Conspiracy.*

6. Peter Kreeft, *Back to Virtue* (San Francisco: Ignatius Press, 1992), 78.

7. Richard J. Foster, *Streams of Living Water: Celebrating the Great Traditions of Christian Faith* (New York: Harper Collins, 1998), 166.

8. See Matthew 25:14–30.

9. C. S. Lewis, *The Abolition of Man* (New York: Macmillan, 1955), 95–121.

10. Foster, *Streams of Living Water*. Foster describes five streams, but for purposes of the discussion here on compassion, the focus is on three of them.

11. Isaiah 61:1–2; Luke 4:18–19.

12. This is a rich stream of Christian participation, with a "family tree" compiled by Richard Foster that includes such diverse people as St. Catherine of Genoa, Helena the mother of Constantine, Roger Williams of the American colonial era, David Livingstone who went as a missionary to Africa, nurse Florence Nightingale, William and Catherine Booth of the Salvation Army, missionary doctor Albert Schweitzer, labor activist Dorothy Day, and civil rights leader Martin Luther King Jr. See Foster, *Streams of Living Water*, 136–83. The Roman Catholic Church has a strong tradition of social justice, which has shaped much of its charitable activity worldwide. Evangelicals for Social Action, headed by Ron Sider, is an example of an organization that links the social justice stream to Protestant evangelical teaching in America today.

13. I am indebted to Ray Bakke for these insights on social justice.

14. John Paul II, "Man Is the Way of the Church," in *Centesimus Annus* (May 1991), 6:58.

15. For John Woolman's story in detail, see Foster, *Streams of Living Water*, 137–44.

16. John Perkins, *A Quiet Revolution* (Pasadena: Urban Family Publications, 1976), 66.

17. Foster, *Streams of Living Water*, 179.

18. Brian Kolodiejchuk, M.C., "The Soul of Mother Teresa: Hidden Aspects of Her Interior Life," *Zenit*, November 28, 2002, 1A:ZE02112820; available at www.zenit.org. Kolodiejchuk is the postulator for Mother Teresa's canonization; she was beatified in October 2003.

19. Ibid.

20. Ibid.

21. Ibid.

22. Ibid., November 29, 2002.

23. Eileen Egan, *Such a Vision of the Street: Mother Teresa—The Spirit and the Work* (Garden City, NY: Doubleday, 1985), 38.

24. Kolodiejchuk, "Soul of Mother Teresa," December 19, 2002, 2:ZE02121922.

25. Ibid.

26. Malcolm Muggeridge, *Something Beautiful for God* (New York: Harper & Row, 1977), 47.

27. Mother Teresa, *A Simple Path* (New York: Ballantine, 1995), 1.

28. Ibid., xxx–xxxi.

29. See Robert K. Greenleaf, *Servant Leadership: A Journey into the Nature of Legitimate Power and Greatness* (New York/Ramsey/Toronto: Paulist Press, 1977).

30. Lawrence Cunningham, ed., *Thomas Merton: Spiritual Master* (New York: Paulist Press, 1992), 426.

31. Nouwen, *Wounded Healer*, 72–73.

32. I am indebted to Peter Kreeft for this image; see *Back to Virtue*, 68.

Bibliography

Aikman, David. *Great Souls: Six Who Changed the Century*. Nashville: Word, 1998.

Allen, W. B., ed. *George Washington: Collection*. Indianapolis: Liberty Classics, 1988.

Bakke, Raymond. *A Biblical Word for an Urban World: Messages from the 1999 World Mission Conference*. Valley Forge: Board of International Ministries, 2000.

_____. *A Theology as Big as the City*. Downers Grove, IL: InterVarsity, 1997.

Barker, Melissa A., and Greg Owen. *Urban Youth Initiative, Inc.: A Support Organization of the Memphis Leadership Foundation*. Saint Paul, MN: Amherst H. Wilder Foundation, 2002.

Barry, John W., and Bruno V. Manno, eds. *Giving Better, Giving Smarter*. Washington, DC: National Commission on Philanthropy and Civic Renewal, 1997.

Bellah, Robert N., Richard Madsen, William M. Sullivan, Ann Swidler, Steven M. Tipton. *The Good Society*. New York: Vintage-Random House, 1992.

_____. *Habits of the Heart*. Berkeley: University of California, 1996.

Bennett, William J., ed. *Our Sacred Honor: Words of Advice from the Founders in Stories, Letters, Poems, and Speeches*. New York: Simon & Schuster, 1997.

Berger, Peter L., and Richard John Neuhaus. *To Empower People: From State to Civil Society*. Edited by Michael Novak. Washington, DC: American Enterprise Institute, 1996.

Beumer, Jurjen. *Henri Nouwen: A Restless Seeking for God*. New York: Crossroad, 1997.

Bradford, M. E. *Original Intentions: On the Making and Ratification of the United States Constitution*. Athens: University of Georgia, 1993.

Caldwell, Kirbyjon. *The Gospel of Good Success*. New York: Simon & Schuster, 1999.

Carey, George W., and Bruce Frohnen, eds. *Community and Tradition: Conservative Perspectives on the American Experience*. Lanham: Rowman, 1998.

Carlson, Deanna. *The Welfare of My Neighbor: Living out Christ's Love for the Poor*. Washington, DC: Family Research Council, 1999.

Center for Civic Education. *American Legacy: The United States Constitution and Other Essential Documents of American Democracy*. Calabasas, CA: Author, 1997.

Cnaan, Ram A., et al. *The Invisible Caring Hand: American Congregations and the Provision of Welfare*. New York: New York University Press, 2002.

Colson, Charles. *Loving God*. Grand Rapids: Zondervan, 1987.

Cunningham, Lawrence, ed. *Thomas Merton: Spiritual Master*. New York: Paulist, 1992.

Donaldson, Dave, and Stanley Carlson-Thies. *A Revolution of Compassion: Faith-Based*

Groups as Full Partners in Fighting America's Social Problems. Grand Rapids: Baker, 2003.

Dreisbach, Daniel L. *Thomas Jefferson and the Wall of Separation Between Church and State.* New York: New York University Press, 2002.

Dubay, Thomas. *Fire Within: St. Teresa of Avila, St. John of the Cross, and the Gospel—On Prayer.* San Francisco: Ignatius Press, 1989.

Eberly, Don, ed. *Building a Healthy Culture: Strategies for an American Renaissance.* Grand Rapids: Eerdmans, 2001.

———. *The Essential Civil Society Reader: The Classic Essays.* Lanham, MD: Rowman & Littlefield, 2000.

———. *Restoring the Good Society: A New Vision for Politics and Culture.* Grand Rapids: Hourglass-Baker, 1994.

Eberly, Don, and Ryan Streeter. *The Soul of Civil Society.* Lanham, MD: Lexington, 2002.

Egan, Eileen. *Such a Vision of the Street: Mother Teresa—The Spirit and the Work.* Garden City, NY: Doubleday, 1985.

Encyclopedia of Catholic Doctrine. Edited by Russell Shaw. Huntingdon, IN: Our Sunday Visitor, 1997.

Evans, M. Stanton. *The Theme Is Freedom: Religion, Politics, and the American Tradition.* Washington, DC: Regnery, 1994.

Fertman, Carl I. *Project 40: Challenges and Opportunities for Youth Ministry.* Pittsburgh: University of Pittsburgh, 2001.

Ford, Michael. *Wounded Prophet: A Portrait of Henri J. M. Nouwen.* New York: Doubleday-Random House, 1999.

Foster, Richard J. *Streams of Living Water: Celebrating the Great Traditions of Christian Faith.* New York: Harper, 1998.

Garcia, Freddie, and Ninfa Garcia. *Outcry in the Barrio.* San Antonio, TX: Freddie Garcia Ministries, 1988.

Glenn, Charles L. *The Ambiguous Embrace: Government and Faith-Based Schools and Social Agencies.* Princeton: Princeton University Press, 2000.

Goleman, Daniel. *Emotional Intelligence: Why It Can Matter More Than IQ.* New York: Bantam, 1997.

Greenleaf, Robert K. *Servant Leadership: A Journey into the Nature of Legitimate Power and Greatness.* New York: Paulist, 1977.

John Paul II. *Fides et Ratio.* September 1998.

———. "Man Is the Way of the Church." *Centesimus Annus.* May 1991.

Jose-Kampfner, C. "Post-Traumatic Stress Reactions in Children of Imprisoned Mothers." *Children of Incarcerated Parents.* Edited by K. Gabel and D. Johnston. New York: Lexington Books, 1995.

Kirk, Russell. *The Roots of American Order.* LaSalle, IL: Open Court, 1974.

Kreeft, Peter. *Back to Virtue.* San Francisco: Ignatius Press, 1992.

Larson, David B., and Byron R. Johnson. "Religion: The Forgotten Factor in Cutting Youth Crime and Saving At-Risk Urban Youth. *The Jeremiah Project Report 98-2.* New York: Center for Civic Innovation, 1998.

Lewis, C. S. *The Abolition of Man: How Education Develops Man's Sense of Morality*. New York: Macmillan, 1955.

Linthicum, Robert C. *Empowering the Poor*. Monrovia, CA: MARC-World Vision, 2000.

Loconte, Joe. *Seducing the Samaritan: How Government Contracts Are Reshaping Social Services*. Boston: Pioneer Institute, 1997.

Lutz, Donald. *The Origins of American Constitutionalism*. Baton Rouge: Louisiana State University Press, 1988.

Mallory, Sue. *The Equipping Church: Serving Together to Transform Lives*. Grand Rapids: Zondervan, 2001.

Miller, Perry, ed. *The American Puritans: Their Prose and Poetry*. New York: Doubleday, 1956.

Minassian, Roger. *Gangs to Jobs*. Lafayette, LA: Alpha, 2003.

Mother Teresa. *A Simple Path*. New York: Ballantine, 1995.

Muggeridge, Malcolm. *Something Beautiful for God: Mother Teresa of Calcutta*. New York: Harper & Row, 1977.

Murray, Charles. *In Pursuit of Happiness and Good Government*. New York: Simon & Schuster, 1988.

Nisbet, Robert. *The Quest for Community: A Study in the Ethics of Order and Freedom*. San Francisco: ICS, 1990.

Nouwen, Henri J. M. *In the Name of Jesus: Reflections on Christian Leadership*. New York: Crossroad, 1989.

_____. *Reaching Out: The Three Movements of the Spiritual Life*. New York: Image-Doubleday, 1975.

_____. *The Wounded Healer*. New York: Image-Doubleday, 1979.

Novak, Michael. *On Two Wings: Humble Faith and Common Sense at the American Founding*. San Francisco: Encounter Books, 2002.

Olasky, Marvin. *Compassionate Conservativism*. New York: Free Press, 2000.

_____. *The Tragedy of American Compassion*. Washington, DC: Regnery, 1992.

Perkins, John. *A Quiet Revolution*. Wentzville, MO: Urban Family Network Unlimited International, 1976.

Pittsburgh Leadership Foundation. *Mustard Seed II Kingdom Venture Fund: Investing in the Future*. Pittsburgh: 2003.

Putnam, Robert. *Bowling Alone*. New York: Simon & Schuster, 2000.

Rai, Raghu, and Navin Chawla. *Faith and Compassion: The Life and Work of Mother Teresa*. Shaftesbury, Dorset, UK: Element, 1996.

Robinson, Lynn D., ed. *Does Free Enterprise Help the Poor?* Wilmington, DE: ISI, 2002.

Roepke, Wilhelm. *A Humane Economy: The Social Framework of the Free Market*. 3rd ed. Wilmington, DE: ISI, 1998.

Sandoz, Ellis. *Political Sermons of the American Founding Era: 1730–1805*. Indianapolis: Liberty, 1991.

Sherman, Amy. *Collaborating for Employment among the Poor: The Jobs Partnership Model*. Indianapolis: Hudson Institute, 2001.

_____. *Establishing a Church-Based Welfare-to-Work Mentoring Ministry: A Practical 'How-To' Manual*. Indianapolis: Hudson Institute, 2000.

_____. *Reinvigorating Faith in Communities.* Indianapolis: Hudson Institute, 2002.

_____. *Restorers of Hope: Reaching the Poor in Your Community with Church-Based Ministries That Work.* Wheaton, IL: Crossway Books, 1997.

_____. *Workbook and Supplemental Guide: Applying the Principles Found in the Welfare of My Neighbor.* Washington, DC: Family Research Council, 1999.

_____, ed. *Empowering Compassion: The Strategic Role of Intermediary Organizations in Building Capacity among and Enhancing the Impact of Community Transformers.* Indianapolis: Hudson Institute, 2002.

Sider, Ronald J. *Just Generosity: A New Vision for Overcoming Poverty in America.* Grand Rapids: Baker, 1999.

Sider-Rose, Michael J. *Taking the Gospel to the Point.* Pittsburgh: Pittsburgh Leadership Foundation, 2000.

Spalding, Matthew. *The Founders' Almanac: A Practical Guide to the Notable Events, Greatest Leaders, and Most Eloquent Words of the American Founding.* Washington, DC: Heritage Foundation, 2002.

Streeter, Ryan. *Transforming Charity: Toward a Result-Oriented Social Sector.* Indianapolis: Hudson Institute, 2001.

Templeton, Sir John. *Agape Love: A Tradition Found in Eight World Religions.* Philadelphia: Templeton Foundation, 1999.

Tierney, Joseph P., and Jean B. Grossman. *Making a Difference: An Impact Study of Big Brothers Big Sister of America.* Philadelphia: Public/Private Ventures, 1995.

Tocqueville, Alexis de. *Democracy in America.* Translated by George Lawrence. Edited by J. P. Mayer and Max Lerner. New York: HarperPerrenial-Harper, 1969.

Voegelin, Eric. *The New Science of Politics: An Introduction.* Chicago: University of Chicago, 1987.

White, Randy. *Journey to the Center of the City: Making a Difference in an Urban Neighborhood.* Downers Grove, IL: InterVarsity, 1996.

Willard, Dallas. *The Divine Conspiracy: Rediscovering Our Hidden Life in God.* San Francisco: HarperSanFrancisco, 1998.

Woodson, Robert. *The Triumphs of Joseph: How Today's Community Healers Are Reviving Our Streets and Neighborhoods.* New York: Free Press, 1998.

Index

Also available from Templeton Foundation Press

Equipping the Saints

A Guide to Giving to Faith-Based Organizations
By Barbara J. Elliott
1-932031-88-x $15.95
To order: www.templetonpress.org   1-800-621-2736

This book is an indispensable guide for anyone who has ever considered giving money to a faith-based organization. *Equipping the Saints* will assist a potential donor in evaluating a program and help to eliminate donor's remorse. It offers sage advice on what makes an effective program, the qualities of good leaders, and the methods of evaluating outcomes.

Based on hundreds of interviews with donors and civic leaders, this book distills wisdom into hands-on recommendations. Barbara Elliott draws from years of experience working with faith-based organizations and the donors who support them to provide a candid look at the unique strengths and weaknesses of these groups. *Equipping the Saints* is packed with useful tools such as a donor's interest inventory, a checklist for making a site visit, and tips on reading nonprofit financial statements—all authored by professional philanthropic advisors.

ADVANCE PRAISE

"Any donor with even a hint of interest in exploring investments in the work of faith-based organizations (FBOs) needs this book. It is packed with practical information about how to understand and assess FBOs. Its numerous examples of real-life donors making real-life differences through partnerships with faith-inspired community healers ought to stimulate much creative brainstorming among philanthropists."

—*Dr. Amy L. Sherman, Senior Fellow and Director, Faith in Communities Initiative of the Foundation for American Renewal*

"Barbara Elliott's *Equipping the Saints* is an important and helpful tool for serious donors. The first book of its kind, it makes the case for supporting causes motivated by faith, and then provides a rich mosaic of information on just how to do that. Since giving among the faithful is such a large segment of American philanthropy, this book is long overdue. Immensely readable, and laced with numerous illustrations and helpful tools, this practical volume is packed with wisdom. Elliott is right on!"
　　　　—*Calvin W. Edwards, Founder & CEO, Calvin Edwards & Company*

⫶⫶⫶

"An excellent guide for philanthropists seeking to unleash the power of faith in healing troubled souls and transforming troubled neighborhoods."
　　　　—*Adam Meyerson, President, The Philanthropy Roundtable*

Advance Praise for *Street Saints*

"Read *Street Saints* for spirit-tingling proof that faith-filled organizations and people are making an unmistakable difference in our world. Written with imagination and joy, this book portrays an inspiring army of 'saints' who have been moved by God's love to practice on the street what they have professed in the sanctuary. *Street Saints* will bless you!"

—*Dr. Virgil Gulker, Founder and Executive Director of Kids Hope USA*

⁝I⁝

"Barbara Elliott has a genius for identifying America's most effective faith-based healers of troubled souls and troubled neighborhoods."

—*Adam Meyerson, President, The Philanthropy Roundtable*

⁝I⁝

· "No one tells the stories of the nation's Good Samaritans with more warmth and intelligence than Barbara Elliott. Few grasp as clearly why faith commitment is crucial to family and social stability. In *Street Saints* we now have the most thorough treatment available of how religious groups of every stripe are revitalizing America's streets, neighborhoods, and cities."

—*Joe Loconte, William E. Simon Fellow in Religion and a Free Society at The Heritage Foundation; author of* Seducing the Samaritan

⁝I⁝

"One definition of vision is simply 'seeing.' This book is a wonderful gift of sight . . . the capacity to get the lens on those who each day are the heart, hands, and feet of a compassionate God who particularly loves the poor. In reading it, I received bursts of sheer joy."

—*Reid Carpenter, President, Leadership Foundations of America*

⁝I⁝

"Elliott's tour of America's soft underbelly in *Street Saints* is inspiring, because it depicts how sufferers have become transformers, bringing renewal to distressed individuals and neighborhoods. The colorful description of effec-

tive models and handy guide to key lessons learned will help anyone interested in tackling community problems to obtain a handhold on how to get started."
—*Dr. Amy L. Sherman, author,* Restorers of Hope: Reaching the Poor in Your Community with Church-Based Ministries That Work

{|:|}

"Barbara Elliott's *Street Saints* is a wonderful compilation of the way faith-based initiatives and faith-based communities are providing hope for those who are seeking help in their lives. These lived out experiences of the Christian message motivate us to seek the well-being of all."
—*Most Reverend Joe S. Vásquez, Auxiliary Bishop of Galveston-Houston*

{|:|}

"Mother Teresa of Calcutta held that poverty in the United States is more severe than anywhere else in the world because, in this, the wealthiest nation on earth, poverty is not only acute, but also humiliating. In this engaging book, Barbara Elliott shows that American poverty is right now being addressed in our neighborhoods and cities in an American way—through faith. Read it and be heartened by what is occurring under our very noses; read it to discover what works, and why."
—*Rev. Michael Sweeney, O.P., President, Dominican School of Philosophy and Theology, Berkeley, CA*

{|:|}

"The strengthening of civic life is central to the quality of private and public life in the United States. Barbara Elliott has her finger on the pulse of faith-based initiatives and offers wonderful insights into the way faith-based communities are contributing to the renewal of American life through civic responsibility and participation in the common good."
—*Rev. Donald S. Nesti, CSSp, STD, Director of the Center for Faith and Culture, University of St. Thomas, Houston*

{|:|}

"*Street Saints* gives us a carefully researched bird's eye view of the extraordinary variety of faith-based social initiatives in this country which are changing the lives of thousands. After reading Barbara Elliott's inspiring account of how the creative compassion and faith of ordinary citizens is changing the face of their communities, you'll find yourself asking: What can I do?"
—*Sherry Anne Weddell, Co-Founder of the Catherine of Siena Institute*